Feeling particularly perceptive one afternoon, I made it my mission to find the mastermind behind the recent cyber-attack on our society. As if we didn't have enough problems already, this attack had only added to the daily struggles we face. Who would be so callous as to orchestrate such a thing? I was determined to find out. Lying down, I concentrated all my attention and began my investigation.

Honestly, I wasn't even expecting to "find" anything. Soon enough though, I came across the suspect. What the "***," you are not human? Those were the words I found myself uttering in my head. It turned to face me, its expression one of surprise. And based on what happened next, it was not expecting to see "me" either.

ABOUT THE AUTHOR

Elly Flippen was born into the family of artist, astrologer, psychic, and Remote Viewer Ingo Swann. Through her time with Ingo, Elly gained unique insights into his creative processes, spontaneous psychic experiences, meticulous personality, and the lively community of visitors who frequented his home.

She has been deeply involved in preserving and chronicling her uncle's multifaceted legacy as an author, creator, and pioneer in perception and consciousness exploration. She facilitated her mother's donations of Ingo's artwork to the American Visionary Art Museum, the Leslie Lohman Art Museum, One Archives at USC, and Edgar Cayce's A.R.E. She and her mother have also given his archives to the University of West Georgia (UWG) and One Archives at USC.

To inspire further research into the depths of human consciousness, Elly and her mother have established fellowships and scholarships at UWG.

Elly earned her bachelor's degree from Vassar College and her MBA from Columbia University. She wrote, edited, and provided the art direction for the book **Stardust Highways: Ingo Swann's Art of Entertaining**, which showcases not only Ingo's artistic abilities but also his flair for cooking and entertaining.

She manages the X account @estateingoswann and website ingoswann.com, with the hope of inspiring future generations to embark on their own journeys into the marvelous wonders of the human biomind.

CONJUNCTION.WORLD

A JOURNEY THROUGH THE MIRROR

A BIOMIND SUPERPOWERS BOOK
PUBLISHED BY

Swann-Ryder Productions, LLC
www.ingoswann.com

Copyright © 2024 by Swann-Ryder Productions, LLC.

All rights reserved. No part of this book may be used or reproduced in any manner whatsoever without written permission. Cover art Mirror © 愚木混株 Cdd20 and interior art Mirror Vine © BiancaVanDijk from Pixabay.

For more information address: www.ingoswann.com.

First edition BioMind Superpowers Books.

ISBN-13: 978-1-949214-86-4

This memoir is a genuine account of events that took place in the author's life. Certain conversations have been recreated, and some individuals and their specific details have been altered for privacy purposes. The contents of this book are meant solely for informative purposes, and are based on the author's own experiences, viewpoints, and understandings of the subject matter. The book covers a broad range of topics and may encompass thought-provoking themes that could be overwhelming or triggering for some readers. There are elements such as violence, strong language, sexual content, controversial religious ideas, and other potentially challenging subject matter. Readers are encouraged to use their discretion while interpreting the content. Neither the author, the publisher, nor any associated parties shall be held responsible for any consequences arising from the opinions or interpretations expressed within this book. Although the author and the publisher have made every effort to ensure that the information in this book was correct at press time and while this publication is designed to provide accurate information in regard to the subject matter covered, the author and the publisher assume no responsibility for errors, inaccuracies, omissions, or any other inconsistencies herein and hereby disclaim any liability to any party for any loss, damage, or disruption caused by errors or omissions, whether such errors or omissions result from negligence, accident, or any other cause. Fair use is a use permitted by copyright statute that might otherwise be infringing. All rights and credit go directly to its rightful owners. No copyright infringement is intended.

CONJUNCTION.WORLD

A JOURNEY THROUGH THE MIRROR

For the most part, life on planet earth is lived out chasing fantasies or believing in them; it is only the fallout from these that bring about the realities.

Ingo Swann, **Anacalypsis: A Psychic Autobiography**

CONTENTS

AUTHOR'S NOTE
(ii)

THE RUN-UP
(00)

CONJUNCTIONS
(38)

THE WIND-UP
(162)

HISTORICAL TIDBITS
(180)

APPENDIX
(248)

BIBLIOGRAPHY
(296)

Author's Note

The following stories recount a collection of bewildering experiences I have encountered and my endeavors to comprehend them, presented in the order they occurred. These events are not figments of my imagination, but real incidents that have happened to me exactly as I have recounted them. However, to protect the privacy of those involved, some creative freedom has been taken with one specific story – the one about the San Diego Mountains. In this chapter, the real-life individuals and circumstances that brought me to the desert there that day have been reimagined into fictionalized versions.

The book begins with a section called The Run-Up, which serves as an introduction to what is to come. After my stories, there is a section called The Wind-Up, where I reflect on the lessons and insights gained from my journey. In this way, The Run-Up section sets the stage for my motives and approach to my adventures, while The Wind-Up section expands on the valuable knowledge acquired along the way.

After The Wind-Up, is a section called Historical Tidbits. The name is a nod to Ingo, who often used this phrase in his own writing to provide context for topics under discussion. In this section, I cover four main points: theories surrounding non-human entities as either extraterrestrial or interdimensional beings; my account of the potential advancement in technology that could explain the presence of anomalous aerial and aquatic vehicles; a brief background on Ingo and the evolution of the Remote Viewing program; and the possible correlation between Remote Viewing and UFOs and non-human entities.

I created these for myself to better grasp the multifarious circumstances surrounding "the situation," an surreptitious reality I believe exists in conjunction to us but is obscured by what I can only describe as a reflective barrier. The metaphorical mirror-like surface pointed at us, creating a sense of separation and ambiguity. We call this situation the paranormal. The prefix "para" originates from the ancient Greek language. It is derived from the dative preposition παρά (pronounced pará), which has various meanings such as, "beside," "next to," or "against." The term paranormal therefore holds within it the power to shatter our understanding of reality, exposing a world beyond what we have been conditioned to accept as truth. Its very definition conveying something in existence besides, next to, or even against, what we have been taught to believe is normal. As such, these documents provided an avenue for me to dissect the complexities of the overarching story and encapsulate my personal musings, perspectives, and comprehensions.

Prior to beginning The Run-Up, I strongly suggest reading the Historical Tidbit notes in sequential order. Although these are simply my own understandings and interpretations, I do believe they act as significant guideposts for my experience.

The final section, the Appendix, features Ingo's complete chapter on the Lourdes apparition from his book **The Great Apparitions of Mary: An Examination of Twenty-Two Supranormal Appearances**. It is also advisable to read this before continuing with my story about Lourdes. Additionally, the Appendix contains a chapter from Ingo's book **Resurrecting the Mysterious: Ingo Swann's 'Great Lost Work'**. This passage offers essential background information to better comprehend Ingo's perspective on the current societal attitudes – or lack thereof – towards psychic abilities.

Moreover, as the pages of this book lack vivid colors, I have turned to an artificial intelligence (AI) image generator to bring my experiences and the contents of the Historical Tidbits sections to life.

For a more unmediated experience of my encounters, some of the photographs and documents referenced in the pages ahead can be found on the website conjunction.world, along with additional details about the places I visited.

THE RUN-UP

We Are Not Alone

In June of 1972, my uncle Ingo Swann,[1] who would later become one of the US Government's top psychic spies, crossed the threshold into Stanford Research Institute (SRI), a renowned West Coast think tank and covertly funded haven. From that point on he became ground zero for what he called "ultra-ultra-ultra-secret" missions. Eleven months later, in May of 1973, he sent out a meticulously crafted letter, containing fragments of his mind-bending discoveries so beyond human comprehension it seemed to defy all laws of reality. Though cryptic in nature, his later writings went further and hinted at a complex web of players involved in inconceivable clandestine operations. But in this dispatch, he spoke openly and boldly: we are not alone on this planet. Decades later in his enigmatic disclosure, **Penetration: The Question of Extraterrestrial and Human Telepathy**,[2] he revealed a shocking truth, Earth was a battleground for two warring races of unearthly creatures. And we, mere pawns in their deadly game, were being manipulated and

---

[1] To learn more about Ingo and the creation of Remote Viewing, refer to the section titled "Ingo Swann" in Historical Tidbits. If you want a deeper understanding of his experiences, visit the website ingoswann.com.
[2] For a short summary of the book, check out the section titled "Exploring the Link" in Historical Tidbits.

controlled by these shadowy entities. As if that wasn't terrifying enough, Ingo's close friend and renowned author of **The Mothman Prophecies**, John Keel, delivered a chilling statement: "Perhaps the planet earth is nothing more than a gigantic farm. We unfortunately are the crop."

Despite the messages from Ingo, the unsettling fact we may be living alongside and under the control of unseen forces is not a recent discovery; it is a long-standing situation that has haunted us since time immortal.

In fact, I would argue what is being called "catastrophic disclosure" in the UFO/UAP[3] community, that would be the disclosure of information about the non-human origins of anomalous technology and these beings' involvement with us, if released to us, having significant implications for humanity on a cosmic and political level, happened nearly 50,000 years ago thanks to paintings on a cave wall in Indonesia – and maybe even earlier but we just haven't stumbled upon it yet.

In ages past, ones from this "catastrophic disclosure" world or worlds or world within worlds, we might call it the multiverse, existing alongside of us, were called such things as gods, ancestors, star people, travelers, saviors, and monsters. This "phenomenon" has been ingrained in ancient history, spanning across the world. Evidence of some other beings' existence with us can be found in oral traditions passed down through generations, religious texts, intricate stone carvings, mythical tales, cautionary fables, and whispered campfire stories. Void, however, of any concrete evidence, we now perceive these tales of otherworldly beings as mere figments of imagination.

Yet, these stories of their existence traces back to a select group of individuals who claimed to have experienced such encounters firsthand, the transcenders. These individuals possessed a profound understanding of the connection between all living beings through potent "magic." Ones who saw themselves as emissaries to the transcendent space.

---

[3] The abbreviation UFO was officially coined in 1952 by the US Air Force, inspired by pilot Kenneth Arnold's report in 1947 of seeing mysterious objects flying. In 1987, the mass media started to use the term unidentified aerial phenomena (UAP) after reporting on a meeting of Ufologists at the "International Symposium on Unidentified Aerial Phenomena." The Pentagon even established a task force specifically for UAPs in 2020. After that, UFO was often associated with extraterrestrial beings, while UAP became the preferred scientific term to avoid any connotations/alignments with things "alien." See the note "Exploring Otherworldly Possibilities" for more information on the origin of these theories.

Early records reveal that individuals would enter an altered state through intense meditation or by consuming hallucinogens, allowing them to visit the invisible land, crossing over into the domain of otherworldly beings with the help of a guide or Spirit Master, passing through temporal openings in rocks and caves. Once inside, an ethereal part of them descended downward, giving us a sense of direction, and explored this shadowy world. When they returned, they depicted their experiences through paintings and carvings on sacred rocks or walls near the caves or portals they had traveled through, which we now label as "outdoor art galleries" or "rock art," but often more specifically as "pictographs" – paintings and drawings – and "petroglyphs" – carvings.

While many consider these installations as reflections on hallucinations, life, or even as boundary markers, they may hold more significance as glimpses into the invisible world. For example, rock art researcher Kenneth Lymer explores the impact of shamanistic imagery in his article, "Shimmering Visions: Shamanistic Rock Art Images from the Republic of Kazakhstan." He notes that the patinated sandstone of the area used for the art not only brought life to the images, but also symbolized the power of the location. The carvings, along with their significant imagery, were believed to be a representation of personal experiences and encounters with "other-than-human" beings during a trance state. This suggests that these petroglyphs had both a spiritual and visual purpose.

But unfortunately, our society has reduced them to mere tourist destinations, with people leaving their mark on the rocks designated for photography and admiration. In doing so, we fail to recognize the true worth that was inherited from those who embarked on journeys of shamanism, prophecy, and divination, seeking to establish a connection with the intangible region to gain "gifts," "protection," and "knowledge."

Fascinatingly, however, these symbols called today by us as rock art go beyond geographical boundaries. Evidence of this can be found in southwest Finland, where a 4,000-year-old snake staff was unearthed. This discovery aligns with nearby rock art depicting human figures holding snake-shaped objects, also dating back to about the same time period. It is believed that the shamans who held these snakes used them as guides into the spiritual realm, both literally and metaphorically. An article from **The Independent** published in 2024 titled "The Thousand-Year-Old Mystery of the Giant Snake Found in Drawings Across the World" asserts that "the widespread presence of snake mythology and religious iconography suggests its ancient origins and the fact that humans worldwide have been compelled to worship and revere serpents for potentially tens of thousands of years." Across numerous ancient cultures, in fact, serpents were known as the guardians of the Underworld or messengers between demesnes. In the **Bible**, Satan, or the Devil, is referred to as the "Ancient Serpent," cast down into and residing within his own jurisdiction, while in Hindu mythology, Shesha, one of the primal beings of creation, was the king of all Nāgas, divine or semi-divine, half-human, half-serpent beings that reside in the Netherworld.

And because to the peoples of ancient times, these "others" with very close connections and connotations with snakes/serpents reached by going down were very real, it appears that they were in some type of servitude to these beings as a result. It seems in exchange for these beings' "gifts," "protection," and "knowledge," an act was required on behalf of the humans. This often involved sacrificing possessions or even lives, sometimes in large numbers, to appease them. This practice can be traced back to civilizations before the Greeks and Hebrews, with evidence found in Mesoamerican and European cultures.

Sacrifice was not limited to one isolated culture, but instead, it was a worldwide custom. Fascinatingly, French comparativist (one who studies comparative mythology to uncover common themes and features) Julien d'Huy has pieced together a possible ancient story involving snakes. In this Paleolithic tale, snakes are closely tied to rain and storms, as well as water sources. They are said to control these natural elements and may demand human sacrifices or material goods in exchange for unblocking rivers or other water sources.[4]

It appears that from the earliest moments of our development on Earth, we have been cognizant of this "other" world lurking beneath us. We associated it with snakes and believed that these creatures held power over us and our surroundings and were willing to offer ourselves to gain whatever benefits we believed they could provide us. And so it was throughout history, that sacrifice and visioning often went hand in hand, for ironically, it was these same transcenders, who once back from their

---

[4] The Zuni, also known as the A:Shiwi people of the American Southwest, have a story about the first humans who were created and lived in an underworld. These people were forced to bring a witch with them to the world above because he had control over rain clouds.

"spiritual journeys," decided who and what and how many of who and what got sacrificed.

In contemporary academia, we refer to the ancient humans' ability to cross invisible thresholds as "supernatural potency," but in the rock art of the ancient San people of South Africa, it was depicted as what we in the western world call polka dots.

For centuries, patterns have served as a bridge between the abstract world and our modern world. And polka dots are no exception; they hold symbolic meanings that trace back to ancient times. In fact, Lesotho in South Africa is where we find an abundance of hunter-gatherer rock art, with detailed explanations provided by a San informant who kept the tradition of painting alive. Numerous efforts have been made to document these paintings over the past few decades, including the Analysis of the Rock Art Lesotho (ARAL) project. The carbon-dating of these drawings reveals their origins in the early second century and their continued use into present times.

The artwork itself is intriguing for several reasons. It portrays boat-shaped patterns formed by phosphenes – possibly the inspiration for the universal abstract art forms and motifs found in cultures around the world, they are often seen as waves, dots, zigzags, grids, and nested curves that appear to our eyes during blackouts or periods of sensory deprivation – snake designs, and therianthropes – creatures that are both human and animal in appearance. It is within this artwork we find these invisible threshold crossings weren't just a one way street. Nor did it always go as planned.

In his academic paper titled "Dots and Dashes: Cracking the Entoptic Code in Bushman Rock Paintings," Thomas A. Dowson explains how the concept of "supernatural potency" refers to shamans' ability to connect with the spirit world and harness powers beyond the laws of nature within their own body. This is depicted in many rock paintings, where such interactions with the spirit world could have dangerous consequences. In one specific painting, known as ARAL 175 and dated to around 300 CE, researchers have identified a feline figure being pursued by or pursuing several human figures.

The San people viewed felines as powerful and potentially dangerous animals, often associated with shamanic transformations. They believed that during trances, shamans' hair would stand on end, and they may even physically transform into a feline if they were not able to control the dangerous powers from the spirit world i.e., became possessed. This interpretation is reinforced by the presence of tiny red dots scattered throughout the scene, which are thought to represent supernatural potency according to Dowson.

In the past, there have been numerous indigenous cultures that have left behind intriguing evidence of otherworldly beings entering our dimension, either by possession – taking over a shaman's body – or on their own. These ancient peoples have depicted hybrid animal figures emerging from a "flying boat" or an area of invisibility and at times, too, tall human-like figures that suddenly emerge from fissures in the rocks.

They also described beings who could take on the form of an animal while wearing a human skin cloak – possibly shamans, but also supernatural shapeshifters. The Indigenous peoples of the American Southwest have even depicted harmful entities known as Skinwalkers who could transform into or possess animals, giving them the ability to travel quickly and remain hidden. Similarly, ancient Mesopotamians believed in powerful demons that were part human and part animal, coexisting with them and affecting their daily lives. These entities were often represented in stone engravings resembling those found in ancient Egyptian depictions of gods as part human-like and part animal. Today, the winged image of Baphomet[5] – with a goat's head and feet and a human body – has become synonymous with Satanic representation.

Throughout various cultures and eras, these otherworldly creatures, depicted as half animal and half human, have been a recurring phenomenon. They appear in different forms and at different times, not just as isolated symbols within a specific culture. In an article titled "Archaeologist Finds Striking Similarities Between Prehistoric Rock Art In Iran And America," a comparison is drawn between two winged human-like figures: one etched onto a rock face in the remote Teymareh valley near Khomein, Iran, dating back thousands of years, and another carved

---

[5] Although the term first appeared in relation to the Knight Templars in their trials in the 11th century where they were accused of worshipping a heathen idol by this name, as an image recognized as today's occult icon, that happened in the 19th century with a two-volume book **Dogme et ritual de la haute magie (Transcendental Magic: Its Doctrine and Ritual)**, written by the French occultist Éliphas Lévi. The image, one of binary opposites showing the being to be both male and female and representing the occultists' ideas of as above so below, is volume two's frontispiece drawing named by Lévi as a "Sabbatic Goat."

into a rock formation in Yellowstone National Park, in the United States believed to be just as ancient. The resemblance between these two figures is too remarkable to dismiss.

Which brings us back to those paintings in a cave in Indonesia. There is no evidence the cave was used to live in, consequently the use of the cave to express the drawings seems purposeful. In accordance with this, there are expressions of figures on this cave's walls; they are depicted as part animal and part human. According to Adam Brumm, co-author of a study published in the journal **Nature** and associate professor at the Australian Research Centre for Human Evolution, the depiction of therianthropes in ancient art within this cave may be the earliest indication of our ability to conceptualize beings that do not exist in the physical world.[6] This fundamental concept has played a significant role in shaping modern religion. Therianthropic figures can be found in the folklore and fictional stories of various cultures around the world, often revered as deities, spirits, or ancestors in many faiths.

It seems even pre-historic humans were influenced by creatures that straddled the line between the physical and phantasmal realms. Yet there is another element to these 50,000-year-old cave paintings that cannot be ignored. The mysterious depictions of creatures with both human and animal features may symbolize a hunting story, suggesting the beings in the artwork were hunters while people were their prey. We may pass this scene off as part of an imaginative tale or myth being told, but what if it was not?

Nestled inside this idea is the uncanny valley concept, one of the most well-known and intriguing philosophical musings of modern times, proposing a significant dip in human emotional response when encountering an artificial object that closely resembles a human but isn't — this would be the negative response that people have towards realistic robots. It was first conceptualized by Masahiro Mori, a Japanese robotics professor, in 1970, who coined the term "bukimi no tani gensho" or

---

[6] These illustrations are older than the well-known "Lion-man" from Germany, which depicts a human figure with the head of a lion and is estimated to be 40,000 years old. Interestingly, a continent and ages away, in ancient South African San tradition, if shamans amid a violent trance were not taken care of, it was believed that they would transform into a lion. This lion was thought to have supernatural abilities, able to take on various forms to deceive people and strike fear into them. It even had the power to transform into a human.

"uncanny valley phenomenon." This phenomenon can be observed globally and raises questions about the evolutionary history of humanity.

There are many theories as to why this is, and one known as the predator theory, offers a more supernatural explanation for this response. It suggests humans evolved to be cautious of beings resembling humans due to a past encounter with a humanoid predator.

Across various cultures and myths, stories of these creatures have been passed down, including the Skinwalkers I previously mentioned. These widespread beliefs point to some truth behind the predator theory and its influence on human perception and emotions towards human-like beings.

Even Ingo observed, "We have to remind ourselves that in most premodern societies the supernatural did not refer to illusions or delusions, as has been taught during the modern period."

All that being said, Ingo declared in **Penetration**, "If one meditates on all of the above, it can become somewhat clear that the existence of the UFOs [and thereby whatever is operating them whether such objects are hallucinations or real technology] is not what is being covered up – because they ARE seen, photographed and videotaped." So maybe the real truth lurking behind "catastrophic disclosure" is what is feared is not that the entities exist, and we have obtained technology from them, but rather just like those transcenders of old, the ones in charge of who and what got sacrificed – the cost of the "gifts" and "knowledge" – it was what we did, or should I say decided to sacrifice, to acquire those technological endowments or even maybe for some to stay off the menu, so to speak?

Versions of Them

In the past and in these other beings' presence, there was both wonder and dread as they possessed immense power and held great significance in the lives of those who encountered them. Today's media industry thrives on these legends and myths filled with mysterious occurrences and extraordinary feats: bloodcurdling thrillers that make us seek shelter under blankets or cling to someone for comfort; fantastical adventures that take us to other realms. But in the reality of our modern society where logic reigns supreme, we often dismiss such experiences as mere faith or elaborate fantasies – figments of our wild imaginations – or even symptoms of insanity.

Nonetheless, this world of faith, imagination, and perceived madness continues to confront us and as the lines between these concepts blur and bend, refusing to be easily categorized or explained, the undeniable truth becomes harder to ignore.

Thus, if the idea is even considered as a potential reality, using the anthropomorphic term "they" are depicted in seemingly infinite variations without any constraints. The depictions are getting increasingly extraordinary, each one surpassing the last with its connections to either our potential salvation or destruction – but sadly this too is not new.

Over the ages many versions have been crafted to represent them, each one unique and enchanting in its own way. In modern times, the foundation of our interpretation of these beings is often linked to the provinces of the supernatural and otherworldly, with a particular emphasis on their connection to UFOs. This depiction usually presents them as either aliens from a distant planet or multidimensional beings who have crossed into our world from alternate dimensions or higher realm[7] or even both.

Lately, there has been another layer added to this complexity – a return to an age-old dilemma: are these beings "good" like angels, or are they "evil" like demons, with us caught in the middle? And even more troubling, could they be deceiving us by appearing benevolent when they are nefarious and malevolent entities? There may also be malevolent forces at work, preventing us from seeing these beings as anything but benevolent. Some even speculate we are seeing astral bodies of other humans or more confounding that we are trapped in a simulation. Of course, these beings could simply be time travelers from the future or the past, as that may one day become or once was possible.

Our Reality Management

In late June of 1992, anticipation abounded as Ingo arrived at a meeting of "interested" individuals. They were gathered to discuss the enigma of UFOs and their occupants – a topic that had long perplexed them. As Ingo began speaking, his words carried weight and urgency. He spoke of a telepathic boundary between these entities and us, and how their nature was intertwined with psychic phenomena. But what truly

---

[7] See "Exploring Otherworldly Possibilities" in Historical Tidbits.

made them conundrums, he explained, was that they did not conform to our understandings and realities. We try to interpret and understand them through our own limited lenses – science, astrophysics, technology, politics, psychology, culture, religion, philosophy, sociology – but their realities remain just out of reach.

Ingo's theories were forged from a horrifying truth – an electrifyingly frightening encounter experienced by a growing number of us known as "the abductees." These individuals are snatched against their will.[8] Once targeted, these unwitting participants often find themselves subjected to unimaginable horrors – physical abuse such as scars, burns, and unexplained injuries; changes in their psyche and way of thinking; and heavy doses of missing or unexplained time. They may also experience abrupt sensory changes, night terrors, and an onslaught of hallucinations and voices they cannot explain or understand. And despite their best efforts to protect themselves – leaving cameras and recording equipment around them while they sleep, surrounding themselves with light and noise as a defense – nothing seems to work. Time and time again, they are taken – mentally and physically abused, often sexually – in a manner that leaves no evidence behind.

These victims have begun now to question whether what has been portrayed to them – and to the public – as mere hauntings or alien encounters – notably involving little grey men with spaceships – may be something far more sinister. And when we can no longer brush these abduction experiences, these inconvenient truths, aside, a new explanation of and for "it" or rather "them," is needed. That's why I believe we're currently being bombarded by them and what I call their human helpers with an endless stream of information about their identities, actions, and desires.

The intricate process of constructing a fresh understanding and explanation – fittingly dubbed "a new reality" by Ingo – for these phenomena, who they are and their agenda, particularly those involving abductions, demands three essential tasks that all require exceptional information-management abilities.

First, facts, evidence and information that support the desired reality must be highlighted and taught as absolute truth to prove its validity. Second, any facts or information that could dismantle or discredit the new

---

[8] See Historical Tidbits under the note "Exploring Otherworldly Possibilities."

reality must be carefully disposed of. And finally, useful illusions need to be strategically introduced when the first two tactics fail to maintain consistency and creativity within the new reality.

Ingo dubbed this process "spin doctoring," which has become increasingly successful because we, as humans, tend to favor illusory information over other types. As he noted, "illusory information can serve quite excellent purposes" due to the lack of desire among the masses for any other type of information.

Essentially, spin doctoring is comprised of two main components: creating illusory information that aligns with what people want to hear and eliminating any inconvenient information. This is made easier by our natural inclination towards an "information comfort zone," where we are resistant to having our realities or visions tampered with. In fact, most people only accept information that fits into their established perceptions and ignore anything that challenges them.

And too, Ingo recognized this inherent human behavior allows for the manipulation of reality by a select few on behalf of the majority who are seen as easy to control. In short, it's a method known as "reality management," used by those in power to maintain their dominance over the masses.

But who exactly are these select few?

In his book, **Resurrecting the Mysterious**, Ingo explores the powerful forces that contribute to our collective ignorance and warns against underestimating their influence. He refers to these forces as the "Equalizer" or the "establishment." According to Ingo, this group is primarily driven by a desire for power and money, which leads them to manipulate and control others for their own gain. Unfortunately, many individuals are willing to betray their own kind in pursuit of these desires, making it easier for the Equalizer to maintain its hold on society. The manipulation of illusion is used to fulfill personal desires and perpetuate false ideas that serve the Equalizer's agenda. In contrast, there are also unseen energies said to guide humanity towards a higher state of being. However, their invisibility has always been a mystery, which Ingo argues can be understood once we unravel the workings of the Equalizer. Defeating the Equalizer is no simple task, as it disregards truth and facts in favor of conformity. And when all else fails, death becomes their ultimate solution – whether it be death of ideas or even physical death itself.

The Run-Up

To reveal the players operating behind this equalizing establishment mask, we must embark on a voyage through some of Ingo's written works.

Among Ingo's literary outputs is a unusual piece, or rather a manifesto, titled **What Will Happen to You When the Soviets Take Over**.[9]

Published by Ingo's own company, Starform, in 1980, it is certainly a departure from his previous and subsequent productions.[10]

In this book, Ingo lays out an overview of the Soviets' plan to conquer America and subsequently the rest of the world, while also focusing on how it impacts various professions. The bulk of his work provides a comprehensive guide on what we can expect under Soviet rule.

As for a personal note on this book, Uncle Ingo was adamant that every member of our family had their own personal copy of the book. We were required to read it and constantly quizzed by him on its content. As a result, when I was a freshman in high school and had to give a book report on politics in American history, I used this book as my main source.

I don't remember much about the report itself, but I do recall receiving a lot of strange looks from my classmates and even having a visit from the school guidance counselor to check on my home life. Two years later, in 1984, the movie **Red Dawn** was released, which depicted a fictional World War Three invasion of the US by an alliance of Soviet and Latin American states. It was incredibly popular at my high school. Personally, I felt vindicated as everyone was now interested in guerrilla/resistance fighters – known as "Wolverines" – against communist actors like the ones in the movie but the stigma of my report remained in my high school social history, nonetheless.

One aspect of this book that stands out to me is Ingo's resolute conviction in America's inevitable domination – not as a mere possibility, but as an unavoidable reality. This idea was referenced by illustrator Tom Joyce in **Stardust Highways**. Given the strained relationship between the US and Soviet Union during the book's creation, along with Ingo's intense abhorrence towards Marxist beliefs, this concept holds significant meaning. But I am convinced that there is a deeper meaning encapsulated

---

[9] A free PDF of the mechanical art for this book, meaning the pages that were sent to the book's printer, can be found on the website ingoswann.com.

[10] The book's illustrator, Tom Joyce, brought his own vibrant touch to my book **Stardust Highways** by sharing his story of how he joined forces with Ingo to add his illustrations to Ingo's Soviet book.

within this, something that cannot be understood at face value, something that must be perceived in a more conceptual and symbolic way.

Based on this, let's now examine Ingo's thoughts on the Soviet Union in his online serial memoir **Remote Viewing: The Real Story (RVRS)**: "Having had good reason, as of 1967, to research Marxism, I knew a great deal about it and international Communism, and even about the KGB." Continuing a few paragraphs later, he states, "Once one got into the dimensions of international Marxist-Communism, well, here is a big and very important part of human history." Despite appearing very late in the book, "Chapter 40," these quotes and an earlier reflection in "Chapter 13" of **RVRS** I find are connected.

In "Chapter 13" of **RVRS**, he mentions a book that discusses a shadow government[11] operating within the CIA. This secret network includes members from various intelligence branches such as State and Defense Departments, Army, Navy, and Air Force, as well as experts in codes, propaganda, and espionage. Even seemingly innocent private companies and academic groups are involved. According to Ingo's comments, this shadow government makes decisions without the knowledge or consent of our elected officials. That sounds a lot like what those in conspiracy circles call the Deep State – an alleged covert alliance between federal government officials, specifically within the FBI and CIA, collaborating with influential financial and industrial groups and leaders to wield authority either alongside or within the democratically elected US government.

To confirm Ingo's veiled message in **RVRS**, we must once again decipher Ingo's words. This time, we will unravel his comment about "the dimensions of international Marxist-Communism" and how it is a significant aspect of human history, notice not just modern history. Oh, so something from a different dimension perhaps which has been with us as a species a very long time?

To do this properly, we need to establish a clear framework and break down each component to fully understand its meaning. Let's start with first quote "investigate Marxism, knowing a great deal about international Communism and the KGB." Putting aside how he came to acquire

---

[11] The authors of **The Invisible Government** refer to it as such. They note that former CIA director Allen Dulles was the main individual responsible for shaping the Invisible Government. In fact, they argue without his influence the rise of the Invisible Government to a position of unparalleled strength would not have been possible. See "Ah, Yes!" in Historical Tidbits for more about Dulles.

information about the secret operations of Soviet Russia despite his very overt claim he had no direct involvement in such clandestine operations for a series of "fictional" stories I plan to write soon, his intention with mentioning the KGB in this sentence is to highlight the presence of a covert organization operating in secrecy and exerting influence on events from behind the scenes.

The connection between these undercover agents and what initially appears to be a global Communist ideology is best explained by rephrasing "international Communism" as its official name: Communist International, also known as the Third International or Comintern.

In essence, it was an insurgent organization that promoted both local and worldwide violence in pursuit of revolution, specifically to overthrow capitalism and replace it with their own form of economic control. This meant destroying all forms of democracy and implementing their own version of economic governance.

The modern iteration of this group's main objective, according to Ingo in his Soviet book, is to implement a grand strategy that includes controlling the entire planet, eradicating any ideas of freedom, directly manipulating decision-makers, and de-individualizing the population. How will they achieve this? By eliminating military opposition, getting rid of those who are educated or knowledgeable, installing a puppet government, and subjugating the masses.

And who oversees this? A Ruling Élite. Who exactly makes up this Ruling Élite? They are a select few who hold all the power and enjoy special privileges that come with their position. And how do they maintain their authority? By implementing strict systems of control and oppression to suppress any resistance or progress from the people. Groups of conspiracy theorists, who may not seem so far from the truth given what is happening in the world today, are familiar with them too, labeling them as The New World Order, with the Deep State acting as their lackey.

Ingo used a unique term in his Soviet book to describe them: "nachal'stvo," roughly the establishment. He explained it as the privileged few in control, ruling over the slaves beneath them. However, this term held a slightly different meaning in the Soviet regime. As Moshe Lewin explains in his essay contained within the book **Stalinism: Essays in Historical Interpretation**, they were essentially puppets who were constantly under scrutiny and control by those above, leaving them with no security or power of their own. By making this observation, Ingo is reminding us that they are mere human operators, ultimately under the control of those with real power – the ones he claims come from a different dimension – but also in terms of the nachal'stvo, ultimately just another group in a long line throughout history.

This then ties to what he wrote in **Penetration**: "Of course, we assume we are the ones constructing our realities." The notion of cover stories regarding these non-human figures and their hidden identities registered in my mind as he espoused, "If ENOUGH information based in identified and proven factoids is assembled and aligned," a startling revelation may surface – the true identity of those constructing our realities remains a mystery. I would certainly say this is definitely a significant and crucial aspect of human history.

As I pondered these ideas, a feeling of immense uneasiness engulfed me. Ingo often considered, as mentioned earlier, that our blindness to the truth was not due to randomness, but rather intentional manipulation and control. He viewed this perception of us and them as a "reality dilemma" that plagues humanity, probing into the disconcerting realization that our perceived reality is only a carefully constructed façade in his book **Reality Boxes: and Other Dark Holes in Human Consciousness**.

He believed we are trapped in an endless cycle of ignorance and denial and vividly described the struggle to break free from this metaphorical prison, comparing it to a frantic escape from a cell. And like a prisoner needing to understand the layout and workings of their jail to successfully escape, one must also deeply examine the nature of this reality box – specifically in terms of us and them – to truly break free from its constraints.

Unraveling the complexities of "our reality" is not a simple task, especially when there are numerous influential and connected individuals exerting tremendous power involved. However, there are often other hidden forces at work in the shadow world.

There is A LOT Going on in the Shadows

Ingo often regaled me with tales of fairies and gremlins, when I was a young college grad, filling my mind with images of fantastical creatures and supernatural energy beings. It did not take me long however to discover these stories were more than just fanciful musings – they were foraged from corporeality. The air inside Ingo's home at 357 Bowery[12] was always thick with a playful energy, as if the walls themselves were alive. But there were also darker energies hanging about within, ones with sinister intent that made my skin crawl – I'll go into those later. Ingo, nevertheless, remained firm in his belief that ghosts did not exist, at least not in the way I had assumed. Little did I know that one day, far in the future, I would find out the truth for myself.

It was the year 2009, and our ghost conversation took place during one of my weekly trips to New York for work. I worked in a transitional role, which required me to stay at 357 Bowery during the week and return home on weekends. My preferred mode of transportation was Amtrak, a train service that offered me the most direct commute from my home in Virginia to New York City. On Friday afternoons, I would take any available seat on my way down to Washington, DC, but on Mondays, I always made sure to secure a spot in the quiet train car. As I traveled from DC to New York in the early hours of the morning, this quiet car provided the perfect opportunity for some much-needed sleep – at least until we reached Trenton, New Jersey. By then, the rush of commuters flooded the train car and finding an empty seat became nearly impossible. From that point on, even with the car's strict rules against talking or phone calls, it was often filled with commuters who did anything but.

As the train rumbled along the tracks from DC to Trenton, I dozed fitfully, always waking up at stops. Being situated in the only path of entry or exit for the train car, I could hardly afford to be asleep when people passed by. At the Wilmington, Delaware stop, a man dressed in a long trench coat and weathered hat strode past me, proceeding further into the car. His demeanor was somewhat off, and it was hard to ignore his unusual choice of attire for the weather. My senses were always on high alert, carefully taking note of the people and happenings around me ever since the moment Ingo had taught me to pay attention to my surroundings when I first moved into his home almost two decades prior; it had become ingrained in me. Regardless, I pushed aside my unease and tried to focus on the other passengers around me. There was quite an

---

[12] Ingo welcomed me into his home, a building in Manhattan's East Village, on three separate occasions during his lifetime. The first was after I finished college, the second after I graduated from business school, and the third as a convenient place to stay during my work weeks in New York City.

assortment of interesting characters on board, and he was the least of my concerns.

But I did find it hard to get rid of the feeling something was amiss as he took a seat a few rows ahead. Now fully awake, I found myself unable to drift back to sleep after the train departed from the station. Seeking some solace and distraction, I turned to gaze out the window and watched as dawn gradually illuminated the nearby landscape.

As the train came to a halt at its next stop, Philadelphia, I was drawn into the chaotic activity surrounding me. People hustled on and off the train, pushing and shoving as they did. That is when I noticed someone take trench coat man's seat, only I hadn't seen him pass by me. Curiosity piqued; once the train pulled out of the station, I was unable to resist my urge to investigate. I began walking up and down the rows of seats, searching for any trace of him. But everything seemed normal, no bags or luggage left behind, no abandoned trench coat or hat. It was as if he had never even been there in the first place. Yet something told me that wasn't the case.

That night at dinner with Ingo, I eagerly recounted the story from beginning to end, leaving no detail unspoken. Ingo's attention was captured, his mood noticeably lighter than it had been in recent weeks as he sipped on his vodka and soda and puffed away on his cigar. His words flowed effortlessly, offering a perspective that was both erudite and intriguing. "You saw a ghost," he stated confidently, though quickly backtracking to add, "but of course, there is no such thing." My eyebrows rose in confusion, but I waited for him to continue. "What you saw was an energy trail," he explained. My mind struggled to comprehend this concept until he clarified further. "It could have been the man's last moments, replaying themselves over and over again in an endless loop like a billboard message on repeat." Ingo paused, taking another draw from his cigar before adding, "I could sense those energy vibrations, and my mind translated them into a kind of movie trailer." Years later, I would discover this phenomenon is known as a residual haunting.[13] But in that moment, with Ingo's words still ringing in my ears, I found it hard to not think I had been plopped into the midst of such an enduring energy loop.

---

[13] It is believed such a haunting occurs from a traumatic or stressful event during which energy is dispersed into the environment, causing the imprinting or recording of the event into and onto the environment. This energy imprinting is then replayed over and over.

Without taking even a moment to gather his thoughts, Ingo's voice carried on. As he spoke, the weight of his words lingered in the air, heavy and attention-grabbing. "If one were to catch a glimpse of a ghost, there are several possibilities," he explained with confidence. "Perhaps they are simply seeing trails of energy left behind by those who have passed on as I just explained. Or it could be a meeting with the consciousness of a living person, or even someone who has departed from this world. And then there is the chance that it is not human at all – never was, and never will be." His tone was matter of fact as he continued, "You see, using the term 'ghosts' is completely inaccurate."

Leaving aside the non-human entity situation for now, with time, I came to understand the intricacies of the meeting of consciousness as Ingo called it and how it is intertwined with the astral realm. As a firm believer in reincarnation, Ingo examines systematically the astral plane and one's journey towards reincarnation and enlightenment in his book **Resurrecting the Mysterious**, a book edited by journalist and author Nick Cook. It was published posthumously after Ingo's passing but written intermittently between the late 1980s and early 1990s.

After reading all of Ingo's books, including several unfinished works, I began to grasp the complexities of this precinct. Here, there are two distinct situations at play: 1) those who consciously or unconsciously ride the tides of the astral space through an out-of-body experience (OBE), perceiving the world from a location outside their physical body; and 2) those who may have died but are unable to find their way to the singularity – known by many names such as heaven, nirvana, the source, etc. – or be reborn through reincarnation.

As for those departed souls who linger in the astral sphere instead of moving on to their designated afterlife or starting a new life, there are various speculations as to why this may be. Some believe they may have died traumatically and unexpectedly without fulfilling their life's purpose. They may not even realize they are dead and instead engage in hiding or even merging with objects or individuals to control or take over said people or things. Emotions also seem to play a role in this state – loved ones holding onto them or vice versa, for example.

In this book too, Ingo wrote about the concept of empathy between individuals. He proposed that we are constantly and unconsciously connected on a telepathic level. He stated assertively: "All thought is telepathic – whether it be in our conscious, subconscious, or supraconscious states. It is impossible to shield our thoughts and beliefs from radiating outwards, as all things are intricately interconnected in diverse forms and ways." These telepathic thoughts and beliefs have the power to manifest into their own vessel or entity, if given enough focus and energy, he explained. In this capacity, these thought-forms might also be the "ghosts" people perceive.

A Perception Problem?

As to Ingo's ideas on thought-forms, the more I reflected on it the more a new understanding dawned upon me. Suddenly, it hit me – we have dismissed their, these other's, existence due to our inability to perceive them.

Recent headlines, such as "James Webb telescope confirms there is something seriously wrong with our understanding of the universe," shed light on the possibility these beings are indeed present. The advanced technology of the James Webb telescope allows it to read and translate frequencies and light beyond what was previously possible, uncovering more of the previously unseen world.

And if a man-made instrument can achieve this feat, why not a human being? After all, our bodies are complex bioelectric instruments, equipped with sophisticated awareness systems. Surely, we have the potential to tap into these hidden frequencies and decipher their secrets. But as Ingo warned, in **Penetration**, we are caught amid a fierce power struggle over our very existence. And although these forces may have their differences, he noted, they all share one common goal: to ensure humanity remains oblivious to its own inherent psychic abilities. "What a scenario, huh?" Ingo wrote. "Talk about being on the outermost fringes! Fringes so outermost one didn't even know where the fringes were in relationship to anything else." Then later adding, if we were to truly unlock this ability and discover "they" are real, the consequences would be beyond our imagination.

To me, once modern humans came into their own advancements whereby knowledge of our bodies and of our extraordinary perception abilities on a more proliferated scale seemed a possibility, something about our relationship with this hidden world changed and a new course of action was undertaken by a group or groups of them possibly with human actors. In fact, in my search for answers about this, a friend threw out to me a beguiling passage in the **Bible**, specifically from Genesis 11:6-7 regarding the Tower of Babel:[14]

> And the Lord said, Behold, they are one people, and they have all one language, and this is only the beginning of what they will do. And nothing that they propose to do will now be impossible for them. Come, let Us go down, and there confound their language, that they may not understand one another's speech.

Who are the mysterious "us" and why do they want to scatter, isolate, and confuse humans? Ingo addressed this in **Penetration**, stating ETs – or non-human entities – would be exposed if humans were able to penetrate them. They know this, so they actively work to prevent humans from developing psychic abilities. Ingo called this our "psychic castration." This is why ALL forms of psychic research are suppressed or minimized, as they may lead to the dreaded telepathic powers. The only exception is when certain approaches to telepathy are discovered and either proven ineffective or used as a smokescreen to distract from potential success.

Under the surface, and very early on in his career, Ingo figured out we as a species must have some pretty awesome bodies and abilities if "they" are working overtime to keep us from knowing about them, and more importantly how to use them.

To him, the constant effort to conceal this knowledge only confirmed its existence, stating in **Resurrecting the Mysterious** directly that society is governed by Equalizers. We must come to terms with this undeniable truth.

This was reiterated in three concerns Ingo spelled out in a **FATE Magazine** article published in 1992:

1) Our species has developed a complex way of dealing with this terrifying phenomenon: we either ignore it completely, laugh it off as nonsense, argue about its validity, or fall prey to media outlets

---

[14] A story in the **Bible**. Following the flood, the people turned away from God and doubted His plans. Without seeking His guidance, they began constructing a tower to reach heaven. This tower was known as the Tower of Babel, but it was a false temple. God was displeased with their actions and decided to confuse their language so that they could not communicate effectively. As a result, they were forced to abandon their construction of the tower and were scattered all over the earth by God to create different communities.

that dismiss it entirely. The government may also be intentionally spreading misleading information. This subject is not something that can be easily accepted or understood; our reactions are often divisive and chaotic.

2) It may be inferred that the reason why psychic research is dismissed and discredited does not originate from us. This could lead to the conclusion "they" are more involved in our affairs than most realize.

3) These beings are completely vulnerable to human psychic abilities, and they know it. In fact, they seem to actively hinder humans from developing such powers.

Has this been their plan since the beginning of time, promoting a better life by rejecting our abilities and submitting to strict quasi-spiritual beliefs? And all the while, leaving ourselves vulnerable to the control of "them," whoever or whatever they may be, which as far as I can tell has not benefited us in any way.

Maybe we start by understanding two sides of the same coin: one that reveals how our world holds deeper meaning beyond what we can see with our own eyes, as exemplified by the groundbreaking James Webb Telescope. On the other side, we confront the concept that we are capable of perceiving far more than society has allowed us to believe.

Wake Up

As I survey the world around us, it strikes me there is a situation unfolding that we may not even be aware of. Regarding this, within the pages of Ingo's uncompleted and unpublished **Maverick Starbuster**, I come across some poignant words that ring true: if you desire to truly live and thrive, then shake off the drowsy, weighty veil of slumber, and awaken from your stupor!

Still, the depth and complexity of it all felt overwhelming, like trying to untangle a massive web of deceit. And yet, to have even an inkling of understanding meant acknowledging the far-reaching infiltration of our lives by these beings. It was a realization that was hard to take in, for it meant our beliefs, ideologies, cultural norms, and even our technological advancements could have all been influenced or created by them. The thought was both terrifying and maddening. What if they had been manipulating history, steering it towards their own agenda? The betrayal would be incomprehensible. And to add another layer of complication, what if we are also being watched and controlled on an interstellar level by others beyond just them?

Further, it seems this entanglement has been fueled by the resurgence and rebranding of 20th century Spiritualistic[15] ideas, where contacting spirits through seances and Ouija Boards became a popular trend. These ideas have been repackaged into catchy buzzwords and social media jargon, emphasizing the pursuit of communication with non-human entities. It is a predicament which is gaining momentum as organized religion steadily declines in influence.

It is pervasive, not just in the ecospheres of UFOs and otherworldly beings, but also within the Remote Viewing community where connecting with "higher intelligences"[16] is currently trending. This idea has also permeated new therapies and quasi-spiritual organizations that promote a complete, all-encompassing sense of connection and immersion.

When it comes to "contact," for example in the RV world, there has been a shift away from Ingo's protocols for Controlled Remote Viewing, or what Ingo referred to as an intellectual means of obtaining information from a distant location in stages, to using it as a front for establishing communication with non-human "higher" intelligences, i.e., channeling or engaging in mediumship.

Perhaps this is not surprising, as Ingo himself stated that Earth psychics were essentially the enemy. After all, if you want to take control, you must eliminate your adversaries.

In these types of situations, individuals often enter experiences and meeting places without fully comprehending what it means to be a channeler or medium. Unfortunately, they are typically not educated on the risks of being possessed or attacked by malevolent beings while in this state. Some may even be unaware that they are even entering a

---

[15] See "Exploring Otherworldly Possibilities" in Historical Tidbits for an explanation of Spiritualism.

[16] The term is commonly used to refer to advanced "Extraterrestrial Intelligence." In Ingo's opinion, our understanding of "higher intelligences" is limited because we only use a small portion of our brain's capabilities. Therefore, it would be challenging for us to recognize and comprehend the intelligence of more advanced beings. We may think we understand their level of intelligence, but it is difficult to truly grasp what "advanced" intelligence entails.

designated "hijacking"[17] by a hitchhiker location as these spots can be hidden or disguised, making those who do wander into them susceptible to the dangers hiding in the shadows.

Ingo was familiar with this course, as he had served as a medium before and had also traveled on his own as a psychic explorer, connecting with other dimensions and beings.[18]

He had studied the early Theosophists and was well acquainted with their Ascended Masters.[19] He had close connections to Andrea Puharich[20] and his Council of Nine.[21] [22]

---

[17] Spiritual hitchhikers are entities that attach themselves to living persons. It's possible for a person to be accompanied by these unseen presences without even realizing it until they experience strange occurrences or disturbances, especially at home. In some cases, hitchhikers may only remain active for a short period before disappearing, while others can persist and require intervention such as spiritual cleansing to repel or disperse them.

[18] Documents pertaining to his last such adventures called "Moon Recon II," are available on the website conjunction.world.

[19] See "Exploring Otherworldly Possibilities" in Historical Tidbits.

[20] Not only was he a medical doctor, but he also had a reputation for being able to create convincing belief systems. His connections with the wealthy elite on the East Coast and their ties to government agencies like the OSS (CIA's predecessor) and Naval Intelligence helped his work gain attention from the Pentagon's new psyops program head, Lt. Colonel John Stanley. In 1952, Stanley extended an invitation to Puharich to speak at the Pentagon's Research Branch of the Office of the Chief of Psychological Warfare. The topic? Puharich's research with mediums. As a result of his lecture, Puharich and his channeling of entities endeavors were granted "parapsychological" funding by the US government – a note about this can be found in "Ah Yes!" under Historical Tidbits.

[21] In ancient Egypt, there was a tale passed down through generations known as "The Council of Nine." Referred to as "higher intelligences" or evolved gods, who saw humans as a lesser species and used their advanced abilities to control them mentally. Puharich was a believer in this legend and had his mediums contact them. In subsequent channeling sessions where Uri Geller acted as the medium, the "Nine" revealed that they were the source of the unidentified flying objects that people had been reporting.

[22] In a 1998 interview with **Alternate Perceptions**, William Belk shared his thoughts on the paranormal. Belk had established his own research foundation dedicated to studying the unknown. He was a supporter of Puharich's work. In the interview, he described the Council of Nine as unseen beings who control our planet from another dimension. He also mentioned he had seen individuals

The Run-Up

He counted several mediums as close friends, friends with ties to what are called contactee cults and/or UFO religions[23] such as Harold Sherman's emergence within Urantia[24] and to masters of learning such as Viola Pettit Neal's Master Jupiter.[25] Not to mention his dictated from "someplace else" books, **Purple Fables** and **Master of Harmlessness**.

But in the end Ingo's message, as encapsulated in his unpublished surrealistic porn manuscript **Pink Neon**, about all of this was clear: Once in, there is no turning back. It is a transformation, a shedding of one's former self and taking on a suit of "a thousand voices." The fabric is tight, adorned with intricate embroideries of nebulas, stars, and planets, each symbolizing a different facet of this new existence. And with it, one must don a scarlet cape, a bold statement that declares their allegiance to the dangerous life they have chosen.

For within this strange poetry lies a violent rage that courses through the cities and planes of the mind. It obscures the lines between killer and savior, lover and energy, puritan and deviate. Everything is inverted, turned on its head, creating a twisted world where nothing is as it seems. In the distance looms a grand throne, standing tall amidst holy avenues and blocked approaches.

The spiritual traffic jams are evidence of the chaos that reigns here. "His" representatives cling to lampposts of faith, their minds hazy with intoxication from the various dogmas they hold onto.

But in this place, even these devout followers can be transformed into something dark and grotesque. This is not a place for the faint-hearted or the weak-willed.

Off in the distance stands a tall, he tells us, imposing pyramid made of dark, ominous stone. Its peak is crowded with figures – adepts,

---

possessed by entities from other dimensions, some of whom were confined in insane asylums. According to Belk, mediumship was simply renamed as channeling (today it's called "contact") for marketing purposes, but it is essentially the same practice that has existed since ancient times when Hebrew prophets communicated with higher powers. A link to the full article can be found on the website conjunction.world.

[23] A set of beliefs that acknowledges the existence of extraterrestrial beings and UFOs as real entities, along with groups that supposedly facilitate communication between humans and these beings.

[24] See the website: https://haroldsherman.com/urantia/.

[25] See the book **Through the Curtain** by Shafica Karagulla and Viola Pettit Neal.

hierophants, magicians, and enchanters – all engaged in their arcane rituals. Amid it all, blood flows freely as they feed upon each other's throats, their faces twisted in ecstasy or agony. A pyramid of spiritual vampires!

As I watch both the entanglement with them and the chaos around them intensify, it has become clear to me this might be one of "their" intended purposes. Our reliance on technology only serves to add fuel to the already raging fire. In our data-driven world, we have become detached from our true selves, lost in a sea of endless information and distractions. We have forgotten how to connect with each other and ourselves, caught up in the endless pursuit of progress and productivity. We have forgotten the intricate web of connections that bind us to the world around us, guided by invisible threads that keep us in tune with our surroundings. Instead, we rely heavily on cold, hard facts and statistics, dismissing our intuition and inner guidance. Ironically, these facts and figures can be easily fabricated and manipulated at alarming rates. To me, blindly waiting for data to validate our beliefs is like hoping for a ship to Neverland to dock.

With all this floating in the back of my mind, I turned to trying to understand where one can even begin to comprehend the vast complexities of our world, our reality prison, especially if we hope to free ourselves from the entanglement which keeps us snuggly inside of it, one which is growing stronger with each passing day. We may have been conditioned to believe in beings or entities that appear more advanced and intelligent than us, but how can we be sure of their true intentions?

This is why I turned to Ingo's teachings found in his book **Psychic Literacy** and his belief in the coming Psychic Renaissance – a time when we will embrace and utilize our innate psychic abilities instead of relying solely on external sources for information and knowledge.

As human beings, Ingo maintained, we possess the abilities to reason, observe, reflect, and remember – referred to as our intellectual strengths. Additionally, we are aware of our visceral experiences such as emotions, sensations, feelings, sentiments, and instincts, which interact with our intellectual processes.

But despite this, there is a lack of understanding when it comes to our powers of intuition, extrasensory perceptions, connection to future or past events, other dimensions, and memories that predate us. While individuals may have personal experiences with these attributes, without a deeper understanding of them, they can only be fulfilled minimally or sporadically.

It is not enough, though he continued, to simply gather information about these "mystical" traits; we must also understand their significance, a combination of information and meaning. Moreover, it is important to dispel the belief that these attributes are only possessed by a select few individuals, as this misconception can create a sense of isolation from these human experiences. Instead, we should recognize, he profoundly stated, that these abilities are commonly shared among the larger population.

Therefore, I could see, the responsibility falls on our shoulders to have faith in ourselves rather than blindly placing it in external sources coming to us through the words of modern day prophets, substackers, podcasters, YouTubers, or talking heads – and who knows if those talking heads are even real or just AI-generated – that may be manipulating us.

Self-Knowledge

When once questioned about the contents of a sealed envelope, Ingo responded with a sly grin, "if you truly want to know, then open it yourself." Firsthand experience was Ingo's perpetual drumbeat. Journalist/writer Cook concluded himself self-knowledge was Ingo's key message, his ultimate takeaway from **Resurrecting the Mysterious** as the book's editor.

In his opening remarks, Cook emphasized the importance of firsthand experience on the consciousness journey and how it is the only way to access a life beyond the mundane. This sentiment is echoed in Ingo's words throughout the book itself, directing us towards a deeper understanding of ourselves and our true potential.

Out of the countless individuals, Ingo discussed, who enter the center of learning, only a select few ever stop to ask themselves this question: what unique qualities and talents do they bring to the table? Do they approach learning with a passive, armchair mentality that relies on secondhand information, or do they possess a creative essence that demands firsthand experience to fully grasp the learning process?

Our Western society, Ingo argued, stands out for its abundance of armchair intellectuals. They can be found everywhere, in various states of decline and decay. No other culture has reached this level of saturation with these individuals. To make matters worse, this state of armchair intellectualism is highly praised and elevated within our culture. If one tries to discuss the importance of firsthand experiences, they may face unexpected ostracization in vague ways because no one knows how to respond.

In our society, there is a lack of appreciation for the personal experiences of everyday people. Only those who are deemed qualified have their firsthand experiences considered valid. For example, if someone like Joe Schmuck witnesses a UFO landing in his backyard and has a conversation with its occupants, his experience is not given much weight until it is acknowledged by authorities who are considered experts in the field of UFOs.

Continuing, Ingo said, our society places greater trust in secondhand experiences because they are easier to understand and align with consensus knowledge. For every one or two individuals who claim to have seen a UFO, there are thousands who have not – leading us to discount their claims. Plus, learning through secondhand sources is more comfortable and convenient, as it can be done from the comfort of an armchair.

Although certain details may hold some truth, any information that is passed down secondhand is mere speculation. The individuals sharing this information have not personally experienced it themselves and are instead interpreting it based on their own viewpoints.

Sadly, much of our education relies heavily on learning from others' secondhand experiences, so we must reflect on whether or not this approach can be effective and how often we should utilize it.

Most importantly though Ingo argued, studying the paranormal purely through secondhand analysis is not advisable. It's like walking into quicksand for your mind, and you'll end up as a wrecked psychic in the end.

Instead, he put forth, consider this: truth is apparent to those who are open to seeing it. Truth cannot be controlled, only lies can be manipulated.

As we prepare to enter the third millennium with a damaged planet and troubled minds, he acknowledged, searching for answers that cannot be found in the past, it is crucial to acknowledge the power of psychic realization. This innate ability must be preserved from the relentless pursuit of materialism and spirituality. And like all genuine truths, it cannot be attained solely through intellectualization – which is often disguised by layers of complexity – but must first be experienced on a personal level.

As Ingo said in **Everybody's Guide to Natural ESP**: "Self-experience is the only way to know true reality. It is self-experience that leads to common sense, which is always superior to label manufacturing. In fact, self-experience and enlightenment go hand in hand."

Hence, it is up to us to self-knowledge ourselves.

Reality's Seam

It has been referred to as "a realm beyond the veil," the Goblin Universe," a "parallel dimension," and "a place of cultural mythologies: complex systems of beliefs centered around deities." It is a mysterious place, shrouded in myth and legend, of entities or beings, or perhaps even just energy or frequencies, who can cross some type of barrier into our own world and intertwine themselves in our lives. The range of experiences associated with this dominion is truly awe-inspiring, capable of evoking feelings of both elation and terror. Some may even find themselves overwhelmed with a sense of reverence and gratitude, while others might see it as material for lucrative horror films and video games. But despite all the speculation and fascination surrounding it, one question still lingers: is it real? Can such an implausible place truly exist?

There are moments when I crave to live in a world of my own imagination, where the harrowing events and encounters of my past can be dismissed as figments of my innermost fears and desires. But truth always brings me back to earth, reminding me there are some things I cannot simply dismiss as inventive musings. My uncle's presence in my life alone has been enough to bar me from such blissful ignorance. As I've grown from a young adult into motherhood and now being over 50, these incidents continue to weave in and out of my life, taking the most convoluted routes. I thought I could simply label them as mere "experiences," but then something else happened – it began with a dream. It was then that I knew these occurrences were more than just random happenings; they were intertwined with my very being, leaving a mark on my soul that could never be erased.

The dream was meant to alert me, and it did so with a jolt. It began in the basement, that dark and foreboding place where I always feel on edge. As I made my way down the steps, a feeling of disquiet crept over me. I couldn't shake the feeling I had left something open down there, a door or window perhaps, but it was hard to make out in the dim light. I hate these dreams; they always leave me feeling vulnerable and exposed. The thought of leaving something open when I know I shouldn't have in dreams has always been to me unsettling. But as I searched through the darkness, my fear turned to confusion. There, in front of me, was an open window that looked more like a door. In my dream state, it seemed completely real. In a panic, I set about locking the window-like door, my dream mind racing with questions. Had something already made its way through? Was it too late? The weight of uncertainty hung heavy in the air as I frantically secured the opening, praying that whatever lurked outside hadn't already entered.

The next thing I knew I was within the confines of a bustling marina. Boats, of all shapes and sizes, bobbed in the water, some sleek and shiny, others weathered and worn. Small groups of people milled about, discussing rentals and routes. My eyes landed on a cluster of floatation devices that looked like they had seen better days. One was particularly flat, and there was no way I could imagine anyone taking it out onto the open ocean – it seemed like a prime target for hungry sharks. I made my way to the makeshift rental hut and approached the group huddled inside. They looked just as weathered as the boats outside, but their tired smiles were welcoming, nonetheless. With a sigh, I told them my destination: Baltimore. That was the last thing I remember before bursting awake. It was before dawn, Sunday morning, February 18, 2024. Rolling over, I reached for my phone to check the time and saw a new message from Rebecca Hoffberger, the dreamer mastermind behind the American Visionary Art Museum (AVAM)[26] in Baltimore, Maryland. It had been sent late the night before.

Despite her official retirement from the directorship of the AVAM, Rebecca's passion for the museum and its mission still burned strong. At her retirement party hosted by the eccentric John Waters and attended by a diverse array of artists and political figures, including myself, two years prior, she had shared her desire to solidify the museum's endowment; she was back at the AVAM working on just that. The dream came into focus; in my mind, Rebecca and Baltimore were inseparable entities.

---

[26] The AVAM has several of Ingo's metaphysical paintings on display.

The Run-Up

Her text message detailed her "unplanned nap in front of the TV." She had awoken to a different program playing, one that she didn't remember choosing before dozing off. The new show was about a second group of Russian teenagers who had ventured into Mansi territory, an Indigenous people residing in the Ural Mountains of Western Russia and surrounding areas. She believed that the same tragedy had befallen them as it had for another group in 1959. But what really caught my attention was her sense of urgency, which stemmed from a marking on a tree.

I did some quick internet sleuthing. It turned out the second group had been lost but joyfully found; it is the first group, all of whom had died, which has twisted minds ever since. I dug into that.

The tale of the first group is known as the Dyatlov Pass Incident, a cautionary and chilling story of nine Russian college-aged adventurers. Seven men and two women in their early to mid-twenties embarked on a cross-country skiing expedition in the Ural Mountains, where they extend into Siberia, Russia during the harsh winter of 1959. Their journey would meet an untimely and tragic end sometime between February 1st and 2nd. It was not just the fact they had perished, but rather the mysterious circumstances surrounding their deaths that continue to captivate people's attention. Despite being highly experienced hikers and skiers, they succumbed to "a compelling natural force," as described by the 1959 Soviet criminal investigation. The nature of this force, paradoxically, has never been identified.

When the group failed to show up at their destination on time, their families and friends grew worried. It took some time but finally a search party was sent a few weeks later. When the search party arrived at the campsite on Kholat Saykhl, known as "Dead Mountain," in the local Mansi language, they were met with a stymieing scene. The group's tent lay abandoned and in ruins, torn open from the inside and covered in a thick layer of snow. Nine sets of footprints, some barefoot or wearing only socks or a single shoe, led away from the tent and into the snowy landscape. Following these tracks, the searchers soon came upon the first two bodies – two males dressed only in their underwear, their feet bare and exposed to the freezing temperatures. Nearby, they found signs of a small fire that had once been lit, now extinguished and covered in a light dusting of snow. Beyond that, three more bodies were discovered, bringing the total to five. Upon examination, it was determined these five had succumbed to hypothermia – one body showed evidence of a minor head injury that was not fatal in nature. The nearby trees bore marks as if someone had attempted to climb them at one point. The stillness of the area added to the mystery.

A few months later, in May, came a gruesome discovery – four bodies, lifeless and ravaged by unexplained forces. Three of them bore fatal injuries that could only be compared to those of a devastating car crash: shattered skulls, fractured chests, and internal damage beyond repair. Strangely, there were no external wounds to match the severe injuries, as if the victims had been crushed under an immense amount of pressure. Upon further examination, it was revealed that one body was missing its tongue, eyes, lips, and parts of its face were torn away along with fragments of its skull. Another was without its eyeballs, and the third was missing its eyebrows – all signs pointing to a violent and deliberate attack. The investigation into these deaths spawned countless theories, ranging from natural causes to clandestine deeds to political conspiracies. Yet despite all the speculation, no definitive answers have been forthcoming.

Curiously enough, this group had meticulously documented their journey using diaries and film rolls, items later retrieved from the remains of their campsite.[27] As I poured over the recovered materials, two photographs stood out to me. These were the images Rebecca had seen in the show and had texted me about. The first was the final image on the roll, seemingly taken on the day of the group's tragedy. It depicted an ethereal orb against a pitch black background with no discernible objects or landscapes in sight. This photo stands out, appearing to be one-of-a-kind amidst the playful shots documenting their travels that precede it on the roll. The bewildering photo held an air of mystery to me, namely because ethereal orbs captured in photographs are said to be a connection to the realm of spirits. Perhaps this photo is a crucial clue in unraveling the group's fate?

But there is another image that catches my attention: a young man, bundled up in winter gear, standing atop a thick layer of pristine snow, gazing intently at markings etched into a section of tree where bark has been carefully peeled away.

---

[27] Some of the photographs, including the ones mentioned, can be found in an article entitled, "The Grim Theories Behind the Dyatlov Pass Incident" by Aimee Heidelberg. A link to the article is provided on the website conjunction.world.

The Run-Up

The carvings have been identified as Mansi markings, used to count game and mark hunting territories. Some believe, though, these were a warning left by the Mansi people, cautioning others not to enter the territory of the Menk – a Russian version of the infamous Himalayan Yeti. This creature is known as the Abominable Snowman in Nepalese culture and referred to as Metoh Kangmi in Tibetan folklore, a beast described as a mystical being standing at least ten feet tall and dwelling in the snowy peaks of the mountains. This Yeti appears to be a cousin to the American Bigfoot based on the Canadian Sasquatch, the anglicized name of what First Nations peoples of the British Columbia Coast called "Sésquac," meaning "wild man," known as a supernatural shapeshifter. But this comparison to the Yeti may not be entirely accurate.

In fact, Menk are not just one type of monster; rather, they are powerful ancestral forest spirits that have been part of Siberian folklore for centuries. They are said to come from a parallel forest world, coexisting alongside humans but possessing unearthly abilities. These tales originated during a time when paganism and shamanism were still prevalent in Siberia, with beliefs in spirits and the undead running deep among its inhabitants.

Under this prism, these markings may not have been just simple warnings of territorial boundaries or a dangerous creature lying in wait. No, they were, I believe, more like a stark "No Trespassing" sign, a line drawn in the sand between the physical world and the dangerous spirit realm beyond. It was an inflection point, where reality and the unknown met, sending shivers down anyone's spine who dared to venture too close to this threshold. The last photograph of glowing orbs served as a haunting reminder of what this group may have experienced, an encounter with the supernatural forces that claimed the land as their own.

And has it turns out, I know something about that.

As soon as my eyes landed on an image scored into the tree in the photograph, a sense of cognizance spread like wildfire throughout my body. This was what the dream, as conveyed through the doorway, Rebecca, and the disconcerting "Incident," had been trying to piece together for me. The same type of symbol etched into a tree from half a world away had been drawn on a rock deep within the arid landscape of the San Diego Mountains in California; part of a scene permanently incised in my mind – one I had shared with Rebecca at the time. The scene had been a cosmological encounter that defied explanation – but I'll dive into more detail on that in the chapters ahead. It was also quite like a symbol I had drawn back in the mid-1990s as part of yet another unexplainable occurrence – I will unravel that as well in the upcoming pages.

Right then, I finally grasped the true purpose of my firsthand experience – to travel to the intersection of our world and the other side of the silver screen to uncover the truth. Is there an evil influence deliberately creating divisions and fear among humanity? But is there also a good force at work, striving for what we perceive as positive outcomes? Are there powerful figures working in tandem with unseen forces for their own benefit? Or could there be deeper layers to this "situation" that I am not considering? But before embarking on this journey into the lands of non-human entities existing alongside us, I needed some kind of guidebook to help me navigate it once I got there.

A Map

As I mentioned above, throughout human history, there have always been those within clans, tribes, and communities who sought altered states to transcend into realms of divinity and seek knowledge. These individuals were known by many names – prophets, shamans, mystics, medicine men and women, magicians, healers, and witches.

But their practices were not confined to the Western world; they were a universal occurrence in times past. Among the Hmong people of southwest China, the Txiv Neeb or "father/master of spirits" acted as the bridge between the human and spirit worlds. While Bedouin Shamans known as Fugara were masters of desert mysticism with access to the spiritual realm.

In these moments, they would lose their sense of self both literally and figuratively, merging with whatever they were connecting to, the journeys seen as necessary for their people's advancement, livelihood, health, and survival.

This concept of altered states, where one can transcend their own reality and connect with another dimension, has been an integral part of the growing movement to contact higher intelligences, spirit guides, guardian angels, and the like.

Amusingly or not, among Ingo's real-life demonstrations was a simple lesson for me on how to avoid this path. One day in the early 1990s, during a mild weather day, he took me to a small park near 357 Bowery. It was an isolated concrete landscape with scattered benches; a refuge from the towering buildings surrounding it. Each bench held a figure or two, slumped over and lost in a heroin-induced altered state. Ingo referred to this place as the cemetery of lost souls. So cross altered states off the list.

As I pondered my navigation route, my mind swirled with questions. How could we ever hope to comprehend something that was beyond our current capabilities? How could we interact with this unknown and create a reality out of it?

Meaning if you have never seen creatures living in the say rain forests, truly the purest way to know these things is to walk straight into the forest's heart, suddenly you will start to see things you never even imagined. Beautiful creatures and deadly ones too, and ones you might be tempted to touch but really shouldn't. But how would you know which creature was what without some sort of interaction with them?

I found myself at a crossroads, caught in between the familiar and the unknown. How could I understand the concept of a prison, or even something beyond our own sphere without stepping into uncharted territories I may not fully understand? I had no desire to venture into the cemetery of lost souls in search of answers, that is I did not want to alter my state of being.

No, I wished to stay firmly grounded in this space, within my body and mind. And then, I remembered something from Ingo's book **Reality Boxes**. Within its pages, he laid out the concept of "strange mind experiencing" and how it differed from altered states – a condition many people cling to instead of facing their true selves.

During this "peculiar" mental state, the normally clear line between being consciously awake and being unconscious is crossed, allowing elements from the latter to seep into the former. One's awareness of their surroundings may fade away completely. Recollection becomes hazy or non-existent, and the person's inner workings become receptive to outside viewpoints.

Some of these perspectives may feel familiar, like intuition or telepathic connection, while others are more extraordinary, such as precognition, heightened sensory perception, especially in hearing and touch, and expanded awareness. This encompasses both the underlying layers and the distant expanses of consciousness, allowing the individual to be attuned to "deep in" and "far out" dimensions.

As to this expanded awareness, Ingo explained how certain receptors in our physical bodies and nervous systems have been linked to telepathy and remote-sensing abilities. These same receptors can also trigger feelings of alarm or unease, even before we are consciously aware of the source. The information from these receptors is transmitted throughout the entire nervous system in the form of bits, which then must be processed by the conscious mind in the neo-cortex – the area of the brain responsible for perception and awareness during waking hours.

One concept that many people do not fully grasp, he resumed, is that information transfer involves a series of subconscious filters and lenses. These filters have the primary function of decoding the bits of information so that they can be compared to stored memories.

If this process is successful, the information is recognized and can be understood in the brain's neo-cortex. But, if no matching memory storage is found, the information may be perceived as "noise" and cannot be comprehended correctly. It may only make sense in a distorted or confused manner. In this way, he said, "much of the information that gets into the whole brain does NOT get forwarded into the cortex, which is the part of the brain that produces the conscious OF phenomenon."

Ingo, using a quote from another author, insisted that we should trust our instincts and follow our gut feelings because they can guide us towards the truth better than our conscious perceptions of reality.

The human bio-mind is a strange and intricate being, especially combined with our bio-bodies that have the potential to perceive beyond the five senses that are typically taught and recognized. When combined, he remarked, they encompass both the depths of our subconscious and the boundless expanse of our consciousness. In this state, Ingo summarized, one becomes acutely aware of both inner and outer dimensions.

I decided I would use my strange mind experiencing combined with a heightened sense of awareness and perception to guide me through, trusting my gut more than anything else. With this as my backbone, I would go to places where things of an otherworldly nature happen, where perhaps the screen, the cloaking, between our world and theirs is the thinnest; where the mirror has cracks. Why not go all in, and voyage myself, not by contacting them, I would only get their side of the story through my understanding of their side of the story, and I wasn't even sure if that would be the "truth" anyway.

The Run-Up

Armed with only my phone's camera and my own innate perception system, I forwent any fancy equipment or idea of a slick production destined for **YouTube**. This was a personal quest guided by my own senses and perhaps aided by a healthy dose of self-protection against whatever may come my way.

But Where?

As to where I would go, well, I certainly was not going to go to the highly classified US Air Force facility within the Nevada Test and Training Range more readily known as the UFO mecca called Area 51 in the barren lands north and slightly west of Las Vegas, Nevada, or Skinwalker Ranch[28] in Northeastern Utah, near the state's border with Colorado to the east and Wyoming to the north. Based on numerous accounts, many who have gone to these places have come to regret that decision, seeking out the help of modern day exorcists and energy healers. I did not want to be one of them.

It is not like we haven't been warned about these places. Area 51 is well guarded for any number of reasons – ones they tell us about and ones they probably never will – while at varying locations i.e., Dinosaur National Monument and McConkie Ranch around Skinwalker Ranch, its name derived from the Navajo legend of vengeful spirits, are some of the most remarkable yet macabre ancient rock art. I call them warning signs

They depict odd and disconcerting figures – some towering in height, others with six fingers or insect-like eyes – along with scenes of chaos and prizewinners displaying severed heads. Just as we heed traffic signs stating, "Do Not Enter," I saw no reason why these ancient rock art warnings should be any different.

Inspired by Ingo and his extensive research on the apparitions of the Mother Mary, I did go to France to visit Lourdes on an arranged Catholic pilgrimage. What is interesting about Lourdes is its proximity, roughly 50 miles, by my calculations, just under 75 if driving, almost directly north, to Monte Perdido, a suspected UFO base in Spain.[29] I did wonder if there might be more to the area than people suspect.

---

[28] For a brief history on the creation of Skinwalker Ranch see the note "Exploring the Link" in Historical Tidbits.

[29] Please refer to the note "Exploring the Link" in Historical Tidbits.

Otherwise, I honestly just started to search the internet using terms such as petroglyphs, paranormal, UFOs, and anomalies in and around the United States, my home. Many times, these locations were labelled "haunted" with a requisite tragic situation attached to them; I sorted those out. I wondered if what I may experience there would be a cross-current of "intentions" from whatever was there combined with those around me. One slight note of contradiction, I do detail ahead what happened to me at 357 in this regard – the origin for my drawing from the mid-1990s.

Likewise, I opted against Bigfoot adventure tours/walks. Either Bigfoot finds you or he/she/it doesn't. I feel certain the outfitters who run these excursions bank on never encountering the creature. But what if you did?

I tried to avoid popular tourist destinations, except for Lourdes, regarded as cursed land and its cousin, vortexes, healing and vile, such as the Sedona desert of Arizona, the former, and the Bermuda Triangle, the latter. This is not to say that I don't believe in the incredible energy present at these locations, I do. My belief instead is that the anomalies found there are a result of both natural and human-infused energies attached to the area, rather than any intersection with a paranormal entity.

In this same vein, I decided to remove places where miracles were said to occur from my list, again, except for Lourdes. After learning about the power of belief and disbelief from Ingo, where he referred to healing and sickness as intellectual processes and how they relate to our abilities to attract or create our own benevolent energies or malevolent forces,[30] I understood these ideas can play a significant role in our perceptions and experiences with these energies.

"The modern definition of REAL," Ingo wrote in one of his many essays, "holds that it is 'of or relating to fixed, permanent, or immovable things apparent in fact, and necessarily existent.' This definition really should be extended to include phenomena – largely because phenomena exist because they exist." My goal therefore was to find places where reality seeps, the places of convergence, of the obscured seams, between us and them; a conjunction. I allowed my instincts to lead me to each, though in one instance, I wasn't actively seeking a "supernatural" encounter; I was simply celebrating Easter and indulging in a holiday buffet with my son.

In this way, conjunction.world is my personal journey.

---

[30] In both **Psychic Literacy** and **Resurrecting the Mysterious**, Ingo elaborates further on this topic.

CONJUNCTIONS

A HAUNTED SPACE
At 357 Bowery, New York, New York
(40)

A BARRIER BETWEEN REALMS
At Anza-Borrego State Park in the San Diego Mountains of California
(52)

A PORTAL
At Judaculla Rock, Cullowhee, North Carolina, and its Counterpart, a Dimensional Bridge at 31/35 North Street, Plymouth, Massachusetts
(60)

TIME SLIPS
At Mountain Lake Lodge, Pembroke, Virginia
(78)

UAPS/UFOS VISION QUESTS
At the Sego Canyon Rock Art Interpretive Site Thompson, Utah and in the La Sal Mountains, Utah
(94)

THE MARIAN APPARITIONS
At Lourdes, France
(118)

MYSTERIOUS HAPPENINGS
In the Chestnut Ridge, Pennsylvania, Pennsylvania
(144)

357 BOWERY
June 1991 – December 1996

A Haunted Space

It happened one day in the spring of the mid-1990s. The day was pleasant, not too hot or cold, when Sandy Wright, the very graceful and extremely elegant founder of the Friends of the Institute of Noetic Sciences (IONS), appeared at 357 with a film crew and a group of individuals I called "New Agers." They were accompanied by a shaman Sandy had brought along. The shaman was to perform a simulated healing ceremony, not on an actual patient, just for the sake of the film crew. The location of Ingo's studio in the basement of 357 added the right milieu.

Because of the weight of the heavy metal door at the top of the basement stairs, Ingo always made sure his studio was easily accessible while he worked below by leaving the door ajar. The door was a thick metal, and solid. Ingo had found a way to prop it open by pushing it forcefully to the left until its bottom wedged firmly against the uneven wooden floorboards beneath. Once stuck, it required significant effort to free it from its hold. Standing just a few feet away from the building's wooden doors, this entrance to the basement seemed almost like a portal to another world. When Sandy and her entourage arrived, Ingo made sure they found the door already in this position.

The basement was divided into two distinct sections, with the back portion consisting of a one-third laundry room/bathroom and a two-thirds bedroom belonging to Ingo. The space was cramped and dimly lit, with a small window providing the only natural light. The upper and lower portions of the window were hidden behind thick bars, resembling a prison cell. Through the cloudy glass, one could catch a glimpse of a desolate alleyway, sandwiched between two towering buildings. A rusty air conditioning unit from decades past hung precariously in the lower portion of the window, its hold on life maintained solely by strips of duct tape. The top section of the window had been sealed shut with glue, but even that wasn't enough to keep out the cold drafts that still managed to seep through – hence the added layer of duct tape to patch up any remaining cracks. It was here the shaman asked Ingo to go with him to.

Ingo's clever use of fans spread strategically throughout the basement kept the air circulating whenever he was down there. With the fan in his bedroom humming softly, the faint scent of Hopi Nicotiana lingered in the air, betraying Ingo and his companion's secret. The circulating smoke added to the already charged atmosphere in the room.

I took my place at Ingo's training table, positioned so that I could observe his painting **Millenium,** his quite large and attention grabbing metaphysical triptych, from a side angle. The anticipation bubbled inside me as I waited for the film crew to set up, their numerous electrical cords snaking through the basement and ultimately leading to one solitary power strip connected to a single extension cord that meandered up the elevator shaft to the fourth floor. This one source of electricity was responsible for powering the entire basement, a fact that had always both impressed and concerned me. As I watched Sandy assist the crew, the rest of her group engaged in lively conversation, filling the air with their voices and laughter.

As Ingo and the shaman emerged from the shadows, their presence seemed to fill the room. Ingo's melodic voice cut through the laughter and chatter as he directed me to close the basement door. We had been told previously the ceremony required complete darkness save for the faint light to be cast by the camera onto the shaman. With the door securely shut, Ingo switched off the lights, and darkness surrounded me, I fumbled my way down the stairs, feeling my way along the metal rod that served as a guide rail, then shuffled along the floor until I reached my seat at the table. The darkness was almost suffocating, but I could make out the shapes of my companions huddled together on one of the sofas or perched on chairs set up around the shaman like a protective barrier. The film crew stood near an extension cord snaking to the power strip, forming a square of sorts around the enigmatic figure in their midst.

As the shaman began their ritual, a sudden and powerful gust of wind swept through the basement, seemingly coming from all places, Ingo's bedroom, shutting down the camera. I could feel the force of it as it passed by me, rushing up the stairs and violently throwing open the door at the top. The strength of this wind was astonishing – strong enough to cause the door to get stuck on the creaky floorboards in its fully opened position. The room erupted into chaos, with the film crew shouting and cursing. Overall, it was kind of unnerving.

After much discussion, it was determined the ceremony would proceed without being filmed. Perhaps it was documented in another manner, but I can't recall for certain. I was sent up again to close the door, which I did but hastily since I was still rattled; there was no rational explanation for what had happened. Once the shaman had concluded, Ingo turned on lights. I retrieved a pen and paper from nearby on the table and sketched the skeletal outline of a fish, as it was still vivid in my mind.

Sandy and her group of friends huddled tightly around the shaman; their eyes alight with wonder as they verbalized their experiences. "I saw rainbows," one exclaimed, while another gushed, "Beautiful lights!" The word "unicorn" was even tossed into the mix, adding to the ethereal atmosphere. It was as if they had found a hidden pool deep in the forest, adorned with colorful rainbows cascading from a nearby waterfall. The shaman moved gracefully among the group, listening patiently to each one's words before moving on.

Ingo, always the life of the party, had opened a bottle of wine and the group eagerly indulged, except for the shaman who remained stoic. Moved, I made my way over to him, only to discover he too had created a fish bone design within his confined space using sticks and rocks. I showed him my sketch. In the dark basement, I hadn't noticed his actions and even if there had been some light, which there wasn't, the table and crowd surrounding him would have blocked my view.

Interest sparked in his eyes as he asked me to describe what else I had seen. I outlined out a figure on some nearby paper, with a semi-circle hovering above it. He rummaged through his belongings and picked out a book. Thumbing through the pages, he showed me an image of a pictograph, a healer, he said it represented. The image was identical to the one I had drawn.

It was a quasi-happy moment, a feeling I was connected in some way, but I didn't have time to dwell on that feeling for long. The shaman quickly pulled me to the side, his expression serious as he asked if I had seen anything else. I shook my head, remembering only the unsettling sensation of the wind earlier. The burst of air had given me an uneasy feeling, but I hadn't seen anything out of the ordinary. With a gentle guiding hand, he positioned me only a few feet from the beginning of the stairs. He stood steadfastly to my left; his figure silhouetted against one of Ingo's overflowing bookshelves. The shelves served as a makeshift backbone for the stairs, stacked haphazardly with books on art, mythology, and Native American portraits – an intriguing contrast to the shaman standing beside them. And in that precise moment, right there in that very spot, he said pointing down to my right, was a dark being, perched like a spectral gargoyle atop the first step. The creature was gaunt, he continued, adorned with a peculiar hat that seemed to mock its surroundings. It was watching us with unnerving intensity. "He" was the cause of the recent chaos – the blowing wind, malfunctioning camera, and forcefully opened door. His voice dropped to a whisper as he spoke again. "The man, or rather entity," he uttered with grave caution, "is evil and he is attached to your uncle. You must be extremely careful."

Before I could even form a response, the shaman was swept up in the group's revelry, leaving me standing alone and mesmerized by the darkened staircase before me. My eyes scanned for any signs of movement, but all that greeted my gaze was the flickering light cascading from behind, casting my shadow on the steps. I let out a deep sigh and I turned away, my mind dismissing the entire scene as nothing more than a fanciful tale conjured up to scare me. Little did I know that I had encountered this entity before at 357 without realizing it. And this wouldn't be the last time either.

When I moved into 357 in 1991, the first floor lay empty and barren. The only sound was the faint hum of Ingo's tools as he tirelessly worked to remodel the space himself. He was aided by Steve, a skilled potter who resided on the second floor with his partner Ellen and their cat. Their floor was a combination of the earthy scent of clay and the sweet fragrance of blooming plants, which adorned every corner of their shared living and work area. Each room held its own charm – Steve's studio filled with colorful pots and sculptures, while Ellen's showcased her captivating photographs. Situated on the third floor was Charlie House, a highly coveted astrologer. The elevator was always wherever Ingo was, and if you weren't fortunate enough to catch Ingo for a ride, the only other option was to ascend or descend the stairs. As I was often where Ingo was not, it was the stairs for me. Frequently as I made my way up or down, I brushed shoulders with familiar faces – celebrities and influential figures I had seen in the news, going to and from Charlie's apartment, exchanging smiles and polite nods as we passed each other, trying not to collide in our haste.

On the fourth floor was Ingo's designated entertainment space, sans an air conditioner but complete with a queen-sized bed in the center and a TV positioned at the foot of it. Ingo rarely slept in this bed himself, but he kept it for guests or anyone who wanted to crash there. At the end of the day, we would relax by watching shows like **Masterpiece Theater** or **Space 1999**, or a rented video from Virgin Records or Blockbuster. I usually sat in a nearby chair while Ingo lounged on the bed. Afterwards, Ingo would retreat to the basement while I made use of my own bed which doubled as a place to sit between the kitchen and dining area.

My days at 357 were filled with glorious and exciting experiences. But there was always a sense of unease lurking beneath the surface. At night, the antique portrait paintings scattered around the front portion of the fourth floor seemed to come to life with a sinister red glow in their eyes. I hated being alone in that section, especially after dark. I made sure not to stay there for too long once the sun had set.

When summer arrived, I would often apartment-sit for Steve and Ellen when they headed off to their house in North Carolina. It was a great opportunity to escape the heat of the fourth floor and enjoy their air conditioning. Along with taking care of their cat, I also watered their plants both inside and outside. Their studio on the second floor had a unique feature – a rooftop patio atop the extension of the first floor.

While apartment-sitting one night for Steve and Ellen, I found myself curled up on their bed, watching their television and accompanied by their cat. Suddenly, the cat's body went rigid, and she froze, her eyes locked onto the wall next to the bed. As I followed her gaze, I felt a chill spread through the room, causing goosebumps to rise on my skin. My heart raced as I saw blood seeping down from where the wall met the ceiling above, staining the brick below. My mind struggled to make sense of it all as I sat there transfixed, just like the cat. But then suddenly, the moment broke, and warmth flooded back into the room. The cat bolted out of the room and disappeared into Ellen's studio, leaving me alone on the bed. I didn't stay long there though. I moved myself to their sofa, turning on every light in the apartment when I did.

In May of 1993, I finally found my own apartment and moved out of Uncle Ingo's building. But even after moving, I still spent most weekends with him, doing the same activities we had grown accustomed to during my stay at his place. Sadly, not long after I left, Charlie passed away at the age of 53. After several failed attempts to reach him, Ingo entered Charlie's apartment and discovered his lifeless body in his bed. Ingo stayed by Charlie's side as various city officials came and went throughout the day before ultimately taking his body away in the evening. It was later determined he had died from a heart attack. A few months afterwards, Ingo rented out the apartment to an artist from France. I met her during one of my weekend visits to 357, and she exuded a vibrant energy and unmistakable French charm.

In August of 1994, I was preparing to start my MBA program at Columbia University and was staying with Ingo for a two-week "Math Boot Camp" before the official first day of classes. Unfortunately, and quite unexpectedly, it coincided with my grandfather's passing. Because it was the end of August no one was around; the city was literally vacant at this time normally. The artist now occupying the first floor studio was traveling the world, Steve and Ellen were in North Carolina, the French artist was in Europe, so it was just me and Ingo, and someone had to look after 357.

We had to always keep the sidewalk clean and clear, a task made sometimes more challenging as the stairs to 357 were a popular sleep it off destination for those too drunk to make it from the bars around the building back to wherever they came from. We also had to take care of trash and recycling, secure the building, and maintain its upkeep. With classes starting soon, Ingo went to Texas to be with my grandmother, and I stayed behind to handle things in the building. This gave me access to something I had never been allowed to do before: drive the elevator on my own. Ingo gave me a training course before he left, and once he left, I took full advantage of having control over it.

It was an ordinary morning as I stepped into the elevator on my way to Math Camp, grateful for the convenience of not having to take the stairs. But as I opened the doors on the first floor, my heart nearly stopped at the sight of a figure standing there. It was the French artist, dressed in all black with a haunted look in her eyes. I gasped in shock. I wasn't aware she had returned. She had been out shopping and was struggling with several packages, so I offered to give her a lift to her apartment. She accepted gratefully and we rode up together. Upon reaching her floor, I helped her unload and as she turned to thank me, my eyes were drawn to her latest artwork hanging on the wall – a morbid depiction of death. The theme seemed to match her gaunt appearance. But it was when she turned to face me and glared, not in gratitude but in warning, I realized perhaps there was more truth behind her pieces than just artistic expression. Trying to brush off the unease creeping over me, I quickly bid my farewell and made a hasty retreat, leaning on my need to rush to class.

Ingo's absence lasted three months. When Steve and Ellen returned in September, Steve took on most of the physical labor tasks, but I stayed to ensure everything was running smoothly. After that initial encounter, I never crossed paths with the French artist again. Eventually, I was able to fully settle into my Columbia apartment. It wasn't until later that I found out about the French artist's passing from cancer.

Whenever I had a free moment, I would make the journey to 357, usually on weekends. Ingo and I worked together to prepare the third floor for its new tenant. He carefully laid down new tiles in the shower, opting for a tranquil shade of green with hints of gray. Despite our efforts, the apartment never quite felt like a home to me. Eventually, a young, seemingly happy couple moved in. But, as time passed, their once blissful demeanor turned into frequent arguments and shouting matches. On some evenings when I stayed over for dinner, establishing myself in the chair while Ingo sat on his bed, our meal was often accompanied by the sounds of their heated altercations echoing up through the floors below us.

After completing my MBA program in 1996, I believed I had my job situation under control. Unfortunately, things fell apart due to what Ingo later described in astrology as my Saturn Return. Without any clear direction or prospects, Ingo kindly offered for me to stay at 357, and so I did. In the meantime, I took on a temporary job at the New York Stock Exchange while waiting for my Saturn Return to resolve itself.

However, back in the early part of 1995, I arrived at 357 one day to learn that in a tumultuous frenzy, the once blissfully enamored young couple had hastily packed their belongings and left.

Now that the third floor was once again vacant, I suggested to Ingo perhaps it needed cleaning, and not the housekeeping kind. That is how Paula Roberts came into our lives.

Paula, a well-known psychic and "ghost" hunter who had recently been featured on the popular TV show **Unsolved Mysteries**, arrived at 357 after being recommended to Ingo by a friend. Armed with nothing but Ingo's hastily drawn map of the building's third floor, she confidently stepped into the elevator. We ascended to her destination. Depositing her there, we returned to the basement. As we awaited her return, Ingo and I exchanged anxious glances and whispered speculations about what Paula might discover. When Paula finally emerged from trek, her expression was of bemusement as she gave her report.

She spoke of a dark presence embedded in the wall on the third floor she had sensed. I noted the location she marked on her map was not far from above where I had seen the blood oozing down and just below those unnerving portrait paintings hanging in the entertainment space of Ingo's floor above. Ingo reluctantly confessed that when he first moved into the building in the mid-1970s, the third floor was occupied by a mysterious pair. They were rumored to be practicing dark magic and had painted an intricate, upside down pentagram on the wall of their apartment. The very spot Paula had marked. She continued, listing off the numerous other events she had experienced, all of which were connected to the building's past as a factory.

As we listened intently, Ingo opened a bottle of wine and poured her, and then himself, a very full glass, attempting to lighten the mood.

But as the night went on and the wine flowed freely, Paula and Ingo became increasingly "happy," and decided to perform a spiritual cleansing ritual using salt to drive out any negative energy. I watched in amusement as they stumbled around, spilling salt everywhere on the third floor while chanting incantations in slurred voices. I did wonder though as they did if perhaps the dark presence Paula had sensed was calling its friends with thoughts of "Come see these two fools, they're quite entertaining." In hindsight, I learned a valuable lesson: never leave intoxicated individuals unattended near containers of salt used for spiritual purposes.

It was the autumn of 1996 when I embarked as Ingo's research assistant on my latest project for him – my job was to transcribe his and his student Robert (Bob) Durant's planetary probes, psychic wanderings shrouded in secrecy.[31]

Little did I know these sessions were nothing more than a ruse, a trap that would ensnare Ingo in a few years' time in yet another cycle of relentless psychic attacks, choreographed by murky powers. He could already anticipate the familiar question that would accompany the onslaught: "Okay, I see a pair of eyes. What are you? Who are you?"

Many years later, as I sat with my recollections of the past, of a wall that seemed to bleed, two mysterious deaths on the third floor, and an ominous atmosphere that drained all happiness from its inhabitants, to say nothing of the glowing red eyes staring out from Ingo's antique portrait paintings and Ingo's covert "planetary" missions, I attempted to string them together into a cohesive narrative. In doing so, I discovered two things:

1) Ingo had made countless attempts to rid the 357 of malevolent beings, not just with Paula but on his own as well. His archives were overflowing with session notes of his last attempts in the late 1990s and early 2000s. Each page was filled with descriptions of dark vortices, curses from other dimensions, remnants of a dark war that clung to the walls like a disincarnate cloud. He wrote of something evil attached to Charlie's bed, leaving behind a trail of destruction. And then there were the psychic attacks, coming from an obscured dimension that seemed to have a personal vendetta against him. It was no wonder the third floor, with all its history and negative energy, was a constant source of fatigue for him.[32] In the end, I concluded, the unremitting "hauntings"[33] that tormented Ingo and 357 could be traced back to a combination of factors: Ingo's secretive psychic spying missions that led him to forbidden places, his telepathic excursions into dangerous territories, and the summoning of dark forces by others.

---

[31] Documents pertaining to the project, "Moon Recon II," can be found on the website conjunction.world.

[32] Ingo's psychic attack notes are available on the website conjunction.world.

[33] Known as hitchhikers, these anomalous events are believed to be evil spirits that attach themselves to those who have encountered UFOs, experienced abduction, or visited "haunted" places.

2) The shaman's sighting of such a creature was not limited to my uncle alone. Little did I know, there were others who have encountered a being just like this, hiding in the edges of awareness and preying on victims far beyond the reaches of 357. This elusive creature has an impressive resume, its work spanning across countless human lifetimes. In our modern world, it is categorized as one of the shadow people – dark, spectral beings with hellish intentions that cross over into our realm. The purpose of this particular entity seems to revolve around its insatiable desire to feed off the energy of fear and terror it inflicts upon its chosen victims; to it, we are nothing more than a demonic charging apparatus. Often described as wearing a fedora hat and a dark dress suit, sometimes adorned with a gold pocket watch or piercing red eyes, it skulks in the corners of rooms, hiding in mirrors, and lingering at the edge of beds with ominous intent. But sometimes, it chooses to attack, leaving deep and lasting trauma upon its unfortunate victims. These "sightings" and attacks often occur during deep REM sleep, rendering the victim paralyzed and completely vulnerable to its grasp. Known as the Hat Man, this entity is believed to be a stand-in for the Devil himself.

A
COSMOLOGICAL
INTERSECTION
November 20, 2023

Conjunctions

A Barrier Between Realms

We drove down the dusty desert road, a constant stream of fine grey powder blowing up and over our SUV as we inched forward. The road was primitive at best, filled with bumps and holes that forced us to swerve and maneuver around them, careful not to hit any prickly objects scattered on the ground around us.

Jessie met us after we, Valerie and I, left Tucson, Arizona, the two leftovers from a girls' pre-Thanksgiving reunion at a wonderful spa resort there, picking her up along the way, having just visited some friends, Jessie said, and needing a ride back to where we were headed, which would be north of Los Angeles. It was Jessie, a friend from college, now an energy healer, Valerie told me, who had directed us to this dusty road in the middle of nowhere as part of a place called the Anza Borrego State Park, the one we now traveled being tossed around as we did, offering only that it would be "fun." The only thing I can remember thinking at that point about the desert, and our drive in our rented SUV across it, was how utterly unfun it all was. But Jessie was directing the adventure, which she taken us to from our highway travels, so we went further and further along the road to nowhere.

With no signs of other travelers in either direction. I remember Valerie's tense comments to Jessie, who brushed them off casually as if she had some sort of magical power. I sat in the back seat, relinquishing my role as navigator in the passenger seat to Jessie. From the corner of my eye, I could see Valerie giving Jessie skeptical glances as we inched along. After all, it was Valerie behind the wheel, not Jessie. As our journey continued, we sporadically spotted a lone camper van parked among the dry scrub brush. It seemed out of place in this desolate landscape, leaving me to wonder why someone would choose to park there. The dry, empty expanse offered no signs of civilization or amenities.

At last, we reached the top of a small hill and drove down into a sunken area in the desert terrain. Valerie pulled up to the far edge of the area and shut off the engine, relieved to finally be off the road. We all piled out of the SUV, grateful for a break from the endless driving. Suddenly, another car appeared over the same tiny hill, catching all of us by surprise. I could see the worry etched on Valerie's face as she turned to Jessie. Where had this unexpected visitor come from? I found myself wondering the same thing. The car pulled up right behind ours, ignoring the wide open spaces that had been carved out for parking in this spot. Instinctively, I stepped forward, my Capricorn nature kicking in as I positioned myself between our group and the intruding car.

A tall figure emerged from the driver's side of a pristine white Mercedes sedan, in stark contrast to our own dust covered SUV. I immediately noticed his height – he towered over me, his well-built frame filling out strange and mismatched clothing that seemed to span different time periods. With his irregular attire, a sense of impending danger began to creep over me, particularly as he had left his door ajar when he approached us. He calmly asked if we were on the pictograph trail.

I turned to my companions Jessie and Valerie, who seemed content to let me take charge in this situation. Little did I know Jessie had planned a surprise for us at the end of this trail. As I scanned the desert landscape, all I could see was a slight hill leading up to a narrow road where we had parked our car, with a small clearing for parking before it continued into the vast expanse of desert beyond. I had no idea there was a pictograph nearby, let alone an entire trail dedicated to it. I looked back again. Valerie had gathered Jessie closer to her. The man smiled; I think. It was hard to tell since the sun was directly behind the man and I had to caste my gaze into the sun when looking at him. I offered a quizzical look in return. Without a moment's hesitation, the man bolted off towards a trail marker I hadn't noticed until that very moment. He moved with a strange waddle, an odd contrast to his otherwise athletic and imposing figure. Soon enough, he returned, holding something in his hand. It appeared to be a piece of paper. With a sense of inquisitiveness, I reached out and took it from him, as I did, he told me, and I will never forget, go to number seven just seven. He pointed relentlessly at the paper.

As I sat studying the paper, a trail guide for this part of the desert, the man suddenly hopped back into his car with inexplicable urgency. "There's so much more to see!" he exclaimed before shutting the door and speeding back the way he had come. I looked up and saw my companions mirroring my confusion as they too turned to watch the man drive away. His words seemed both humorous and out of place, as even from our current vantage point we could see all there was to see: a vast expanse of grey, powdery desert floor dotted with prickly bushes in every direction. If there was any more to see, it definitely wasn't the way he had just traveled. What made it even stranger was his car never kicked up any dust as it disappeared into the distance, just as it hadn't when it first appeared. And in that moment as I thought about it, neither did the man himself as he waddled over to the sign and back to me. As the car disappeared over the small hill on the road, Valerie's voice rose in agitation towards Jessie. She worried about our tires being slashed or engine tampered with, but Jessie brushed off her concerns and ushered us along the trail. The path was not what Jessie had originally planned, as she had intended for us to venture further into the desert where the "more to see" was. But we followed her lead.

The trail we were on, if you could even call it that, was more like a narrow, winding barely there footpath lined with desert brush and scattered boulders. Jessie, having taken the trail map from me back in the lot, pointed to the first six items listed as we walked along. Valerie and I stuck close together, our footsteps crunching in unison on the dirt below, rather than paying attention to the checklist in Jessie's hand. My heart was racing, I was certain we were being stalked by a venomous rattlesnake, coiled and ready to strike. But even more unnerving was the feeling of unseen eyes following our every move.

As we reached marker six, a rocky slope loomed beside us casting long shadows in the diminishing sunlight. I hadn't realized it until that moment, but the sun was going down and fast. We picked up our pace. Ahead, our next destination awaited, marked by two imposing boulders forming a perfect "V" shape, flanked by steep jagged hills on either side. The symbol we were there to see was painted in black on the left boulder, its distinctive lines standing out against the rough surface. It wasn't a symbol as much as figures which seemed to come alive on the rock, the lower one reaching up to the figure above with outstretched arms. The six-toed foot of the upper figure pointed downward, as if commanding the lower one. I looked up and past it. In the valley beyond, large boulders filled the space like play toys strewn by a giant's hand, no desert plants or cacti to be found within. I looked back at the image and a rush of recognition stirred within me. It was an exact replica of the healer I had drawn many years ago. My mind was consumed with memories as Jessie hesitantly reached out to touch the rock next to the depiction, exclaiming that it was vibrating. Suddenly, fear snapped me back to reality and I scanned my surroundings, half-expecting an earthquake, but everything else remained motionless.

Jessie's words were quickly forgotten as a sense of the most intense foreboding consumed me, and I frantically yelled for us to leave, and to leave right then and there. Valerie didn't need any convincing and turned back without hesitation, her eyes mirroring my own panic. As we hurried back, abandoning our leisurely pace for a frantic one, we all felt a slight gust of wind pass us. In an instant, Valerie expressed her worry for the SUV, afraid once again its tires had been slashed or the engine messed with; we pushed ourselves even faster.

We finally reached the SUV, and miraculously, the tires were still intact. Valerie swiftly slid into the driver's seat and turned on the engine, providing us with a moment of relief. It was short-lived though as I noticed six fingerprint like marks on the side of my door, resembling the six-toed figure we had seen drawn on the rock. It looked like something had been trying to open it. Without hesitation, I wiped away the grey dust. I looked up in time to see Jessie bowing in gratitude towards something in the distance. She urgently instructed me to get in and for Valerie to drive as fast as she could back to the highway where we had turned off onto the dirt road. The sun was already now extremely low in the sky, and Jessie warned us we needed to make it out before it disappeared completely. Jessie and I hopped into our respective seats, and we sped off, with the sun threatening to disappear rapidly behind us.

Exhausted and shaken from our recent ordeal, we stumbled upon a hotel and collapsed, too drained to continue on. Later we huddled around a table at the edge of the hotel's pool eating a makeshift dinner, desperate to forget the events of what had just transpired.

When we dropped Jessie off at her destination the next day, she pulled me aside, holding me in a tight embrace for a moment then letting me go. As the two of us stood next to the passenger's side door of the SUV, Valerie disappeared around the other side to make a call. Jessie's voice was stern as she warned me about the dangers of black magic and dark thoughts. She stressed the importance of turning towards the light, even in moments of betrayal and despair, to let go of pain and find joy in other aspects of life. I was trying to absorb this when she then launched into a dizzying retelling of the chaos that unfolded the day before, referring to it as a cosmological intersection.

She tried to explain, at this boundary between worlds, our first encounter had been with a spiritual guide of sorts. "He" was sent to steer us towards the correct path and away from any wrong turns; essentially preventing us from venturing too far into the "more to see." She didn't elaborate on this, only mentioning her job, I took that to be her energy healing work, had brought her to this place. From what she told me, it seemed like she was led there intentionally for a specific purpose, although she never specified what it was. Nevertheless, she did admit that bringing all of us was a mistake. Things went way differently than she had anticipated and for that she was sorry. According to her, the helper had expended a significant amount of energy to manifest in our vibrational frequency and interact with physical objects. This required him to appear as a normal-looking human, which explained his strange attire, movements, and lack of dust as he moved. The fact he handed me the paper meant he couldn't stay for very long. Next, she unraveled the chilling truth about the ominous pictograph, revealing its true purpose: an inter-dimensional warning sign, a signal to stay clear of what lay beyond it. The image portrayed below was not just a shaman, but a martyr who gave his life to create a formidable barrier at that exact location – one that prevented anything from passing to our side of those two boulders. It was the spirit of this shaman, forever tied now to the barrier, which had been following and watching us. My feeling of being observed now made sense. If we had continued driving, we would have crossed this barrier.

She then told me what she saw as we first arrived at that no trespassing sign: thousands upon thousands of small creatures, about four feet tall, with grotesque appearances. They had no eyes, only empty sockets, and seemed to be workers of evil. Among them were taller figures, much taller and more menacing – the spawn, she called them.

They are the ones depicted as the upper figure painted on the rock. They are warlike, immoral, evil monsters. My eyes must have widened at this point, because she proceeded to explain further. Throughout recorded history, myths and legends have intertwined with tales of half-human, half-god beings, she announced. These demigods were said to be the offspring of "gods," or perhaps what we would call children of fallen angels and humans; a result of the merging between our world and the kingdom of the supernatural. Called the Nephilim in the **Bible**, in the ancient native cultures of the Southwest, they were known as the Anasazi, while in the Middle East they were called the Anakim. Described as fearsome giants, referred to as fallen ones and ancient enemies, and were distinguished by their six fingers and six toes. Despite their intense gaze upon her, they made no attempts to approach her. The moment she touched the surface of the massive boulder, she sensed an invisible barrier that seemed impenetrable. And it was her hand upon bolder which drew their attention not to her but to me. As their intense energy focused solely on me, I felt the urgency to escape this situation. She explained I must have felt subconsciously overwhelmed, and hence why I cried out we needed to leave immediately with panicked desperation.

As we were hustling back, she carried on with her story, one of the enormous creatures, unable to cross the barrier blocking its path, began manipulating the elements around us. We felt it as a slight gust of wind brushing past us. As it did, the spirit shaman immediately chased after it, engaging in a fierce battle at the SUV. This was when Valerie's fear crept in. The shaman emerged victorious, ultimately putting an end to the manipulated energy, but not before it left its imprint on the door I had used. As she and I milled about the SUV the shaman watched us closely. Hence why she had thanked him with a bow, but he was insistent, Jessie emphasized, we leave before sunset, stressing to Jessie our need to depart immediately. "When darkness engulfs the land, dark spirits rise," she relayed. "They are not the ones bound by mortals or the barrier, but ancient beings who claim these lands as their own. And when they find you …" her voice trailed off. We could hear Valerie end her call. Jessie's gaze turned towards me. She leaned in close, her eyes fixed on mine. "If I attempt to replace my own abilities with those of spirits, entities, or other supernatural beings – whether they are benevolent or not," she explained, "the consequences could be severe." The heaviness of her words, all of them, remained with me long after we parted ways.

Judaculla Rock | North Carolina
35°18'05''N | 83°06'36''W

The Trask Museum | Massachusetts
41°57'28''N | 70°39'48''W

SIREN'S SONG
February 20, 2024
November 24, 2016

A Portal

In Greek mythology, sirens, a mesmerizing blend of women and birds, are seductive and dangerous creatures. They haunt the ancient stories of Homer's **Odyssey**, tempting men with promises of pleasure and paradise only to lead them into destruction. They are to me symbolic of the treacherous dangers that lie in wait in the pursuit of temptation. Their method of luring, most notably through song, reminds me of a lullaby, a promise, an offering of paradise, of an enchantment beyond this land, of peaceful wanderings into sweet dreams. But beware, for once under their spell, there is no escaping the perilous fate they have in store.

The mythical creatures of ancient Greece, including the enchanting sirens, playful satyrs, and beautiful nymphs, have all been grouped together to create the captivating world we now refer to as fairies. These beings, also known as the "Hidden People," have been woven into stories across cultures and time. They are believed to be an ancient race, perhaps even pre-dating Christianity, with magical powers and a deep connection to nature. Some have even drawn connections between fairies and other mystical creatures such as the Spanish xanas, beautiful maidens associated with rivers and springs and the Sanskrit Gandharva, divine musicians, singers, and dancers. In the legends of various Indigenous peoples of the Americas, there are tales of "little people" who reside in the forests or mountains. These creatures are said to interact with humans in a variety of ways — from benevolent helpers to devious tricksters and even malevolent demons.

The idea of fairies in western culture can be traced back to the Celtic fair folk, known as the Aos Sí in Irish mythology. These supernatural creatures exist in an invisible realm connected to our own, and they were often portrayed as mischievous tricksters. In contemporary Western literature, they are usually depicted as ethereal, enigmatic creatures with wings.

After settling into 357 in the early 1990s, Ingo shared a zany story with me. He spoke of a mischievous gremlin that resided on the light pole at the intersection of Fourth and Bowery, just steps away from 357's entrance. This little creature had a fondness for causing chaos at the intersection, Ingo said, making it imperative to avoid it at all costs. Instead, he instructed me to walk up or down a block before crossing the Bowery. I often found Ingo waiting on the stoop, perched atop the stairs that led from the sidewalk to 357's door, ensuring I followed his instructions.

As we spent more time together, Ingo also mentioned seeing fairies, but he never elaborated much further. At the time, I was not sure if I truly believed him; perhaps I gave him a skeptical look as he returned it with his trademark Cheshire Cat grin and blew out smoke from his cigar. Looking back now, I really wish I had taken him more seriously.

After my dream and its connection to pictographs sparked my journey of self-knowledging, I decided to begin my quest at a location showcasing rock art: pictographs and/or petroglyphs. To narrow down my options, I created a list of all the rock art sites in the United States, luckily finding many near my home. I decided to do some research on them, but not too in-depth. I just wanted a general understanding of each one. During my internet wandering of these sites, I came upon a location rumored to be a portal to another dimension. I knew, without a doubt, that was where I needed to go.

Hidden deep within the Great Smoky Mountains, a subset of the Appalachian Mountains, in the remote countryside near Asheville, North Carolina lies a sacred site known to the Cherokee people as Judaculla Rock. With a surface area of about 240 square feet, the rock is carved with over 1,500 enigmatic symbols, more than any other known petroglyph boulder in the eastern United States. According to Cherokee legend, the rock and its intricate designs existed long before their arrival. Archeologists have confirmed this belief, dating the rock back to a time before the Cherokee inhabited western North Carolina. Although, the exact origin of the rock remains a mystery, the current estimates place it between 3000 BCE and 1000 BCE.[34]

It is described by the Discover Jackson County website as a massive boulder located in the area, covered with ancient carvings that have puzzled historians and archaeologists. These petroglyphs are believed to have been created by Native American tribes possibly thousands of years ago. The rock is commonly referred to as Judaculla Rock and is made of soapstone, with multiple symbols etched all over its surface. It holds significant meaning for the Cherokee tribe, who have a legend about a powerful spirit, a hunting god named Judaculla associated with the rock. Like many Native American cultures, the Cherokee believe in the influence of the spirit world on the physical world, and view all living things as having their own spirits. They also believe in gods that control these spirits, requiring mediation between the two realms.[35] For the Cherokee, Judaculla Rock was a sacred place associated with their hunting god.

Judaculla is the English translation from the Cherokee Tsul-ka-lu (Tsu' Kalu or Tsul`kälû') interpreted as Great Slant-eyed Giant. In the legends of the Cherokee people, he was revered as a hunter beyond compare and one of their most powerful mythical characters. According to tradition, he resided on the southwestern slope of the highest peak of the nearby mountains, his kingdom encompassing vast reaches of land. The rock itself is said to be a marker of his territory, and is believed to hold the giant's handprint, his palm marked with an indentation where seven fingers once pressed into the stone.

The site holds an insidious allure I found. Rumors whisper of supernatural forces at play, with some theories even suggesting the presence of UFOs and electromagnetic anomalies. The Cherokee believed Judaculla himself used the rock as a conduit between realms. But for the

---

[34] As legend has it in Crow Nation folklore, the Pryor Mountains located in Montana are inhabited by mythical beings known as the Nirumbee or Awwakkulé in the Crow language. These creatures, a race of little people, are described as demons. They are believed to be the ones responsible for creating the petroglyphs on rocks within the mountains.

[35] The legend of the Zuni witch, mentioned earlier, speaks of a powerful figure who held control over life and death. It was said that he could manipulate reality, bringing people into the world of daylight or erasing them from existence.

European settlers who dared call this land home, it was known as the dwelling place of the "Indian Satan," a malevolent and calculating force.

Based on what I read, it appeared by looking at a map the rock was located about three hours away from my home by car. As it had been on my perspective go to list, I had read up about how to get there and what to expect parking and facility wise once I did. Basically, not much, and certainly make sure to use the restroom before going since there are no facilities. That was the extent of it, oh, and do not go after dark. But one morning, I suddenly felt an overpowering desire to be there at exactly noon. Determined to make it on time, I left early and carefully planned my route. However, Google Maps suddenly redirected me onto a side road for a moment. It only cost me two extra minutes, but it felt like an eternity. I arrived at 12:02pm. Looking back, I wonder if the timing was intentional, even though it didn't seem so at the time.

The rock site is situated at the end of a half mile dirt road and sits in a remote valley, surrounded by fields on one side and rolling hills and a nearby stream on the other. As I approached the road, my eyes caught sight of a white pickup truck parked to the side. A short distance away, I could see a couple about my age walking along the road. I assumed they were the owners of the truck. The half mile of road was more like a mix of dirt and lose gravel, and itself cuts between two cow pastures before winding along the edge of a mountain. The couple smiled and waved as I carefully drove by, and I waved back. It struck me as odd they were walking on such a rough path when there were plenty of hiking trails nearby. At least I wouldn't be alone, with the couple and cows around, I thought, completely overlooking the significance of a white vehicle parked at the start of the road.

My itinerary for visiting this site was based on a review I found on Trip Advisor. The review stated it was not a typical state park or museum. It was simply a large rock with ancient inscriptions. The recommendation was not to spend the whole day there, but rather take some time to reflect on this unusual attraction and the historic mountains surrounding it. And then leave – at least, that's what I assumed they meant to say – so my plan was for a three-hour drive, brief visit at noon before heading back for another three hours.

I easily located the parking "lot," a small patch of dirt off the road. As I pulled into the lot, the couple passed by on foot, quickly reaching the end of the road where it turned into private property, marked with a "No

Trespassing/Private Property" sign. The couple was already walking away from me when I got out of my car. I didn't get any negative vibes from the location or the couple; in fact, I hardly felt anything at all aside from the warm sun on my skin. Though winter still lingered on the edges, the weather was pleasant and mild enough for the couple to have their jackets tied around their waists as they walked.

I followed a short halfhearted wooden fenced path down to the rock. Situated around the rock itself, which relatively speaking, is quite large, 16 feet long by 11 feet wide, is a semi-circle wooden walkway with guardrails. Two signs saying "please no climbing on the rock" sticking up from the ground near the rock read. Although I am not sure anyone would be any wiser if you did, but I was not going to tempt fate physically or spiritually.

As I stepped on the walkway, I saw the rock was spotted with closely spaced indentations, all of which appeared worn away. I moved to the closest angle the walkway allowed, but even then, it was hard to distinguish each individual one. With my phone in hand, I began snapping photos, zooming in for a better view. But to be honest, I wasn't entirely sure what I was photographing. Once finished, I stood there and eagerly waited for some kind of portal to appear. I imagined a shimmering opening to another world, but as I stood there gazing at the rock, nothing happened. Zip, zilch, nada. I was certain a star gate-like portal was about to materialize at any moment, complete with a visible translucent rainbow and wavering frequencies. But there was nothing – no sign or indication of any kind of portal. Just a large grey rock with mysterious carvings.

In 2016, during Thanksgiving weekend with my family in Plymouth, Massachusetts, I stumbled upon what I can only describe as a dimensional bridge. It was not intentional at all. We had already seen the sights – the rock, the plantation, walked around town, attended services, and had a traditional Thanksgiving meal with actors dressed as "pilgrims."

Yet, I had this strange urge to do something different. So, I bought tickets to the Dead of Night Ghost Tour for us. It promised an eerie walking tour through the streets by lantern light, with stops at haunted locations where ghost sightings were reported. This included a visit to a graveyard and a supposedly haunted house connected to the Trask Museum.

The atmosphere that evening was perfect, with a light drizzle adding to the spooky ambiance. Our family was not alone; two other families looking for a break from all things "pilgrim" joined us, along with a young couple having escaped their own families. We were all having a blast – walking, talking, sharing stories, and snapping photos on our phones and comparing caught images of orbs and streaks of light that appeared in our pictures, the paths of raindrops perhaps, or maybe something else. Regardless, our collective mood was one of adventure, that is, until we reached the museum, the last stop on the tour.

Everyone went inside initially, but most soon came back out – including my family and the young couple. The few of us left decided to venture on – myself and maybe another mom or dad chaperoning their kids. Personally, I found it all rather contrived and cheesy but played along. In my head, I laughed at those who stayed outside, thinking they were just too scared of staged ghosts and jump scares.

As we arrived at the top floor, I stayed behind with one of the tour guides, whom I will refer to as Dave for privacy reasons. The rest of the group moved on with the tour's owner for a closer look at one of the bedrooms. The upper level of the house was pitch-black except for the flashlights each guide held. As Dave and I stood in the hallway, we could hear them pleading for a ghostly appearance. Dave suggested that we move to the other end of the hallway, towards the chained-off stairs leading to the floor below. Using his flashlight to guide us, we positioned ourselves outside of a bathroom, standing on a landing where the stairs let out. Facing the direction we had just come from, we could still hear the voices of our group down the hall. I rolled my eyes at this over-the-top display and Dave caught it with his flashlight, making sure I was safely away from the staircase before chuckling. It all felt like a scene from a ridiculous horror movie; I found it amusing until I didn't.

Suddenly, the space around Dave and I grew even darker and began to shift and twist in an unnatural manner. It was a disturbing sight that made me think, "This is not normal."

My instinct was to shrink away, as if I had a shadow to hide behind. The hallway now felt suffocatingly chilly as the air warped and writhed around me. Without hesitation or communication, Dave and I both turned to face the source of the chill at the far end of the hallway where the rest of our group was located. From my perspective, the hallway seemed to stretch endlessly into the distance. Our voices overlapped in unison, Dave saying "Here he comes" while I said, "Here it comes."

I quickly pulled out my phone and began snapping photos, capturing every moment of this unnerving encounter. As time dragged on, Dave mentioned something about someone standing right in front of me, but all I could see was the never-ending tunnel of darkness. I managed to capture one last photo – a bright white orb trailing it as it retreated down the hallway away from me.

In an instant, the hallway reverted to its original state all the while our group continued their pursuit of the ghostly presence. I glanced at Dave, and the expression on his face gave me all the information I needed. It was clear what I should do next. With quick and urgent determination, I bolted towards the exit, Dave lighting my way. When my family saw me outside, they asked why it took me so long.

Plymouth, however, was a distant memory, a faint whisper in the back of my mind as I stood before Judaculla Rock expecting a majestic and wondrous structure from some fantastical realm. But as I looked around, there was nothing particularly special about this place. It was a sunny day, and the rock was interesting, but did it really hold some kind of mystical power? I questioned why I felt such a strong urge to visit this spot at noon, of all times.

It was then as I was standing there questioning my surroundings, a sense of something behind me caught my attention. It wasn't necessarily good or bad, just a prevailing feeling of interestedness. Behind the wooden semi-circle, there was a narrow path that led to a thicket. To reach it, one had to cross a small wooden bridge over a dried-up gulley that was barely visible at the time. I found myself intrigued by this hidden pathway. Someone must have intentionally created this, leading me to believe there must be something worth discovering at the end of it. That was my reasoning anyway. And so, without hesitation, I made my way down onto the path and into the unknown thicket.

As soon as I stepped off the bridge and into the thicket, a feeling of being watched overtook me. My mind immediately conjured up images of fairy children peering at me from hidden places. I sensed their presence all around me, and it seemed like more were joining in, almost as if they were calling for reinforcements to come witness my arrival. Things darted around me as I ventured further into the thicket. It felt like tiny hands were reaching out to touch me with inquisitiveness rather than malice. Their focus seemed to be on my hair.

While in this strange situation, I didn't feel drained of energy or absorbing anything from them, until suddenly I began to feel a sense of euphoria. It was different from any other sensation I had experienced before – not like drunkenness, but something much stronger and more intense. If this is what being high feels like, then I could understand why people seek that state of mind in the cemetery of lost souls. Despite the consuming bliss, I remained fully aware and present in my mind and body. This all-encompassing wave of euphoria grew, leaving me breathless and buzzing with electricity. I could feel sunlight on my skin, warming and energizing me to the point where I felt weightless. My body hummed with a tingly sensation; it was almost too much to handle. Amazingly, despite being lost in this enraptured state, I was still able to snap pictures.

I was unable to pinpoint the direction, but I caught fragments of a conversation from the older couple. The words seem to waif down to me and were muddled and confusing. Suddenly, a voice in my head warned me it was time to leave; mustn't stay here for too long or linger any longer, I had 15 minutes max. I admit, I was a little angry at the voice and may have stumbled in an attempt to calm it down. But my actions had no clear purpose, so the voice persisted and this time it was sterner. Reluctantly, I pushed my way out of the thicket.

Arriving at the semicircle walkway, I snapped five quick photos of the rock, but made no further progress beyond that. Instead, I nonchalantly leaned against the railing and scrolled through emails deleting them without really paying attention to what I was deleting. But then, I started to feel something behind me creeping closer, not initially sinister but growing more ominous with each passing moment. I acted as if taking selfies while secretly aiming my camera at the feeling, hoping to capture whatever it was.

The voice in my head urged me to hurry up and leave, telling me I had used up most of my 15 minutes. So, I retraced my steps towards the parking lot, snapping some photos of the surrounding area along the way, including a Cherokee medicine garden I had seen on my way in. When I reached my car, I saw the couple from earlier were already far down the road.[36] It was perplexing how I could hear their voices in what was to me mere moments before, and yet they were so far away.

A few moments later, I was in my car, driving down the road. I waved to the couple who had also been waving as I drove past them, right where

---

[36] As I compiled the photos, I scrutinized the ones I had taken of the garden before departing, I zoomed in on the road in the background but there was no sign of the couple, or their white pickup truck parked at the beginning of the road.

we first saw each other earlier. The feeling of enraptured bliss stayed with me for a while before fading away. And when it did, it left behind a dark void in its wake.

After an hour and a half of driving and feeling the full effects of withdrawal, I stopped at a rest stop along the highway to regain my bearings. As I scrolled through the photos on my phone, I was surprised to see most of them were filled with orbs and streams of light in various directions – up, down, left, right, diagonal, you name it. When I came across the "selfies" I had taken of the feeling behind me, I noticed a strange small shadow in two out of the five photos. It was unlike any of the other shadows from branches or trees around it; instead, it was contorted and knotted in a different direction. Looking back at the photos more closely, I saw the initial photo of the path into the thicket had a very distinct shadow compared to the others. While the shadows from trees and branches flowed from left to right, this one seemed to be going more up and down. It started at what would be noon on a clock, then curved at an angle before making a sharp turn at about five o'clock. Upon closer inspection, it almost looked like it was drawn onto the photo – as if it were sitting on top of the image. In hindsight, it could have been the dividing line between reality and something else altogether.

Once I returned home, I began looking at the photographs I had taken more closely. In examining my very first photograph of the rock that day and comparing it to others online, I realized I had unknowingly captured the giant's handprint. As I studied the photo further, I noticed the handprint was located beside a circular image. The core of this image was surrounded by an outer ring shaped like a "U," with a passage connecting it to a smaller concentric circle inside.

Interestingly, my first photo after leaving the thicket happened to capture this specific scene. A sign at the site interpreted the image differently, stating that instead of connecting to another set of circles, the line extended to the right and connected to what appeared to be a door. Either way, the meaning I gleaned from it was clear: this was a sign of a portal.

I then began to mentally sift through the events that had transpired there. My mind drifted to Homer's mythical land of Lotus Eaters. The inhabitants of this island nation were said to spend their days indulging in the narcotic effects of the lotus flower, causing them to lose themselves in a haze of pleasure and forget all practical concerns. Intrigued, I turned to the orbs and streams that appeared in my photos. In those moments I had immediately associated them with fairies, so I decided to stick with that notion.

Drawing on Irish and Celtic lore, these entities seemed to possess magical abilities such as enchantment and teleportation, with a penchant for abducting humans – especially children – and bringing them into their territory to propagate their bloodline.

This concept reminded me of the Djinn, Arabic demons, who were also accused of kidnapping people for various purposes including marriage and sexual relations. It was intriguing to note that even the legend of Judaculla itself involved him choosing a bride from a Cherokee tribe and refusing to release her back to her family after she entered the spirit world with him. The legend says he killed her brother after the brother's attempts to bring her back failed. Nevertheless, afterward Judaculla allowed others from the tribe to pass through his rock portal into the spirit world to visit her. What struck me was the similarity between the Judaculla legend, the various fairy stories, and modern accounts of "alien" abductions, where individuals claim to have been subjected to violating experiences involving their reproductive systems. Could there be a connection between these seemingly disparate cultural tales?

Ingo himself provided one such account,[37] although it was not his intention to do so. The year was 1987, and Ingo was collaborating with Dr. Gerald Epstein, a renowned psychiatrist known for his expertise in mental imagery. They were working towards the goal of accessing Ingo's "inner realities" through a state of wakefulness, almost like lucid dreaming. This from a session on March 18, 1987:

> A bunch of indistinct dreams, but then a sequence in which myself and two others (who they were, I don't know) were kidnapped and taken to a room encased in steel which was a kind

---

[37] It was a secret he kept hidden, never spoken about. I only discovered it in 2017 when Dr. Gerald Epstein and his wife gave my mother the files from their research on waking dreams with Ingo during the late 1980s and early 1990s. Among these documents was a recording by Ingo of his memory of an abduction. If my mother had not received these files, I would have never known about it. This narration, based on his recollection, is available for download as a free PDF on the website conjunction.world. It also includes the excerpt from **Penetration** which I suspect was a substitute for his actual encounter.

> of clinic/prison in which people were tortured by having syringes plunged into their jugular veins in order to try to force changes in them, as well as other forms of torture...In the dream, a little hypnopompically, it seemed quite clear I was a prisoner of some kind....and needed to look into this.
>
> Followed by a write up by Ingo on March 30, 1987:
>
> This is a rather delayed write-up of the waking dream sequence that was based upon the "kidnapping" dream of 18 March 1987 -- delayed because...well, because all this is rather "psychotic-making," and I guess I'm avoiding it all.... This part of the waking dream was clearly a memory and not a dream. I was watching this memory...then it started to unfold when Gerry said get into the room in the kidnapping dream and tell me what you see. Well....here goes, right into a .... (I don't really have any words for it.) It suddenly became clear that the "room" was in a spaceship of some kind, and that by some means I had been rendered unconscious...and taken into that spaceship.

During his time aboard the spaceship, Ingo remembered waking up as a young child to a moment of pain before losing consciousness again. It wasn't until later he realized his genetic material had been taken from his reproductive organs without his consent. The next thing he knew, he was back in the same place he had been taken from.

The events of 1987 likely shaped his perspectives in the article he wrote in 1992 for **FATE Magazine**, which I referenced in "The Run-Up." In this case, though, he expanded on his earlier statements I referenced, by declaring, "Evidence of UFO-ET abductions suggests that we humans are being used for our genetic materials against our will and for unknown purposes by these extraterrestrial beings." This echoes the sentiments expressed by his friend Keel, also mentioned in "The Run-Up": Is it possible we, humans, are nothing more than products grown on a vast farm called Earth?

The thought of fairies and aliens following the same modus operandi triggered a memory I had of messages "given" to psychic medium Mark Probert in the late 1940s and early 1950s. These messages, Probert said, were from ethereal beings who claimed to know more about another set of beings, ones who travel in UFOs.[38] The message said this UFO set likes to not only take some of us but also large groups of us and experiment on us. But even so, they are benevolent. This has been documented in **The Coming of the Guardians: An Interpretation of the Flying Saucers as Given from the Other Side of Life**. Based on these messages, it appears they engage in such activities on a continuous basis with no intention of stopping. It's not just experimentation they subject us to, according to Probert's revelation. They also have a habit of keeping some of us indefinitely.

This hints at the existence of another group of abductees – those who are never returned and essentially disappear without any knowledge of their abduction or their current state.

It is interesting to observe that initial reports of UFO encounters in the years following World War II depicted those framed within the UFO motif as peaceful and spiritually advanced. They were regarded as our "space siblings" and there was no mention of any experiments, despite Probert's messages.

But this perception shifted in the late 1960s when reports began describing hostile interactions and abductions by monstrous creatures. The term "abductees" also emerged during this time. Even with these frightening experiences mounting, these "extraterrestrial" beings were still portrayed as having good intentions towards humanity and nothing to fear. As more stories surfaced, the idea of "missing time" was used to explain memory loss or implanted false memories. This led to the concept of a "close encounter of the fourth kind," where an individual is taken aboard a UFO and examined before being returned.

In 1981, Ufologist Budd Hopkins proposed a new theory: that extraterrestrials may have a specific need for human beings, potentially related to our genetic structure. This sparked accounts of experiments and multi-generational abductions including children, and of invasive sexual experiences and extraction of bodily materials or implantation of devices. By the 1990s, there was a return to the belief that these encounters were blissful and spiritual in nature, with the beings viewed once more as benevolent guardians watching over us.

---

[38] Please refer to the note titled "Exploring Otherworldly Possibilities" in Historical Tidbits for further information.

Today, everything mentioned above is in motion, and it appears to be orchestrated chaos. Some who have experienced negative interactions with entities now describe them as peaceful and enlightening, while others who started off positively struggle against malevolent forces. However, no one seems to link these events to disappearances[39] until David Paulides, a former police officer and paranormal investigator, begins his own investigations into what he dubs "The Missing" in the early 2010s. Through his books and documentaries, he explores the possibility that some of the most puzzling missing person cases may have ties to the paranormal. In 2022, nearly 70 years after Probert's messages, Paulides releases **The Missing 411: The U.F.O. Connection**, a documentary diving headfirst into this theory.

In my own exploration of Paulides' mysterious missing cases, I came across a multitude of natural explanations and instances of animal predation or human intervention. Yet, amidst the noise, one case caught my attention – that of Everett "Carl" Higdon Jr. This case made headlines in the 1970s, drawing the interest of both media outlets and UFO researchers. In 1978, it was even featured on the TV show **In Search of...** and Higdon's wife wrote a book about it in 2017. It all began roughly a year after a well-publicized UFO encounter involving a rancher not far from Higdon's home in Wyoming.

The highly respected oil rig worker was out hunting when he suddenly found himself being abducted by non-human beings. They took him to a tower lit up with blindingly bright lights, where they conducted tests on him before ultimately returning him because he did not fit their needs. Under hypnosis later, Higdon was able to recall these details.

---

[39] Although there are hundreds of thousands of reported missing people in the US each year, most cases are resolved quickly. This number, however, does not accurately reflect the global statistics as there may be various reasons for disappearances that go unreported or cannot be tracked, such as war, conflict, drug use, and political instability. According to the National Missing and Unidentified Persons System (NamUs) database from the US Department of Justice, there are currently about 20,000 individuals listed as missing and another 14,000 listed as unidentified bodies in the United States as of May 2024. It is believed this number greatly underestimates the actual situation. Some experts estimate the true number could be four or five times higher than what is reported. Additionally, the NamUs system is unable to determine if violence played a role in these disappearances.

Meanwhile, his friends had formed a search party when he didn't return home as expected. When they finally found him, he was sitting in his truck – but it was now parked far away from where he had originally left it. He appeared semi-conscious and disoriented, unable to remember what had happened to him. Fearing a medical emergency, his friends rushed him to the hospital where doctors were baffled by his amnesia-like state and the burning sensation in his eyes. Despite thorough examinations, no medical explanation could be found for his symptoms. Strangely enough, however, the scars from tuberculosis that had once marked his lungs were now completely gone. As if all of this weren't bizarre enough, a bullet was discovered in Higdon's pocket – one he distinctly recalled firing while hunting. Yet, upon closer examination, it was clear the bullet had hit something and then flattened itself before falling to the ground. A forensic team which examined it could offer no explanation for this strange occurrence.

In Paulides' investigation of the case, he revealed Higdon's theory that his vasectomy was the reason he was returned by the mysterious forces that took him. As Higdon recounted his harrowing experience of being thrown out and tumbling down a hill upon his return, Paulides emphasized the gravity of this moment. Having investigated countless occurrences involving missing persons or recovered bodies, Paulides knew when someone had been deliberately discarded like trash. This wasn't an accident or a mere slip – it was a calculated act of malicious intent.

But there is a captivating twist to this story that was not widely reported when it occurred in 1974. It was not mentioned in the **In Search of...** segment or by Paulides, but I discovered it in an article from the **Tampa Bay Times** in 1975. In this article, a debunker mentions the case and remarks that Higdon stated he was not the only human at the testing facility; there were other Earthlings present as well. This detail was also mentioned in his wife's book, where we learn more about these other humans. According to Higdon, there were five of them – one adult and four children or teenagers – at the testing facility. In a YouTube interview from 2022 titled "Then and Now ~ Carl Higdon talks about his alien abduction during hunting," Higdon recalled the other humans as a man and perhaps three or four children. He even speculated those running the facility may have been androids instead of actual aliens.

Conjunctions

This reminds me of what Ingo, Pat Price, and other Star Gate RV'ers witnessed at similar facilities, leading me to recall Tom McNear's categorization of such places as prisons.[40] Based on media reports from that time, it does not seem like any of these other humans Higdon saw was returned.

In this too, I immediately recognized the similarities between Higdon's experience and Ingo's childhood memory of being abducted by a UFO. Just before losing consciousness, Ingo saw two other people with him – one older and one still a teenager – just like Higdon did in his encounter. This is on top of Probert's message about them targeting groups of us.

The thought was chilling, as it meant there could be abductees we may never know about, ones who have been taken captive, and are powerless and helpless, enduring endless cycles of unspeakable torture and violation for hours on end. And for children or teenagers, this could mean a lifetime of imprisonment until they are no longer useful, subjected to the same heinous acts as the stupefying mutilated cattle and other animals we find – brutal penetrations that leave them forever scarred, until they are simply discarded and disposed of like garbage.

In this too, the idea of the Lotus Eaters stayed at the forefront of my mind and led me back to the creatures that had enveloped me. I had christened them as fairy children, but I knew deep down they were more than innocent creatures; their seductive charm was like the sirens' song, luring unsuspecting victims to their doom. Once engulfed in this dreamy state, it would be easy to understand how one might plead with these fairies to never leave, willingly following them wherever they may go.

But what those who have succumbed to the fairies' intoxicating ways don't count on, recalling that Trip Advisor review about contemplating the strange rock but not staying long, thanks to a clearly manufactured ecstasy and thus are prevented from ever really knowing about, is also encased within this "heaven" a dark shadow concealed, perhaps the "Indian Satan," the one which had followed me. Leading me to think what happens to those who stay and linger too long, disappearing perhaps into that stepping stone between realms and vanishing within forever, might not be very blissful at all.

---

[40] Please refer to the note in Historical Tidbits titled "Exploring the Link."

There are all sorts of possibilities to investigate.

Ingo Swann, **The Windy Song**

THE MOUNTAIN'S TIME

March 31, 2024

Time Slips

On the drive back from our Christmas dinner buffet at Church and Union, a restaurant operating within a converted church on Union Street in Charleston, South Carolina, I made a promise to myself. I declared this would be the last time my son and I would ever do a holiday meal buffet. The food was delicious, but the chaos of the restaurant was too much. It seemed like they were understaffed and overbooked, especially with the torrential rain outside. Everyone wanted to come in, regardless of their reservation time.

Facing an hour-long wait, despite our reserved time, and being starving, we negotiated for a seat outside on the restaurant's back patio under a sagging tent collecting water. We had to brave the continuing downpour between our table and the back door of the restaurant to get to the food, but it was worth it. My tall son was able to push some of the water out from under the sagging tent to keep us dry while we ate. Once we were full, we left. As we walked past the same group of people who had arrived when we did, I made a silent vow never to participate in another holiday buffet again.

The concept of swearing off a holiday buffet lasted exactly two months. Without hesitation, I made a reservation for an Easter buffet. My son was still in college, so I searched for restaurants on Open Table near his apartment.

There was only one option, and it happened to be close by: Mountain Lake Lodge. I booked a table for two at noon, within the brunch hours of 11am to 3pm, assuming he would still be asleep when I arrived. All I knew about the place was from its name – it was a lodge up in the mountains with a lake and they were serving an Easter buffet. After making the reservation, I visited their website to see what dishes might be available. The website boasted of a quiet and peaceful atmosphere, top-notch cuisine, and a variety of indoor and outdoor activities to enjoy. It seemed like the perfect choice even if it was the only choice.

Utilizing Google Maps, I calculated the distance from my son's apartment and planned my arrival time accordingly. I factored in an extra 30 minutes to allow for some exploration of the surrounding Lodge area. As my son is an enthusiastic fisherman, I thought it would be a great spot to visit during our sporadic summer weekends together, especially since he would be staying in the area for summer classes.

The drive to see him took two and a half hours, and it turned out to be uneventful. There were the usual annoyances of slow trucks blocking the left lane on the two-lane highway, but traffic was mostly light. But then there was one moment that made me jump out of my skin. A flock of birds suddenly swooped low over the highway right as I was approaching. In the mix of birds was a dark one, possibly a crow, but everything happened so quickly I wasn't sure. As the bird flew towards my windshield in what felt like slow motion, I screamed, knowing I would be powerless to brake on the busy highway. Miraculously, at the very last second, the bird was lifted away from danger by some kind of wind tunnel above my car. "Thank goodness!" I exclaimed in relief. Regardless of any superstitions surrounding black birds, I just wanted it to live.

I arrived a bit ahead of schedule, and after a brief examination of my son's living quarters – for which I will refrain from comment – we departed. He drove my vehicle as we climbed up to Mountain Lake Lodge, situated amid the Blue Ridge Mountains within the Appalachians of Southwest Virginia, at an elevation of nearly 4,000 feet above sea level.

As we made our way along the winding mountain road, a Turkey Vulture suddenly appeared, startling me as it flew out from the side of the lane. I let out a scream, and my son shot me a disapproving look. The road was already treacherous enough without my hysterics, his expression seemed to say. We watched in silence as the large bird took flight, feeling like an eternity had passed before it finally disappeared. My son had slowed the car down significantly, and we were now inching forward. Thankfully, there were no other cars behind us. After that close call, my son picked up some speed but still drove cautiously around each hairpin turn. As we approached another turn, we noticed a hawk perched on a nearby tree branch, staring at us intently. This time, it was on my son's side of the car. We drove by slowly as the bird and I made eye contact; it was the third bird encounter of the day for me – a sign that something was in the air. But I didn't catch on.

At last, we reached the top of the mountain and came to the end of the road. To our left was a large stone building, the main structure, while on our right was a wooden building slightly ahead. We followed signs for parking and found a narrow but not yet full lot. As we drove in, families of all ages were walking towards us from various cars. My son carefully navigated through the crowded lot until we found an open space. He pulled into it, leaving enough room behind my car for another vehicle to park. We both got out and he asked if he had pulled forward enough, leaving enough space behind my car for a long bed pickup truck.

"Sure, but what truck?"

He paused, as if he were gazing at the vehicle in question, but then corrected himself. "The one," he said, gesturing towards the empty spot. "It's going to be here."

He seemed particularly concerned about leaving enough room for this vehicle, so I obliged. I chuckled and replied with something along the lines of, "There's plenty of room." My car was a compact size, and he had pulled forward significantly.

Our next stop was the lake. I had mentioned it while we were driving up the road, talking about how it might be a great spot for fishing during the summer. As we left the parking lot, we followed the signs pointing towards the boat ramp, but when we finally reached the path and could see our destination, we exchanged looks of confusion. Where was the lake? We continued to trust the signs and on we went. But said lake was nowhere to be found. In our state of confusion, we did what I imagine anyone would have done in our situation: we continued walking up the boat ramp, passing by metal cleats spaced out for boats to tie up to. We descended its steps and onto a sunken area in the ground, now overgrown with rocks, trees, grass, and bushes, but completely devoid of water. To our disbelief, the lake had disappeared, and not recently either. We were completely unable to comprehend how or why.

In the distance, we spotted a deep pit filled with water. It reminded me of a rock quarry that had been partially filled in, although "partially" was being generous. With our minds set on reaching this mysterious lake, we walked across what used to be the lakebed towards the water in the far-off hole. We eventually stumbled upon a pontoon boat stuck in the earth, with trees growing around and through it. Standing next to a towering pine tree, I asked my son to search online for an explanation. That's when we both discovered two things:

1) If you've watched **Dirty Dancing**, you've seen the lake. The Mountain Lake Lodge was used as the iconic setting for the fictional Kellerman's Mountain House in the scenic Catskill mountains of upstate New York. It was in these waters, now absent from sight, where Johnny (Patrick Swayze) famously lifts Baby (Jennifer Grey), forever cementing their dance moment in movie history.
2) It is one of Virginia's only two natural lakes and has an inexplicable habit of cleaning itself out and refilling every few hundred years, for reasons unknown. According to predictions, the next refill is expected to happen in the next 50 years.

At that moment, my son looked at me and said what was on both of our minds, "Won't be fishing here."

"Nope," with a contorted smile was all I could muster.

Standing there not knowing really what else to do, I suggested he take a picture of the landscape without the water and proposed he keep the photo and in 50 years, bring his grandchildren to this spot, display the photo while they gazed out at the water. He obliged but skeptically. As it was nearly noon, we gave up on our lake aspirations and made our way back. We both pondered how the Lodge, with its lake-themed name and cabins scattered over the gentle hills near the main structure, managed to survive despite now offering a view of a desolate landscape.

As we made our way back to the Lodge, we began to understand how. Signs were scattered around, pointing out different features. One read "The Lift," drawing attention to the cinder blocks Swayze used to lift Gray out of the water in the movie. Sure enough, there they were, looking just as I had imagined – like abandoned ruins in a desert. The Lodge was capitalizing on its past as a movie set, I thought. They were unquestionably taking the "fake it until you make it" mantra to heart.

The Lodge is certainly an impressive sight. It took some effort to find the entrance, climbing up a steep set of stairs. Once we reached the top, we were greeted by a cozy bar that felt like a typical lodge. As we continued walking, we entered an inviting drawing room with a large fireplace as its centerpiece. Straight ahead was the entrance to the restaurant. The hostess asked if we wanted to sit on the heated patio. But after glancing around at the empty space and noticing some dark clouds rolling in, calling forth memories of our previous rainy outdoor Christmas dinner, we said, "No thank you."

We were directed to a separate room attached to the main dining area, designed for those lucky enough to find a seat with a view of the lake, when the lake is there. My son and I were placed at one of these coveted tables by the window. A narrow walkway separated our table from the ones against the outer wall of the main dining room.

We had developed a strategy during Christmas: one of us would stay at the table while the other went to get food. We used this same tactic here, with my son going first. He returned with plates filled with prime rib, ham, and trout. I had to laugh. Trout really, it certainly seemed like they were in denial. He warned me about the carving station being managed by an unhappy woman who struggled with larger cuts of meat. With this knowledge, I ventured into the dining area. Except when I arrived at the carving station, it seemed as though it had just been set up and there was no one manning it. I hesitated, unsure if it was self-serve or not. Like many others around me, I decided to load up on sides like cheesy cauliflower, mashed potatoes, and green beans instead. When I returned to our table, something caught my eye about the family sitting across from us by the actual dining room wall, but I couldn't quite figure out what it was.

My son raised an eyebrow as he noticed the arrangement of side dishes on my plate, "No prime rib?" he asked.

I shook my head. "There was no one there to serve it," I replied.

"That's strange," he commented.

Before I could answer our waitress brought over some sparkling water for us. "Can I clear your plate now?" she asked me politely.

"Thank you but I haven't finished yet," I replied, pushing the plate aside to make room for the new glasses.

"Oh, sorry," she apologized, "I thought you were done since the plate had been there a while."

It was an odd statement, considering I had just sat down and only moved the plate when she arrived with the glasses. But she didn't seem defensive; in fact, she appeared quite pleasant and attentive to our table. Meanwhile, my son headed back inside.

As he took longer than expected, I scanned the area and landed my gaze on the family sitting across from us once again. Except this time, there were six of them. Confused, I wondered what happened to the family of four that was there before. I could have sworn there were only four people at that table earlier. Not only that, but they were now dressed in different clothing than what I remembered seeing earlier.

I began to survey our surroundings with greater scrutiny and take note of the people present. The more I focused, the more I became aware that something was off. It wasn't a disturbance, per se, but rather a feeling of being out of sync with time. Just as I started to process this, our waitress returned to refill our glasses of water. Worried I may be hallucinating, I asked her specific questions about the lake, and she cheerfully provided detailed answers and her opinion on when it might be refilled.

My son returned to the table after our waitress left, informing me that groups of people had suddenly appeared out of nowhere. I chuckled, "That's just how buffets are sometimes." I glanced at his full plate as he sat back down. "Looks like the woman finally gave you some decent sized slices this time."

"Yeah, I had to ask her though," he replied. "She wasn't super happy about it, but I stood there and waited until she did it."

I shared with him the conversation I had with the waitress about the lake and her ideas. He responded with an interesting observation, "You were testing her to see if she was real."

I was surprised, "How did you know?"

He shrugged nonchalantly, "Just a guess."

"Mom, I saw a table with twelve people when I walked in, but on my way back there were only six and no sign there had ever been more. And then all these people suddenly appeared out of nowhere, and the tables that were empty before were now full."

"I have the same feeling," I replied.

I entered the dining room, thinking about the table with twelve people that my son had mentioned. But as I passed by again, there were only eight people sitting there as if they had always been eight. Something strange was definitely happening. I went straight to the carving station, but instead of finding the woman who was supposed to be there, a man was carving the meat. He happily handed me thick slices and I made my way back to my seat. The dining room seemed unusually empty compared to before.

As I took a moment to assess the situation, it became apparent my son and I were experiencing completely different realities. Everything seemed tangible and real to me; I even had conversations with people around me while waiting at the carving station. It was as if we were moving through events in a compressed timeline, jumping back and forth between past and present. This became even more evident when my son mentioned a conversation he overheard while I was away – a waiter detailing his interaction with the couple who were sitting behind me. But when I had observed that area earlier, there was no couple but instead a family sitting there. We were experiencing vastly different things in time at the same time. Suddenly, my earlier exchange with the waitress about clearing plates made much more sense.

I made one final trip to the dessert station, and I noticed the large party of twelve had returned. The man who had carved slices for me was now chatting with a group at a nearby table while the woman was busy carving meat. When I returned to our table, I found the family of six was back down to four. My son and I quickly finished our desserts, eager to leave. After paying the bill, we hastily left the dining room. Once again, it was filled with patrons, and the party of twelve was back to the one of six. My son pointed at their table as we passed by it.

We both used the restrooms off the lobby and then hustled passed the bar and down the stairs, quickly covering ground in the parking lot. We got to the car.

My eyes trailed over to the long bedded pickup truck parked behind my car, the one apparently my son had expertly maneuvered my car ahead in the spot to leave enough room for.

"Your pickup truck," I said, pointing in its direction, not even registering its color, white, at the time.

"Yeah, I know," he replied, "can we go!"

And back down the mountain we went, grounding ourselves shortly thereafter in the familiar aisles of the local Wal-Mart.

After getting home, I decided to do some research on the internet for answers. My search parameters were "Mountain Lake Lodge" and "paranormal." That's when I stumbled upon a 2012 YouTube video by

SuperNatural-Media titled "Mountain Lake Hotel Investigation: Full DVD." It was an hour-long video of a ghost investigation and analysis, seemingly approved by the resort's general manager at the time, Buzz Scanland, who appears in the video.

The investigation begins in the drawing room I mentioned earlier, with a large fireplace. The lead investigator, Dan Morgan, stands before the fireplace and comments on the electrical energy vibe coming from the rock walls throughout the hotel. They appear to be using an electric and magnetic fields (EMF) device/reader and a Ghost Box to capture Electronic Voice Phenomena (EVPs or spirit voices).

As they move around the drawing room, they note high activity near the front desk. Another investigator, David Henderson, enters wearing a t-shirt that reads "Have you seen my Zombie?" I made a mental note to get one of those shirts. Holding an EMF reader to the mantle, he mentions the stone has a high quartz content which can act as a conductor. They eventually realize their readings near the front desk are likely from wiring for the lodge's alarm system rather than spirits. Throughout their investigation, they debunk some claims but also find evidence for others. Towards the end of the video, they mention picking up distinct voices from different time periods – something that caught my attention.

After watching the video, there were three key points that stood out to me: There seemed to be a high level of electrical energy in the dining room, the Lodge – then called a hotel – was made of a specific type of stone with a lot of quartz, and several investigators reported hearing voices from different time periods throughout the building.

The next video I watched was an interview with the owner of the Lodge at the time, an elderly woman named Mary Moody Northen. The footage appeared to be from the 1970s, or even the late 1960s, well before the Lodge gained fame from the movie **Dirty Dancing**. At one point during the interview, the camera pans around, capturing the lake in all its splendor as it sparkles in the distance. Moody Northen and the reporter make their way down to the boat house, with the water still in view. The reporter brings up a local myth about trees at the bottom of the lake, hinting the lake may be relatively new. Moody Northern dismisses this notion, claiming there haven't been any visible trees for a long time. I catch myself laughing out loud.

This video, though, provided valuable insight into the history of the place. The area itself has a rich native past, in fact for over a hundred years, people from all walks of life have been drawn to this location, including Indigenous peoples who used it as a hunting territory. It became a "resort" when the land surrounding the lake was developed for stagecoach lodging in the mid-1800s.

The original hotel was a large wooden structure, but it was torn down and rebuilt with native sandstone quarried from the land in 1936 due to fire concerns. In between World War I and the Great Depression, it was a popular destination for entertainment. Moody Northern herself spent many summers there as a child, often traveling alongside pack horses up the mountainside to get there. Despite the long journey, she found the beauty of the lake and its surroundings worth every effort. Her father, William Lewis Moody, a successful businessman who had been a guest at the hotel since he was a young child, purchased it in 1930 when she was in her forties. After his passing in 1954, she took over ownership until her death in 1986. It is now managed by an estate connected to her family. The ghost of Mary Moody Northern was a focal point during that 2012 paranormal investigation.

I used this background to start investigating the geological structure of the land and stumbled upon a website detailing the topography and geology of the region. According to this source, the area surrounding the lake consists of a layer of Rose Hill sandstone at the surface, followed by varying depths – ranging from 50 to 100 feet – of Tuscarora or Clinch sandstone, then 200 feet of Juniata sandstone, all atop a massive 1,500 foot layer of Reedsville-Trenton shale, also known as Martinsburg shale. After breaking down the components of each layer, it's clear the overall terrain is comprised entirely of sandstone infused with veins of quartz running throughout.

My exploration continued, broadening my search to include terms like quartz, time, and paranormal. One term caught my eye: "time dilation." It described the phenomenon of experiencing time differently due to varying gravitational fields, such as between someone on Earth and someone in space.

This concept is often seen in science fiction, where it is portrayed as logical, through concepts like space folding or traveling through wormholes at accelerated speeds of light. In the realm of paranormal, this idea of altered time exists alongside another term: "time slips." According to **Psychology Today**, this theory suggests each moment creates a new universe with its own timeline, potentially leading to an infinite number of universes. It could also explain the occurrence of time slips, where individuals or groups inexplicably travel through time without understanding how or why it happened. These experiences are often referred to as time anomalies or more readily just lumped under the indescribable banner of paranormal episodes.

Next, I watched an academic presentation titled "Geological Analysis of Quartz in Time Slip Cases." The video reiterated the high quartz content of sandstone and explained time slips as paranormal events where a person or group experiences a sudden shift from their current time period to another while remaining fully conscious and interacting with their surroundings. The presentation discussed two theories to explain this phenomenon: the Stone Tape Theory, which suggests quartz can record and play back information from its environment, and the Place Memory Theory, which proposes that residual energy left by individuals can be accessed through extrasensory perception due to the environment's ability to store it.[41]

Putting those two together, a time anomaly with a place memory seemed to sum up our experience in the restaurant. It was as if there was a tear in the fabric of time, causing our experience to be altered. Perhaps it was due to some sort of energy field that surrounded us, transporting us to and from recorded memories from the past.

The presentation also references an academic paper titled "Using GIS to Analyze Relationships to Explore Paranormal Occurrences in the Continental United States." According to the paper, haunted locations are considered to have paranormal activity that is recurrent and associated with a specific place. The study focused on analyzing correlations between reported haunted locations, based on the show **Ghost Hunters**, and geological and hydrological features.

The results showed a strong likelihood that paranormal activity could manifest in areas with certain features such as faults, streams, quartz-containing rock units, limestone deposits, large, localized deposits of quartz, and high concentrations of magnetite.

Based on these results, the researchers created a map of the entire United States using these parameters to predict areas where paranormal activity was more likely to occur. As I scanned the map included in the

---

[41] Visit the website for this book, conjunction.world, to discover academic papers discussing these two theories.

report as "Figure 5. Paranormal activity predictive map," I take note of the deep orange shading over southwestern Virginia, indicating a high potential for paranormal activity. Could it be, I thought, that the quartz-rich mountain, layered with sandstone that goes hundreds of feet deep and forms not only the building but also the landscape itself, acts like an amplifier? When combined with the presence of the nearby lake, whose water levels constantly fluctuate, it's as if this area operates on its own unique time frame.

So, what about the essence of time and its connection to unexplainable occurrences? In a way, it was something that I had encountered 11 years earlier.

During my junior year of college, while studying at my desk in my dorm room, I noticed a small ball of white light moving towards me from the corner where the ceiling met the wall. Before I could even process what was happening, I was transported to a field of wheat. The wind was fierce and threatened to push me back, but I stood my ground against it. In the distance, dark storm clouds loomed, resembling tornadoes and emitting powerful winds. A young girl approached me, appearing more childlike than adult. I was struck by the color of her hair; it was almost white. She was visibly afraid, telling me "they" were warning her not to come near me. Behind me, the sky was clear and bright with warm light radiating outwards. I encouraged the girl to ignore "them" and instead head towards the light. She expressed her hesitation and fear about going against their warnings, but I reassured her it would be the right decision.

As I urged her forward, the storm clouds grew darker, and the winds intensified. Despite this, she eventually made the choice to walk around me and into the light. Suddenly, I found myself back in my room sitting at my desk without a single thing out of place or disturbed.

I was unsure of how to interpret what had occurred. The experience left me feeling uneasy, but it wasn't the actual event that bothered me; it was the way I was taken to that stormy field and then just returned. I mentioned it to some friends, and we all dismissed it as just another "college experience," even though I hadn't consumed anything except for a Diet Dr. Pepper.

As time passed, the memory faded into the back of my mind. With everything going on at 357, I never thought to tell Ingo about it. There were so many other things with life and work and Ingo's life and work which seemed more important to discuss. From there it just faded into memory.

After Ingo's passing, my mom and I uncovered a bundle of paintings wrapped in dirty plastic. It seemed Ingo had hidden them away in his sub-basement in the late 1970s. Among the collection were paintings from the early 1960s, including a portrait of a nude young woman sitting in a wheat field. Her white hair is swept back by a strong wind, and she sits motionless with her legs crossed, looking back over her shoulder. The sky behind her is painted a golden hue, while storm clouds cover the other side, the side she is looking back from. Fear radiates from her eyes.

As I stared at the painting, memories of my college days washed over me. I was unable to fathom what I was seeing – it was an exact depiction of the experience that had happened to me in my junior year. My mom stood next to me, a worried look on her face as she wondered if I had been exposed to some toxic substance from the artwork. My thoughts were racing with unanswered questions while my inner voice screamed in shock and confusion.

How was this possible? It was impossible. The painting, created in the 1960s, depicted an event that took place 30 years later – and from my own past, no less. I began to shudder. I was lost, questioning the fabric of time and reality. My attempt to explain this to my mom only resulted in jumbled words and confused expressions. Sensing I needed a break, she suggested going for a snack and led me to Ingo's art studio. As she stepped into his office, I could hear her washing her hands and possibly searching for the number of the CDC. But before she could make any calls, I quickly reassured her everything was fine and there was no need to contact anyone. I forced a smile, trying to convince myself as much as her.

Was Ingo involved in something I had yet to experience? Or was this a memory from his past I was somehow drawn into? Or were we, irrespective of the other, pulled into something in which time seemed irrelevant? If it were a message from him in the past to me in the future, he would have left some kind of indication; that was always his way. We found the trash bag filled with paintings by pure chance. It was more likely to end up in a dumpster than for us to open it and discover its contents. So, this was different, outside of his normal actions. As I analyzed it through the concept of time, as an intrusion into our separate realities, beyond the constraints of time itself, I began to realize there are mysteries that surpass and maybe even transcend time itself.

According to Ingo, we are capable of directly perceiving other levels of awareness, which can yield the same results as our five physical senses. He described this as being connected to the universe through a "web of electromagnetic energy." Expanding on this concept, he stated we are not limited to only our five senses, and how our bio-electromagnetic bodies possess numerous exceptional senses through intricate systems of receptors and sensors at the cellular, nervous, chemical, and bio-electromagnetic levels. To understand this more fully, one can imagine each cell, and perhaps even each atom, in our physical form as a receptor or sensor. In this way, he argued there are natural explanations for many forms of Psi functioning that are being ignored by society, both in terms of factual evidence and potential implications.[42]

Taking a broader view and pulling on the loose threads from various directions, an aspect of my own re-examining came into view. Perhaps there are certain locations where the line between realms, or frequencies, is thinnest due to geological factors. These places amplify our innate powers and heighten our senses beyond society's acknowledged five, allowing us to tap into invisible frequencies and fields where memories are stored. At these thin lines, time may become extraneous and irrelevant, bringing us closer to things we cannot easily explain or understand. Because of this, I think, paranormal, or what we perceive as paranormal, occurrences at these places can be quite inadvertent, affecting people differently, adding to the phenomena's complexity, and ultimately making what happened very hard to explain or at least explain using concepts of time and space as we currently know them. And when things occur outside of accepted knowledge they tend to get dismissed entirely.

---

[42] From Ingo's **New Scientific Discoveries Regarding the Existence of Certain PSI Faculties Synopsis of a paper presented on 21 March 1994 at the United Nations to members of the Society for Enlightenment and Transformation**. The full document can be found on the website conjunction.world where it is available for free along with his other essays on unleashing the full potential of the human biomind.

It will take time to unlock it.

Ingo Swann, **Your Nostradamus Factor**

HOLY COW
April 16 - 19, 2024

~~UFOs/UAPs~~ Vision Quests

Ingo voiced to me once: "The monstrous entity known as UNCERTAINTY feeds on chaos and thrives in the shadows of our reality." And in the realm of anomalies, unidentified flying objects (UFOs) and unidentified anomalous phenomenon (UAPs) reign supreme. They are rivaled only by our obsession with stories of portals to hell and haunted places in media such as shows, movies, and video games. It seems we have a fascination with fear, if it stays within the confines of fiction.

UFOs/UAPs are the ultimate enigma. Are UFOs simply a figment of our imagination, a creation of our minds? Or is it something far more menacing – a telepathic invasion, or perhaps a non-human entity manipulating us? And then there are the UAPs, technology that defies all rational explanation and shatters our understanding of physics. A technology, Ingo remarked in **Penetration**, that boldly reveals itself even to the lenses of cameras around the world.

They, whether an elusive phantom or technology beyond our understanding, have continually drawn us into their mysterious web ever since unidentified objects flying at breakneck speeds bursting onto the scene after World War II. From that point on, they have been a constant source of fear and fascination, their indefinable nature shrouded in mystery.

While communities dedicated to unraveling their secrets have been and continue to be rife with opposing beliefs and warring ideologies, each vying for dominance in the search for "the truth." Ingo, wise in his observations, recognized there was more to this however than meets the eye. Like peeling back the layers of a buried artifact, one would uncover a carefully crafted web of camouflaged information and deliberate misinformation being disseminated from powerful sources, all working towards the suppression and obscurity of the true nature of the phenomena. And so now, these communities, perhaps spaces is the more appropriate term, have devolved into something even more ominous – a dangerous minefield where people threaten and dox others to enforce their own version of events. These once inquisitive circles have become tainted by the extreme. It's like trying to navigate through a treacherous swamp.

My initiation into the UFO/UAP ecosphere began in the early 1990s, when Ingo would take me to various events and gatherings focused on abductees and anomalous happenings. As I spent more time at 357, I also became acquainted with his friends who were deeply involved in the world of the "extraterrestrial" happenings. Because of this, I became way more familiar with this aspect of the "paranormal" than I ever did with anything relating to Remote Viewing. So of course, I was going to add this phenomenon to my list.

Where do I even begin? Being abducted and/or engaging in some sort of telepathic game playing with supernatural beings was certainly not at the top of my list. I decided therefore to focus on the technological aspect[43] and seek out any hint of bizarre contraptions soaring through the sky. Using a map[44] from a website that listed UFO/UAP hotspots in the United States based on data collected from the National UFO Reporting Center between 2000 and 2023, I zeroed in on Grand County, Utah. It had a high number of reported sightings compared to its population. I dug some more and discovered Moab, the county's largest city, was ranked number one in the state for UFO sightings. It seemed like the perfect place to see a UFO/UAP. Because such a sighting seemed commonplace, at least in my mind, with a sense of nonchalance, I allotted myself two full days

---

[43] For a glimpse into the depths of Ingo's involvement with "acquired" materials, visit the UFOs/UAPs page on the website ingoswann.com.

[44] The map can be found on the website: https://www.axios.com/2024/02/08/ufo-uap-sightings-us-hotspots-2000-2023.

for this expedition, just in case the first day was not successful. Ludicrous thinking in retrospect but nonetheless my operating expectation.

Salt Lake City, Utah was the closest direct airport, so I booked a flight and arranged for an SUV rental. The trip to Moab from Salt Lake City would take around four or five hours, so I booked a hotel near the airport for the first night. My strategy was to depart early the following day to avoid any potential traffic and complete the drive in one shot. But I still needed a place to stay in Moab itself. That's when I chanced upon Under Canvas, a company offering luxurious "glamping" accommodations near Canyonlands and Arches National Parks. With safari-style tents and even one with a clear panel for stargazing, it seemed like the perfect place for me to search for UFOs/UAPs from my bed at night. I booked a two-night stay and made reservations at a hotel near the airport for my return trip. Everything was falling into place perfectly.

Unfortunately, I received a call the following day informing me my tent had been double booked. The staff offered to upgrade me to a larger tent at no extra cost, but it did not have a clear panel at the top for stargazing. Since that was the main reason for my choice of tent, I saw it as a sign and decided to cancel the reservation. This left me in a difficult position, as I still needed a place to stay from which I could easily spot a UFO/UAP.

I expanded my search and discovered a place I hadn't considered before: Whispering Oaks Ranch. It was a remote 50-acre property with seven cozy cabins, situated at an elevation of over 8,000 feet in the Manti-La Sal National Forest/La Sal Mountain range of the Rockies. Located just outside Moab, on the border of Utah and Colorado, it boasted breathtaking views of the surrounding canyonlands in every direction. If there were any UFOs/UAPs to be seen, this would undoubtedly be the prime location for sighting one, perhaps even coming face-to-face with one. After researching the cabins, I decided to book the Wildflower cabin because it had its own private hot tub – all at a lower cost than my airport lodging. How perfect! I could relax in the hot tub and scan the skies for UFOs/UAPs.

The check-in time was four o'clock, so I knew I would have some time to kill between Salt Lake City and Moab. I wasn't interested in visiting the area's famous national parks; they seemed too chaotic. Time and again my attention was drawn to the high concentration of ancient rock art sites in and around Moab. Although my experience at Judaculla Rock was still vivid in my memory, the allure of the Sego Canyon Rock Art Interpretive

Site was too much to bear; the temptation to witness it for myself was too strong. So, against my better judgment, I tossed caution aside and put it on the list. I checked the map of the area. Given the timing of what I had planned, I could add a stop at a second site, the Courthouse Wash Rock Art site.

Sego boasts famous panels of Ute and Fremont pictographs and petroglyphs from ancient Indigenous peoples of the region, specifically its Barrier Canyon style pictographs. These images are subject to much speculation: some believe they depict encounters with extraterrestrials, while others see them as spiritual visions. Considering my quest to see a UFO/UAP, I convinced myself these were a necessary addition to the trek. But instead of extensively researching them beforehand, I simply searched online for directions on how to reach them.

I came across photos of the "art" but didn't spend much time studying them. I printed out information from two websites – "Sego Canyon Rock Art Petroglyphs" and "Roadside Attraction Sego Canyon Rock Art" – and jotted down the directions in case I lost service on my phone. Because I would be traveling through remote areas, it seemed wise to have a physical copy. From these sources, I learned there were three main panels that could be easily accessed from the road or a short distance away, about four miles up Thompson Canyon Road. A parking area was also available. The only other information I had printed out was the directions to Whispering Oaks Ranch, which provided three alternative routes from Moab.

My flight to Salt Lake City was smooth and uneventful. The airport was impressively modern and efficient, making my short time inside surprisingly enjoyable. I quickly retrieved my luggage and rental SUV before heading to the hotel. After a quick dinner, I collapsed into bed and fell asleep. Despite my intentions for a sound sleep, I was abruptly awoken at two in the morning by what felt like tiny jellyfish stinging me in a circular pattern around my thighs. It was extremely unpleasant, to say the least, and hostile. I was able to quickly rule out the possibility of my legs being asleep. My mind immediately jumped next to bed bugs as I had dealt with them before while at Columbia. But upon turning on the light and examining myself, I found no bites or signs of bed bugs. And yet, the stinging continued throughout the night every time I fell back asleep. The last time it occurred it was accompanied by a clear voice taunting me, "You're in it now!" followed by what sounded like laughter. Something wasn't right here; I didn't go back to sleep after that. Instead, I stayed up eating snacks I had brought with me and reading the internet.

Two hours passed before I checked out and hit the road. After another three hours of navigating through high mountain terrain, noting the possibility of needing tire chains if the weather turned harsher – which was quite likely given the lingering patches of ice – I finally reached the high plains of Route 6/191. The only other vehicles in sight were occasional tractor trailers. I decided to pull over and grab a bite to eat, taking a break from my solitary journey. That's when I came upon the Tamarisk Restaurant, situated along the flowing banks of the Green River. As I sat there watching the river make its way outside my window, I tried to make sense of what had happened in the early hours of the morning. But no answers came to me; none of what I encountered made any sense. After filling up on gas, I hit the road again and about 30 minutes later, turned onto Thompson Canyon Road.

A weathered building, possibly from pioneer days, sports a pictograph sign depicting a figure holding a snake with an arrow pointing forward. It's the only indication you're on the right track, but at least to this point the road is paved even though it is not, as a sign tells you, state maintained. Very quickly, the road leads to the middle of nowhere. Stretching out on either side of the road are barren desert plains doubling as cow pastures kept in check by wire fencing, in varying states of usefulness, running parallel to the road on either side. I pulled over to take a photo of a high mesa in the distance, noticing there were no other cars behind me. I had enough time to get out of my vehicle and capture the perfect shot. The road may have been narrow, but it stretched straight into the horizon, and enabling me to see quite far in all directions.

As I returned to my SUV, I still didn't see any other vehicles on the road behind or in front of me. I pressed onward. Movement up ahead caught my eye. Are those animals? Bears? Baby bears? My mind raced to come up with a plan in case of an attack. But as I got closer, I realized they were just three playful calves crossing the road in front of me. Where is their mother? And then I spotted her standing off to the side of the road. Should I be worried about her charging my vehicle for getting too close to her babies? I slowly inched forward, making sure not to startle or provoke them. Do cows even have triplets? Is this some kind of ambush? These thoughts raced through my head as I passed by them, snapping a photo of one calf lying peacefully on the side of the road and then capturing aspects of the two others with their mother on the other side. I could fully sense the mother cow's annoyance, so I gently accelerated, not wanting to risk an angry cow's charge. Finally passing the group, I let out a sigh of relief, not wanting to disturb the cows any further. I checked my rearview mirror again to ensure I wasn't being chased by an angry cow, but luckily, she was just giving me a stern glare. Glancing back further in the mirror, I saw that no one else had encountered the cows yet.

I paused once more, feeling compelled to take a photo of the striking red and black configuration crawling down a rock outcrop on the mesa up ahead and to my left. I didn't realize it at the time, but this was one of the rock faces I had set out to see, although the pictographs were located much lower than the red and black I seemed mesmerized by. Glancing around there wasn't a single vehicle in sight. I drove onward. The road then quite suddenly transitioned from pavement to dirt at which point I became very grateful I had rented an SUV. A few feet later the road descended at an almost vertical angle, leading to a trickle of a stream that had to be crossed before immediately ascending another steep hill.

Once I reached the top of the hill, I spotted a sign pointing towards Sego Canyon site parking on a sideroad made of dirt. I followed the arrow and pulled into the spot designated for parking and maneuvered to a spot next to some tall bushes. There was also a well-designed shack noted as "restroom" nearby that caught my attention; for some reason, I assumed it contained an actual restroom despite knowing deep down there could be no water lines in such a remote location.

I quickly put on my hiking boots before getting out. As I was about to take a step, I heard another vehicle approaching from behind me. The site is situated in a canyon, so the sound of the vehicle echoed all around me. A blue Jeep began to make its way into the parking area but then suddenly stopped. I could see multiple people inside, not just one person. The Jeep then turned around and drove back the way it had come. Two thoughts came to mind: where did they come from? I didn't see anyone on the road behind me, and why are they leaving? I briefly considered the significance of their departure, but didn't let myself dwell on it for too long.

Once their engine faded away in the distance, I continued towards the "restroom" that stood beyond the dirt lot where I found a short length of wooden fencing. From there, I could view the rock face I had photographed earlier with its mysterious black and red markings. I photographed it some more, only this time I was much closer to it than when I had been back on the road. It struck me as odd that I had been drawn to this spot, but upon closer inspection, it seemed like the fencing was meant to prevent people from falling off the edge of the small canyon. There was a stand nearby, but any information it held was long gone due to weathering. Still, I assumed it must have been a directional sign pointing towards one of the many paths that branched off to the right. So, I ventured down one of these dusty paths surrounded by tall bushes. Before long, I reached a dead end with a steep climb up a sheer rock face in front of me – an unexpected turn of events since I had been searching for pictographs known to be easy to find.

As I contemplated whether to attempt the climb, another vehicle's engine roared in the distance, amplified by the rocky enclave around me. Deciding to backtrack, I crossed back through the dirt lot – where I had parked – towards a picnic table and bench on the other side of the lot just off from the restroom.

But as I was making my way across the lot, an SUV suddenly pulled up and parked near to me. Saying the SUV was "near" would be an understatement. The large vehicle was practically right beside me, even though the dusty lot had technically a lot of space to park within.

I am still fuzzy on if there were two couples or three, but I remember feeling like their SUV was about to run me over before they parked, and the couples exited it. The color of the vehicle caught my attention: white. The recollection of that disturbing encounter in California rushed back to me. The image of the white pickup truck parked at the beginning of the road to Judaculla Rock and the one at Mountain Lake Lodge played on a loop in my mind. Was it all just a coincidence, or was there a hidden significance behind these events? I didn't want to dwell on the latter possibility and made a conscious effort to ignore it.

I turned away from the couples and continued my journey toward the table bench combo, adamant about waiting until the couples finished their meandering. All I wanted was to have some time alone with the "art." Except, I had no clue where the art was located. I secured a spot on the bench and settled down, making sure to keep an eye on the couples' movements to assess if and where they found any "art." However, my view was constantly blocked by the tall brush.

Frustrated, I ventured further into the barren desert landscape which lay beyond the table and its bench, snapping photos of desert flowers and cacti to pass the time. Then suddenly, the sound of another car approaching shattered the silence. I turned just in time to see it pull into the parking lot, adding to the already strange scene. It was white too. The driver emerged from the vehicle and headed towards the restroom shack. I turned my focus to taking panoramic shots of the mesas, but every single photo had those blaringly bright white vehicles in them, no matter how hard I tried to avoid them. Once more, I did my best to ignore any hint of their importance.

Not long after, with the driver's business settled, the white car left. Still, I was starting to get moments where I felt that perhaps something was amiss; I made a conscious effort to push those emotions away too, but they hung on. That is when I noticed the group had lost one of their own, Paul. They were working as a team to locate him, making sure to shout his name as they did. Given there really wasn't much around you could get lost in, thoughts of a different nature crossed my mind. Was Paul a victim of some portal-snatching? The more I observed the area, the more I began to feel something dark and unearthly had happened in this very area along those lines. It wasn't just individuals vanishing without a trace. No, it was more along the lines of shamanic gatherings with malevolent beings in an interdimensional gateway hidden within the towering rocky cliffs guarding the entrance to the canyon. So transfixed by their nature, I photographed them, and the opening between them, more than any other feature that day.

Paul was finally captured and in their possession. However, before they could leave, the blue Jeep pulled up next to their white SUV. A father and his two teenage children stepped out of the vehicle. I would have to bide my time again until I was able to be by myself. I navigated down a slope towards the stream or as I called it, the water lost in the desert, I had driven over earlier, approaching the canyon's gateway.

As I got closer, I felt I was being watched from that direction. It wasn't a reassuring feeling. The rock face to the right of the entrance was unnerving, but the one on the left was particularly ominous. Fervently, I clicked my camera, desperate to capture any sign of a presence attached to the towering rock formations I was feeling. But my photos showed nothing. So, I gave up and turned my attention to the stream, there was something intriguing about it. I walked right up to it and stood by its side, captivated by the sound of the water rushing by my feet. I started to record the sound.

Conjunctions

Not long after I started to film the stream, trying to record its peaceful flow, another vehicle's loud approach caught my attention. It was a white pickup truck. It seemed like someone was sending some kind of signal with their consistent color choice. I tried to brush off any implications I shouldn't be there, but the thought lurked in the back of my mind. This vehicle looked official in some way, and wondered given how far I was off the "beaten trail" so to speak, if I could get in trouble for being where I was. To play it safe, I moved closer to the action happening in the dirt lot nearby. It was a lively party, completely opposite to my quiet time alone with the "art" I was intending.

The pickup truck crashed into the area near the restroom shack, prompting me to question the driver's intentions. But as it turned out, she was there to clean the restroom instead of catching any trespassers. This was a relief, and I returned to my seat at the picnic table, watching the driver of the white pickup truck fiddle with equipment in the back of the truck's bed. I insisted out loud that I didn't need any help and could handle being alone in this remote location. Nevertheless, it seemed like the universe had other plans for me. Soon after, the group in the SUV left. This was followed by the pickup truck driver using that equipment to extract blue liquid from the restroom shack. Suddenly, it hit me – this wasn't a real restroom but a cleverly disguised Porta Potty. I don't know why this revelation shocked me, but it did. The horrid smell and noise caused the family in the Jeep to make a quick exit. I debated leaving too, thinking maybe that was the purpose of the white truck and its Porta Potty extraction. But dammit, I still hadn't seen any pictographs or petroglyphs, and I was determined to find them. I may have even voiced this determination aloud.

I strolled over to my rental SUV and pulled out my printouts, scanning them for any sign of directions to the "art" that was supposed to be easily visible. But so far, I hadn't spotted anything that fit the description. I sifted through the paperwork, searching for any clues. According to what I had printed out, the Ute panel – named after the Indigenous people of this state and featuring depictions of white men, horses, buffalo, and shields – was situated past the wooden fence near the restroom. It is considered the "newest" panel amongst the others. Surprisingly, even though I had been standing in front of it and taking pictures of the area earlier, I had somehow managed to overlook it completely. Digging through my collection of photos, I finally spotted it amidst all the striking red and black elements that had initially caught my attention. It was sitting there, tucked in the bottom corner of the frame, almost as if it was mocking me and my obliviousness.

With the pickup truck driver now retracting the hose used to clean the Porta Potty, I approached the rock face again with a fresh outlook. This time as I stood at the fence, I photographed the panel directly. After the pickup truck had departed and I was finally alone, I followed the directions outlined in the papers to the next panel, which happened to be right beside my rental on the other side of a bush. It was almost comical how I had blindly stumbled between these two panels when I had taken that path to nowhere.

On the second panel, I viewed the petroglyphs known as the Fremont Style panel, dated from the early part of this millennium to its midpoint. I had read these carvings had been made over earlier paintings, but as I stood there looking at them, it was hard to decipher what those original images may have been. Although this panel directly faces the entrance to the canyon, it didn't seem to have any significant impact on me one way or another. Feeling as though someone, or something was hiding just out of sight, I shifted my focus back to the first panel on my left, the one I had just visited moments ago, snapping another photograph. But once again upon review, nothing.

Following the next set of instructions which said, walk out of the lot and into the road and then up it, I did just that. Around the corner I immediately came across the most spectacular of "art," the visions of non-human beings, limbless figures some with huge eyes, others with antennas, some with what looks like helmets. Next to these figures are what I interpreted as energy circles, portals possibly, and snakes or snake-like energy patterns. This panel was featured once on the show **Ancient Aliens** and is the one referred to as Barrier Style. Barrier, as a designation of this type of "art," comes from similar images seen in Barrier Creek in Horseshoe Canyon, formerly known as Barrier Canyon, in the Canyonlands. It is the oldest of the panels, dated between 2,000 to 6,000 years before the common era.

The panel sits directly across, I noticed, from the rock portal area I had been feeling and photographing. I wasn't there but two seconds more before I heard the now familiar echos bouncing off the canyon walls. I heard a vehicle pull in behind me as I was around the corner, I could not see what vehicle exactly had come to join me, only knowing it was there.

I explored just slightly further up the road where my papers said other panels were located; I found one, it was of petroglyphs. The whole time I was on the road, I kept having a feeling about the rocks to the left of the canyon's entrance, somewhat across from the "spectacular" panel. I found myself constantly turning to face it.

As I approached the "spectacular" panel, my mind conjured up the words "vision quest." The closer I got to this mystical rock formation, the more I felt a connection to men from a time long ago. It was as if their spirits were still wandering in this space, and I could sense them surrounding me. The feeling was so intense that I began snapping photo after photo of the left rock face, its counterpart on the right, and the canyon's entrance, the space between them. Pervading me was a nagging suspicion there was something concealed within those images. Yet, when I looked at my photos, all I could see was the landscape in front of me. It seemed impossible, but the feeling persisted despite the lack of evidence in my photographs.

A voice shattered the stillness, causing me to jump and peek around the corner into the dirt parking lot. I saw a familiar silver Toyota 4Runner, much newer than the one I had owned for 15 years before passing it down to my son, parked in front of me. It dawned on me; this was a warning that maybe it was time to go. I gave up my search for a second panel on private property nearby and headed back to the lot. There I found a couple, probably about my age. They seemed just as bewildered and clueless as I had been when searching for the "elusive" art. They looked at me suspiciously, so I lifted my hand and beamed a smile towards them as I made my way over to them.

As we stood near my SUV, discussing the location of each panel, we heard a vehicle approaching from further up the road. The low rumble grew louder as the vehicle barreled down the road. All of us glanced over to catch sight of the blue Jeep, its engine roaring as it passed us. It was heading in the same direction I needed to go. I hadn't realized when they left, they went in that direction, further up the road. I took it as a sign that I had to go, to leave this place quickly just like the Jeep did. Without pausing to consider, I said a quick good-bye to the couple, hopped into my SUV, and swapped out my boots for a pair of shoes. Then, with a sharp U-turn in the parking lot, I headed off down the road.

After a short while, I came upon the mother cow this time without her triplets by her side – I had since sorted out cows can't have triplets, but that is how I categorized them in my mind.

As I passed by her for the second time, she was lying down in the same spot where she had been standing before, the calves were nowhere to be seen. I stopped my car and leaned out the window to take a picture of her. She did not seem too pleased with me. I started inching forward again, slowly, unable to take my eyes off her in the rearview mirror. I could practically hear her thoughts, filled with exasperation and possibly even some choice curse words directed towards me. I offered an apology, explaining I was on an important mission for my project, but it didn't seem to make a difference as she continued to glare at me disapprovingly. I brought the vehicle to a complete halt as I felt a strange connection between us at that moment. Me, looking in the rearview mirror, and her, glaring at me. It was as if we were linked somehow, as if we were having an unspoken conversation between us. I had landed myself in a precarious situation and she, as the mother figure and guardian of this place, had to put in extra effort to assist me. She already had enough responsibilities without me having sauntered in, and enthusiastically too. It felt somewhat along the lines of me having sojourned into the land of stupidness, and her slapping me across the head while simultaneously yelling, rhetorically, "what were you thinking!"

The words "holy cow" reverberated in my mind, taking on a whole new significance. "Fine, I won't go to the Courthouse site," I declared, staring in the mirror at her. But her scowl only deepened, her lips drawing into that all-too-familiar expression of disapproval that every child knows too well. It was the kind of look that cut deep, revealing she knew more than I wanted her to. "And I promise," I continued, "I will never ever go to any rock 'art' site again." Her strong presence lingered in the mirror, reminding me to keep my word. I hastily put the SUV into drive and focused on the road ahead.

A short while later my thoughts drifted. This place was a vortex of colliding intentions and volatile interactions, I contemplated while trying to recover from the feeling that I might have narrowly escaped something much more sinister than I had originally thought. For the remaining four miles on my way back, I didn't pass another soul coming or going.

I returned to the highway and followed it towards Moab. Stopping in a grocery store parking lot, I made some calls to friends and asked about entities, stinging sensations, and jellyfish. No one had answers for me. In hindsight, I'm grateful they let me figure things out for myself. After checking into my cabin, I settled down and tried to make sense of everything that had happened: the strange stings from the jellyfish, the concept of a vision quest, and the possibility of there being something more to Sego Canyon if it required a "guardian." I moved to sit on top of the bed, not under the covers, so I could stretch out comfortably. As the sun set and darkness crept in, I gazed out the window facing the mountain and continued contemplating these thoughts. As I drifted into a state between reality and something else, the idea of a vision quest became even stronger in my mind.

My body was both fully present and detached as lay on the bed, my mind expanding beyond its physical boundaries. A strange, pulsing electricity coursed through me. As I looked out towards the mountain, I sensed hundreds of ethereal figures approaching. They moved with a purpose, guided by their own mysterious agenda, much like the residual images Ingo had described to me. Though not afraid, a sense of marvel mingled with apprehension as I watched, feeling both connected and separate from this unfolding event. Almost like when you watch a movie and you feel so engrossed in what is happening you try to talk to the characters on the screen as though your advice, admonition, direction will have an impact.

As they approached, but kept a respectful distance, they eventually paused outside. A few selected figures moved forward from within the group. I perceived them as medicine women. They encircled the cabin in a loose formation, and I could see forms raise up what I imagined to be arms, releasing what appeared to me as birds: a symbolized circular object flying away. The circle didn't seem to be acting together, each one seemed to be doing their own thing, but it all appeared as one cohesive action. Their presence felt sacred and all-encompassing, beyond my control. This went on for only a few minutes before my memory went blank; the next thing I knew, it was much darker outside.

When I went to look out the window, there was nothing there. But no time to linger on those thoughts; my job of searching for UFOs/UAPs was calling. Despite my excitement and anticipation for a possible UFO/UAP sighting, the cloudy sky revealed nothing but one distant airplane making its way slowly across the horizon. The lights in the valley below, likely from

Moab or another town, were the only sign of life. As the boredom set in, my exhausted mind drifted off to sleep.

As the sky began to lighten, I woke up and headed to the hot tub. Today was my day of rest from searching for UFOs/UAPs. The sky was still covered in thick clouds, and all was quiet around me. The absence of sound made it easy for me to notice the approach of an animal across the small meadow next to the hot tub, even though it was difficult to see in the dim dawn light. Unsure of what to do, I stayed still and observed, hoping for a peaceful encounter.

Gradually, a shape emerged – it was a buck. I felt relieved. Then, another form appeared – a doe. They both moved toward the hot tub as the first rays of daylight hit their coats. Somehow, my scent hadn't reached them yet, even as the buck scanned his surroundings. It seemed like he had picked out this spot specifically and was bringing his mate here for some alone time, or as my son's high school English teacher would say, "special hugs." But then he saw me, and his expression changed from joy to frustration – though he never showed fear. The pair continued their way in search of a new spot. A grin spread across my face, and I didn't even try to stifle the laughter that bubbled up from within me.

As the minutes passed, dawn began to break, and the clouds formed an interesting pattern in the sky. It almost looked like a smiley face. I stepped out of the warm hot tub and grabbed my phone to capture a photo. But as I studied the image, it started to feel slightly ominous. The events at the cabin had been oddly fortunate so far, but now this cloud's smirky formation gave me an uneasy feeling. It was like being caught in a sudden but warm and refreshing summer rainstorm, only to look up and see a looming tornado about to strike without any warning.

Thankfully, the sun arrived, and the first full rays of dawn began to filter through. I set my phone down and sank back into the hot tub. For a while, nothing else happened except for an inquisitorial Mountain Bluebird that flew close to me and perched on a nearby tree, observing me. It reminded me of what the forms had released the night before. I gazed back at it and wondered about its significance. When I eventually got out of the hot tub, the bird flew away. I searched online for its spiritual symbolism and found several meanings such as hope, love, positivity, and renewal. Perhaps this encounter was a sign for me to let go of something and embrace a new beginning. But something didn't quite add up for me.

I decided to do some more research to fully understand the message behind this encounter.

As the day wore on, I focused on my research. In the endless maze of the internet, I unearthed vital information. My understanding of visioning and vision quests was limited to a surface level, but as I dug further, I discovered its significance in the spiritual practices of Indigenous peoples in the American Southwest. It involved communing with the spirit world through a guardian spirit – a ferry boat captain doubling as a life coach in the form of an animal – for guidance and protection in life. This ritual, undertaken by both young men and women, required entering a trance induced through prayer, meditation, fasting, or even ingesting hallucinogens. It was viewed as a transformative experience.

The more I read, the more I realized my own experiences were aligned with this process – from feeling the presence of medicine women to being visited by the Mountain Bluebird. It was no coincidence; our paths had crossed for a reason. Slowly but surely, I began to understand Sego Canyon as not just a remote location, but a sacred space where one could connect with a realm beyond our own. The rock faces looming over me seemed to act as gateways between worlds, but worse was the feeling there was something waiting on the other side. I went back to examine my photos from Sego Canyon, paying particular attention to the shape of its entrance between the two rock faces.

As soon as I saw it, I knew it resembled a "U" shape. Through my research, I found this shape holds great significance in multiple cultures. It is believed to act as a powerful portal or gateway, leading to realms beyond our own.[45] Could it be that Sego Canyon was not only a physical place, but also a spiritual one? Everything I had experienced seemed to point towards this conclusion. I made a mental note to read more about this when I returned home and sent myself various articles for further exploration.

After returning home from my trip to Utah, I eagerly sat down to write this chapter and consolidate all the articles I had gathered while there.

---

[45] The Crow People of Montana had a tradition of using small structures to guide them on their spiritual journeys. These structures were often built on steep cliffs and resembled a "U" shape made from stone. It occurred to me that over time, remnants of ancient rituals may have seeped into modern practices, much like how a river changes its path as the landscape shifts, holding onto pieces of its previous course despite being altered.

Having established a strong understanding about vision quests, I redirected my focus towards learning more about the "art" at Sego. During my excavations in the world wide web, I stumbled upon a brief mention of the second panel I had encountered on my journey – the one decorated with petroglyphs. In this stumbling too I learned about earlier pictographs that were now worn and carved over. Intrigued, I explored more and found higher quality images of the paintings hidden underneath.

Since this panel faced the "U," I quickly searched through my own photos to see if by chance I had captured any glimpses of what lay behind the carvings. And there they were. On the left side of the panel, there is a chain of figures depicted in profile, linked together in what seems to be an act of unity or perhaps subjugation. The first figure in line holds out a round object to a larger figure depicted head-on with outstretched arms and another round object in its left hand. Beside this imposing figure stands another one of equal size, also facing forward but holding what appears to be a person by their neck in their left hand. It was jarring and disturbing, a stark contrast to anything transformative or inviting.

I immediately began to question my understanding of the vision quests that took place there, doubting the validity of what I had previously believed. The memory of the medicine women's circle and their release of birds kept replaying in my mind. It was like a mirrored version of the group depicted in the ancient rock painting, but instead of linking arms they formed a complete circle. And the birds that flew away could have been my mind's interpretation of orbs or spirits freeing themselves from their physical forms. Was the towering figure next to the chain a "Spirit Guide," holding onto the quester's soul or consciousness, the orb, before passing it on to the next figure in line – symbolizing those waiting in the other realm? Was this a warning? Was it possible that instead of providing wisdom or direction, these entities had ulterior motives? Perhaps their true intention was to control or obliterate the very core of those who came seeking them out. Had this been why the holy cow was so mad at me?

A tremor shot through my veins, quickening my pulse followed directly by memories of my first night in Salt Lake City flooding my mind, the excruciating pain of jellyfish stings amplified by the haunting warning: "You are in it now!" With a sinking feeling, I realized they were right, I was undeniably knee-deep in something. At that moment, though, I was unable to fully comprehend the enormity of what was unfolding so I tried to set my questions aside. I moved on to my photos of the "spectacular" panel. My eyes caught something I hadn't zeroed in on previously. Could it be a jellyfish? No, wait...yes? No way, it was a jellyfish! Oh my gosh, I couldn't believe it.

Amid the strange, apparitional images of snakes and portal bubbles, I noticed a small crescent moon shape on its side. It reminded me of a jellyfish with six long tentacles streaming down from its curved edge. Questioning, I searched for more information about this image online and discovered others had also seen it as a jellyfish. In fact, a blogger named Curt Mekemson had even given it that name back in 2017. I then discovered a sub-Reddit discussion about the "Jellyfish UFO" that had made headlines in January of 2024, and how it resembled two pictographs found in different locations: Sego Canyon and Wild Horse Canyon near Moab. These pictographs at Wild Horse Canyon featured a similar jellyfish-like figure with either four or six tentacles, hovering above much smaller human figures.

As I examined these images, it felt like fitting a top to a container that I never would have thought belonged together. Yet now that I saw them side by side, the connection was undeniable. It made me wonder what else I hadn't noticed.

My jaw dropped in shock and disbelief, the words "Holy S***!!!" tumbled out of my mouth. The so-called "spectacular" panel was not a work of art, it was a message board, a warning sign, pointing towards the rock face that stood in front of it, depicting exactly what is on the other side. Its dire message was clear: do not enter this sacred realm beyond the "U." For if you dare to embark on your vision quest or seek wisdom from the spirits within its walls, as the second panel, the one directly facing the "U," now carved over warns graphically, you will be doomed. Crude perhaps, but the way I saw it, true, too.

It all clicked into place. The profusion of white vehicles, the silver 4Runner, were ominous smoke signals I should have heeded, warning signs I had foolishly ignored. All the while refusing to believe I was, literally, by coming to this part of Utah, despite my avoidance of anything near Skinwalker Ranch, in their territory. The dark intentions of these malevolent beings were evident to me. But who are they, these shadows with such insidious plans? The unpacking of that started with what had happened during the final stretch of my trip.

After an uneventful night without any sightings of UFOs, I packed up my belongings and left before dawn. Instead of taking the same path as before, I opted for a different route that would take me north towards Horse Mountain, Round Top Mountain, and Adobe Mesa – popular spots for hikers and tourists. Eventually, this path would lead me to Route 128 where I drove west with the Colorado River by my side. When I reached Interstate 70, I continued west but took a different route than the one I had arrived on. I just wanted to put as much distance between myself and where I was as possible. Plus, the views along this interstate were breathtaking with its varied landscapes of deserts, canyons, and cliffs. The only downside was the lack of "provisions" – not even a gas station for quite aways. By the time I reached Salina – the town with provisions – my gas tank was getting dangerously low. The sign heading into town reads: "You Made It." Yes indeed, if anyone has captured a sentiment more perfectly, it is this town with this sign, hands down.

After filling up my gas tank, I headed to Mom's Café, passing by the local arena. It was hosting a rodeo, which seemed fitting for my mood – as if I were in a western movie, thankful to be out of the desert. As I ate a hearty breakfast at Mom's, a sign caught my eye, and I took a picture of it. Its message reminded me of the simple beauty of living a good life despite chaos. Titled "Life," it said: How far you go in life depends on your tenderness towards the young, compassion for the elderly, empathy for those striving, and acceptance of the weak and strong. Because someday, you will have been all of these. The quote was by George Washington Carver. This moment at Mom's was just what I needed.

I arrived back at Salt Lake City earlier than expected and was eagerly counting down the minutes until my flight the next morning. I had no interest in seeing the shrinking Great Salt Lake, so I dropped off the rental SUV at the airport and took the shuttle to my hotel. Unfortunately, my room wasn't ready yet. The shuttle driver suggested I take a ride on the light rail and do some shopping downtown while I waited. It sounded like a decent idea, and he even told me where to get off for shopping. He made it clear that when I returned, I should call him for a ride back to the hotel. I nodded along without paying much attention. But after being dropped off at the airport station and boarding a train, I quickly regretted not staying at the hotel. There was nothing sinister or dangerous going on; it was just an overshadowing feeling of being surrounded by NPCs (non-player characters) – people who seemed to be going through life without any real purpose or direction.

The outdoor mall downtown felt just as empty and soulless, so I hopped back on the train towards the airport. I got off at a stop before the airport. I had noticed the stop on the way out, and the walk back to the hotel from there appeared to be a fairly simple journey. Yet, as soon as I got off, I regretted that decision too. Despite it only being two o'clock in the afternoon, something about this place made it feel like anything could happen at any time, none of which seemed good. I picked up my pace and thankfully found my room ready when I got back to the lobby for the second time that day.

That night I descended into a dream of swirling winds and towering canyons. I was not interacting with it, just observing it. Around me was a thick tide of spirits, floating forms; above me was the backdrop of the dark sky. In my dream, I interpreted this place as a spiritual dumping ground, where restless souls were herded and trapped like cattle waiting for their inevitable fate. The moment I opened my eyes, I knew I had to leave as soon as possible. I didn't even care if it meant missing out on the complimentary breakfast at the hotel and spending three hours at the airport. At that point, anything was better than staying where I was any longer.

Finally having a chance to decompress after returning home, I spent hours scouring the internet for more information. It was during this time I discovered exactly what I had been up against when I made the decision to go to Utah, specifically the area I had visited. Initially, I was aware of the significant population of Mormons in the region and decided to start my research there. It turns out that prior to settling in Utah, they had been on the run from persecution and chose this location because it was "owned" by Mexico at the time. Additionally, no one else seemed interested in the land, including the Indigenous peoples such as the Paiutes, Utes, and Shoshone.

The reason for the easy surrender of this region remains unclear to me, but during my exploration of the history of Utah Lake in the southern parts, I stumbled upon a legend that may provide some insight.

The Indigenous people who lived nearby believed in water babies — not in the sense of cute ghostly infants, but as malevolent beings that took pleasure in causing suffering. Some pioneers interpreted these creatures as dwarves, others as part reptile or mermaids. Whatever the form, they were known to drag victims down to watery graves.

Perhaps though this is too literal an interpretation. It could also be viewed allegorically – crossing a line when tempted by the riches of the water and area or driven by desires for power and control you turn to these creatures for just that. This reliance on supernatural forces and spirits then leads one on a dangerous path, even if it starts with good intentions. It becomes clouded and difficult to determine where the line is drawn. Once on this path, you have no idea how far you have gone until you are so deep that staying above water is nearly impossible. You either drown or shall I say as the pictograph points out, your life is choked out of you. In this too, what struck me was the Indigenous peoples' refusal to interact with the land. It sparked a memory of a missing persons case where hunters disappeared in an area the nearby Indigenous peoples avoided at all costs. Right then while watching the show that led me to form an IF-THEN equation: if Indigenous peoples refuse to enter a certain place, then you should do the same. And yet, there I went right into the middle of such a zone.

In summing it up, the ancient rock art, I think are more than mere depictions of spiritual beings and symbols, they are warnings. Each generation has its own lure, from revering serpents to worshiping playful spirits to falling under the spell of technology and AI, or even the concepts like UFOs/UAPs. But make no mistake, what awaits you are not guides or gateways to enlightenment. They are deadly traps, placed strategically by those who seek to prey on spiritual seekers.

The first panel, with its carved over warning symbol facing the "U," is a clear message: do not attempt to spirit travel here unless you want to meet your demise. And the second panel, with its grotesque figures and ominous atmosphere, serves as a last warning for those who still insist on entering this forbidden realm. These images have lost their true impact over time, but their message remains unchanged: "they" will turn your journey into a perverted game or worse, snatching your soul away into another dimension where you become nothing more than an NPC. Seek wisdom elsewhere, for here lies only danger and deceit.

In terms of my personal journey to see a UFO/UAP and why I traveled to Utah in the first place, I could potentially interpret the crescent shape with its six trailing strings as a UFO/UAP taking flight. It appears to be leaving behind a trail of energy or jet stream, much like the one that initially drew me to Moab. But I am not alone in this fascination with contact with non-human entities.

As I reflected on the phrase "You are in it now," I began to see it as more than just a physical location where they have the upper hand; it could also refer to a mental state where they manipulate our desires and lead us into delusions. Ingo's friend Keel wrote in his book **Why UFOs: Operation Trojan Horse**, warning of the dangers that come with dabbling in UFOs. "It's like playing with black magic," he stated, "preying on the neurotic, gullible, and immature." He spoke of paranoid-schizophrenia, demonic possession, and even suicide as potential outcomes for those who become too deeply involved in the UFO phenomenon.

And to me, this warning rings true for the current state of the UFO/UAP world, especially surrounding the topic of disclosure. The community is rife with individuals on their own personal "vision quest," desperately trying to unravel the truth from a tangled web of disinformation. For answers, some turn to "trusted sources," others to supernatural entities, only to find themselves consumed by obsession and confusion. After all, as Ingo wrote in **Resurrecting the Mysterious**, "It is then usually only one brief step from belief management to belief manipulation and belief modification with all the conspiracies these latter two demons imply." And so, seekers enter one way, hopeful and eager, but emerge completely changed – broken, lost, and plagued by very formidable powers and forces. Is it any wonder why that ominous cloud was smirking.

It is amazing how much of our loves and lives go on about us, and how much we dream our dreams in the middle of the dreams of others, and yet be unaware of what is really happening about us.

Ingo Swann, **Pink Neon**

The Grotto,
Lourdes | France
43°6'0"N | 0°3'24"W

Chapelle Notre-Dame,
Lestelle-Bétharram | France
43°7'23"N | 0°12'26"W

THE
RIVER GAVE
May 12 - 16, 2024

Conjunctions

The Marian Apparitions

According to Ingo, his love for Mary, the blessed mother of Jesus, can be traced back to 1978. Although I believe it goes further back than that, possibly to his childhood when he had an encounter with what he described as an angelic intervention. Whatever the case, this profound reverence for Mary remained with him until his death. Evidence of this can be seen in the careful placement above his bed of iconic images of her: Blessed Mother, Virgin Mary, Mother of God, Our Lady, and the Holy Virgin, along with depictions of Jesus the Christ.[46]

Before leaving this life, Ingo made sure to give us precise instructions on where his memorial service should take place: beneath the painting **Mother of the World** by Nicolas Roerich.[47] The painting is a depiction of a universal mother sitting on a throne high in the mountains and embodies a feeling of eternal universal love, with constellations adorning her and a river winding around her, symbolizing life. It was fitting for Ingo's memorial, especially given his own painting, **Feminine Rising**, currently on display at the AVAM. While different in imagery, it captures the same sentiment.

---

[46] I think Ingo was also looking for protection from another dimension.
[47] The picture in the "About the Author" section is from this service.

In contrast, his portrayal of Mary in a separate painting, **Madre Dolorosa (Mother of Sorrows),**[48] is not serene or peaceful; it contains elements of her apparitional warnings and dire messages to humanity. Completed in 1986, it too is displayed at the AVAM. The message of Mother of Sorrows is clear: with great love comes great anguish.

Ten years after completing his Mary painting, Ingo investigated the supernatural sightings of the mother of Jesus, known as the Marian apparitions, in which she appeared to seers to deliver her messages. He narrowed down his list to 22 of the most well-known and highly regarded sites where these appearances occurred, naming them "supranormal." With this list in hand, he set out to uncover the context surrounding these occurrences – who saw them, where they saw them, and what was happening politically and socially during that time. This research became the basis for his 1996 book **The Great Apparitions of Mary**, featuring his own painting of Mary on the cover. During this detailed examination, Ingo also noticed a common theme connecting all these occurrences: something important was happening beyond just their individual appearances.

He wrote, as society continues to evolve and reassess its beliefs, a revival of interest in once-dismissed phenomena begins to emerge. One such phenomenon is the infamous "near-death experience" (NDE), which has been documented since ancient times. In these instances, an individual who is clinically dead is brought back to life and shares their journey through various transcendental dimensions or realms while they were "dead." Among the reported encounters during NDEs were reunions with deceased loved ones, orbs of intelligent light, wise guides, protective guardians, celestial angels, and even the divine Savior Himself. These near-death experiences seem to touch upon the sacred realms and dimensions that have long been cherished by religious traditions throughout history.

Enveloped within this aura of divinity, he maintained, the apparitions of the Holy Mother, Mary, Queen of Heaven, Mother of Humanity transcend even the most extraordinary experiences. Witness accounts speak of ethereal visions and prophecies fulfilled, all attributed to the Lady herself. Her messages, whispered with a celestial grace, reach those who

---

[48] The tale of how the painting departed from Ingo's possession and eventually made its way back to join his other artworks at the AVAM can be read in my book, **Stardust Highways: Ingo Swann's Art of Entertaining**.

seek her guidance. And the miraculous cures that follow her visitations are held in awe by believers and non-believers alike.

There are times, he is saying, when a part of us connects with the beyond, his entering transcendental dimensions or realms. In these moments, when we are more connected to this beyond than to our current reality, something from beyond reaches out to us. This often takes the form of something revered, sacred, or holy — but perhaps it is more accurately something we have been accustomed to worshiping. The concept of something reaching out to us in the form of sacredness is not confined to a meeting in a faraway place outside our understanding. It can happen right here and now, in our present reality. And when it does, the implications are profound.

It is a peculiar thing, the way we have intertwined ourselves with an unwavering dedication to the messages and promises that manifest during these extraordinary moments. Whether it be following their guidance or avoiding their warnings, we are bound to them by a fierce sense of longing and belief. And further in our desperation for hope, especially when seeking cures, we cloak ourselves in a shroud of sanctity. But what if this is all a ploy, the most malicious form of deception?

My world collided with the Marian apparitions in 1995, when I joined Ingo in his quest to compile evidence and artifacts for his book on Mary. I watched him fearlessly approach the topic from all angles, including the sobering warnings from the Holy Mother that the Church chose to ignore or downplay. He ultimately crafted a frame around them, using the "Hologram Metaphor" as his tool. When faced with something inexplicable, humans, Ingo expounded, tend to compare it to something that can be explained. This allows us to gain some understanding of the unknown. This is where metaphors come in; they suggest a likeness or analogy between the known and the unknown, helping us to make sense of the inexplicable.

Ingo went on, using holographic techniques, something can materialize where nothing actually exists. These hologram images are visible to the naked eye and can even be captured by a camera as if they were real objects. Despite being intangible in the traditional sense, they can be photographed just like any tangible object. However, the concept of a hologram is not able to fully explain the various sightings and appearances of the Holy Mother.

But what about those who have experienced these apparitions firsthand, the only ones to witness them? In all the cases Ingo studied, the seers were either children or adults with limited education, and these experiences tended to occur in remote locations. Ingo portrayed these enigmatic souls in his book **Purple Fables** as individuals born in the most secluded of places. With their unique talent, they were able to witness events unraveling across vast distances, even peeking through the veil of secrets shielded from others. So, I divided the scenario into two distinct parts: the individuals and the settings. From there, I could easily visualize how the locations, where numerous individuals had reported seeing apparitions, aligned perfectly with my effort to uncover any connections to the land.

I deliberated on which appearance to choose, weighing the parameters of my project. Almost instantly, I thought of Lourdes, France, although personally, I felt a deeper connection to the apparition at Tilly-sur-Seulles, France, which I explain further in "The Wind Up." All the same, trying to trust my intuition, I decided to go with Lourdes. The only information I had about the apparition, which is considered one of the most significant in history, came from Ingo's book.

My recollection, however, of the details was hazy at best. With a few clicks, I opened the digital file of the book and began to read his chapter on the site:[49]

Bundled in tattered clothing, three young girls ventured outside of town on a cold winter day in February 1858. They made their way over a bridge and to a rocky promontory, surrounded by frigid waters from the Gave de Pau. Despite the area having been picked clean by previous scavengers, the girls searched for sticks or brushwood to burn and discarded bones to make soup with. All three were visibly emaciated due to severe malnutrition.

Towards the westernmost point of the promontory, but on the other side of a smaller body of water, stood Massabielle, a massive rock cliff. It had a large opening in its side, known as a cave or grotto, surrounded by some bushes and a dying wild rose bush. The older girl ventured there in search of sticks.

---

[49] To fully understand the situation, it is strongly advised to read the entire chapter on the Lourdes apparitions from Ingo's book, **The Great Apparitions of Mary**. It has been placed in the Appendix for your convenience.

As the two other girls went to search for her, they came upon her kneeling in front of the cave with her face pointed towards the sky. They rushed over, worried that she had been hurt. But when they reached her, they realized she was completely still, and her eyes were wide open and unblinking. They tried to move her arms, but it was as if she was frozen in place. Filled with fear, they started screaming for help.

The mesmerized girl was Bernadette Soubirous, who would soon become one of the greatest seers in history – while the humble cave would turn into the legendary "Grotto." In just two weeks, the small town of Lourdes, with a population of less than 300, would be flooded by over 20,000 pilgrims. And one month later, another 50,000 would arrive.

Bernadette had noticed a faint radiance about halfway up in the cave – the same place she had spotted it on two previous scavenging expeditions. But this time, there was a "beautiful girl" inside of the glow. When the stunning girl gestured for Bernadette to come closer, she became frightened and hesitated to respond.

Although the sources may differ in some details, they all agree on one thing: Bernadette's two companions found her kneeling in a trance-like state. These two girls were her sister and a troublemaker by the name of Jeanne Abadie. They were able to snap Bernadette out of her fixation and she proceeded to tell them about what she had witnessed. She called it "Aquero."

The crowds that gathered later formed an opinion on the identity of Aquero – meaning "that one" in the local language. Most believed it to be the Blessed Virgin Mary.

Ingo, in his own summary of Lourdes, asks, "Who else could Aquero be than the Holy Mother?"

It was a one seer event.

Why was I being directed to go to this place, filled with talk of miraculous cures and seemingly disconnected from my project. It felt like a complete detour from my original intentions. Why was I being led away from a location where numerous people had experienced unexplainable phenomena, where the lines between reality and the supernatural may have distorted? Instead, I found myself directed to a land where only one person had reported a mystical experience and of cures which I believe are attributed to the people, a mind over matter situation, rather than the specific location. It was like visiting an online psychic's office just to see their computer; it didn't make sense to me. Why even go there, honestly? I questioned this very thing out loud. Crickets in response.

With no explanation forthcoming, I decided to add to my minimal amount of pre-knowledging, just so I would have the most basic understanding as to what I would be walking into. I learned Lourdes, specifically the Massabielle grotto or cave, was once a garbage dump and generally seen as a desolate area. Set aside the River Gave de Pau (or simply the River Gave),[50] it is now renowned for its healing waters and miraculous cures, as well as for its seer Bernadette (later known as Saint Bernadette).

The multitude of apparitions and how they occurred, however, have taken a backseat to the site's more famous reputation as the world's most prominent healing shrine. With over five million pilgrims and visitors each year, it has become the top destination for Christian worshipers. Some even watch live streamed videos of the site.

Of course, it had to be the most cliché tourist destination. It seemed like fate was working against me, as if this trip was meant to be everything that I didn't want. But perhaps, instead of fighting it, I should embrace it. After all, there must be organized pilgrimages to this site that I could join. In a moment of surrender, I searched online finding one such pilgrimage.

The company had a selection of weeks available, each with its own designated hotel. After considering the different hotels, I ultimately chose the one connected to the Hôtel Eliséo. The hotel promised a rooftop lounge and showcased images of delectable pastries and modern rooms. It was for the third week of May 2024, and I booked it.

Little did I know at the time, but my timing was lucky; the following week was a major event for Catholic military chaplains from around the world in Lourdes. The city would have been even more crowded and lively than usual with these pilgrims in their elaborate dress uniforms.

While I approached other locations with a focus on figuring out how to access them, this one, being a non-Catholic, required more preparation due to its religious significance. I knew there would be a lot of mass attendance,[51] praying the rosary,[52] and experiencing the stations of the

---

[50] To construct the Sanctuary on the site, a portion of the river was filled in.
[51] The Catholic central communal act of worship.
[52] Used in the Catholic faith, it is a physical string of knots or beads used to count the component prayers.

cross.[53] My first task was to obtain a rosary, which I did. Thankfully, it came with instructions on which prayers corresponded to each bead. I also watched instructional videos on how to use the rosary and recite the prayers on YouTube. On a practical level, I made sure to pack appropriate rainy weather gear for my visit since Ingo had mentioned in his book that Lourdes is often wet. When I checked the location of Lourdes in France, I realized it was literally on the other side of the mountains and across the border from Monte Perdido in Spain, where one of the underground human extraterrestrial collaboration bases was said to be located. It was clear this would be an interesting trip. As the days passed and my flight to Lourdes approached, I felt as prepared as an outsider could be for a pilgrimage to one of the most famous Christian vestiges in the world.

I departed from the United States on Saturday, May 11, 2024, in the late afternoon and arrived in Dublin, Ireland – a marvel of controlled chaos compared to Charlotte's chaotic mess – in the early morning hours of Sunday, May 12, 2024. With just enough time to make it to my next flight at the domestic terminal, I rushed past the bustling international terminal. My next destination was Lourdes, and I had been assigned a seat on Ryanair.

As I settled into my seat towards the back of the plane, I realized that I had unknowingly joined an Irish-sponsored pilgrimage. Out of all the wayfarers, I was the only American. It was a small group compared to some of the larger gatherings I saw around town. The other members were around my age with a mix of older and younger individuals as well. There were adult children accompanying their mothers or grandmothers in wheelchairs, siblings, couples, and a few solo travelers like me. Our tour included a priest and one guide – an expat living in Lourdes whom I shall, again for privacy reasons, assign my established tour guide pseudonym of Dave. Everyone in our group was deeply devout and on their own personal journey. They had no idea about the details behind mine, however. They were all incredibly warm and welcoming, making my time among them truly enjoyable. One thing I learned about the Irish: they love a late party but hate an early mass. Their words, not mine.

---

[53] Called the Way of the Cross or the Way of Sorrows (Via Dolorosa), it is a series of images (can be in varying forms) depicting Jesus Christ on the day of his crucifixion.

Our flight to Lourdes arrived later that morning. The airport was small, and we quickly went through customs and boarded a bus to take us into the town. We were all seated close together, our faces glowing with anticipation and happiness. Then our tour guide climbed aboard. It was at this point I realized the hotel I had been eagerly anticipating for my week-long stay was not actually our destination, a substitution had been made to the Hotel Roissy. While a few of my fellow travelers seemed to be aware of this fact, it was a complete shock to many of us. It was especially "disappointing" for those who had previously stayed at the now substituted hotel and hadn't planned on returning. Quickly some choice words filled the air. Quite an auspicious start I thought.

When we arrived, though, our rooms were not ready yet, which gave us some time to explore before lunch at noon. One of my fellow pilgrims, a friendly widow who seemed to be the most experienced among us, kindly showed me around and took me to see "The Grotto" and its miraculous spring. I hadn't brought my camera with me on this spontaneous trip, as it was just meant as a quick introduction. Before coming to Lourdes, I had only seen a few photos of the sanctuary: a small cave, a church, some benches, statues, and a plaza.

But in reality, the Sanctuary covers over 130 acres and includes 22 places of worship, including three basilicas: the Upper Basilica of the Immaculate Conception, built after the Lady's request during her 13th apparition; the Lower Basilica of Our Lady of the Rosary, which is overlooked by the Upper Basilica; and the underground Basilica of St. Pius X that can hold up to 25,000 people.

There are three main entrances to the Sanctuary, not including key card/coded access points near the back edges and rear of the expanse including one to a very large parking lot at the far end for buses: St. Michael's Gate[54] near the bend of River Gave for the best view; St. Joseph's Gate close to hotels and souvenir shops selling many items like Lourdes water bottles, statues of Mary, rosaries, candles, religious objects, and rain gear; and a side entrance next to the Upper Basilica.

The focal point of the Sanctuary is called The Domaine – it includes all three basilicas, the Grotto, water collection stations – taps and fountains

---

[54] Despite the name "Saint Michael's Gate," and the nearby statue of him vanquishing the Devil, the entrance is "guarded" by the statues of two other archangels: Gabriel and Raphael.

– and Baths. Other buildings on site include an information center, medical facilities, offices for reviewing miracles, statues throughout the walkways and as stations of the cross, and two paths to follow – one is flat while the other includes a steep climb and descent for those wanting a more prayerful experience. Many visitors choose to walk this path barefoot, stopping at each station along the way.

As we turned the corner and approached the Grotto in front of us, my eyes were drawn to the River Gave on our right. I wandered close to the wall separating the river from the Sanctuary grounds, staring into the rushing water and feeling a strange energy. My docent noticed my fascination and quickly directed me to the benches outside the Grotto. She showed me where Bernadette knelt during her first apparition and how to get in line for a closer look. The line starts, if facing it, at the Grotto's left side and winds through its interior, ending at a statue above the cave's entrance. Despite being led away, I kept turning back to gaze at the River Gave behind us. Eventually, we settled onto an open bench facing the Grotto, watching the activities within. After a brief stop at one of the spring water foundations, my cicerone filled her water bottle and let me try some of the cool, pure water before we retraced our steps.

Following our lunch, we were given our room assignments. My room was located on the first floor and had a single twin bed facing a small parking lot, with a sheer rock face just beyond it. I didn't spend much time in my room though. The pilgrimage offered various organized events which we could choose to attend or not, but there was also plenty of free time for self-reflection. This gave me the chance to pursue my own interests if I wished.

Every evening between April and October, at nine o'clock, the Marian procession takes place in the Sanctuary. Pilgrims gather to sing and walk with candles from the Grotto to the Lower Basilica's Plaza. The procession begins with a statue of the Holy Mother, followed by groups carrying banners. I was eager to witness this event, so I arrived early at the Grotto.

As pilgrims prepared the statue for its nightly journey and formed groups, the Grotto area was relatively quiet. I saw this as my chance to join the line to experience the Grotto. Standing in front of me were some individuals touching the water flowing down from the rocks inside the cave. I was about to do the same when I suddenly heard a loud and clear voice saying, "Do not touch that! Leave now!" Every muscle in my body froze as I stared wide-eyed at the scene before me. Right away, my senses heightened, and having learned to pay attention, I abruptly realized this was not an ordinary warning. Without hesitation, I heeded the command and stepped back, resisting the urge to touch the water cascading down the rocks. As I made my way out, heading back the way I had come in, I felt I had narrowly escaped something inexplicably ominous.

I continued walking, passing the growing line behind the statue of the Holy Mother being carried by the faithful. The crowd was swelling and there seemed to be an endless stream of people entering the Sanctuary with lit candles. I made my way through it all, back to my room.

Once I was safely inside, I noticed a low frequency humming coming from the back corner of my room, where the wall faced the rocky cliff behind it. The humming would rise and then fade away, making me wonder if it was just the pipes. But as I started to investigate its source, my phone chimed. Surprisingly, it had service now – something it didn't have even when I was in Ireland. It was Mother's Day in the States, and I checked my messages, sending reassurances to loved ones that I had arrived safely. Lastly, I checked the estate's **X** account and saw a reply to a post discussing whether holy apparitions were simply disguises. This came after rumors the Vatican would announce their position on supernatural occurrences later in the week. What were the chances that on Mother's Day – the very day I arrived in Lourdes to witness the site of an apparition of the Holy Mother – this topic would come up? And sure enough, on the Friday I returned home, the Vatican announced changes in how they handle reports of "apparitions and other supernatural phenomena." It was no coincidence, I thought to myself.

The time was late, and the incessant humming outside my window only seemed to grow louder. I opened the window, trying to pinpoint the source of the vibrations. To my left, there was some equipment belonging to a neighboring building. I waited for it to turn on and make its vibrating-like noise before shutting off again. It was contributing to the humming, but even when it was off, the sound continued. I wanted to make sure, though, so I left my room and headed straight out into the parking lot. As I stood there, mere feet aware from the wall of rock, it dawned on me that this rock face just beyond my window was also emitting a low hum. This rock, I started to feel, carried an immense amount of energy, as if it were being used to absorb and collect it.

A sickening feeling crept over me as I realized this rock, not just a hillside but a solid mass like those in my previous experiences, was being used for something far more disturbing than just energy production. Memories from Salt Lake City came flooding back – "You are in it now!" I pulled up Google Maps to confirm my suspicions: if you followed a line straight from my room through the rock hill passing under the path of the High Stations of the Cross, the Rte de la Forêt (the Forest Road leading from the Sanctuary to a campground), and the end of the Basilica, all elevated above, you'd end up at the back side of the Grotto. This wasn't a one seer event; this was something much worse, that much I felt certain. The words "be careful what you wish for" echoed in my mind as I switched off my phone and tried to get some sleep while keeping a table lamp on for comfort.

After breakfast the next morning, I grabbed my phone and made my way down to the Grotto. On the way, I stopped at one of the many shops and purchased a small glass jar to collect some "holy water" from Lourdes. It had a picture of a young Bernadette kneeling before an apparition on one side. I hesitated for a moment; after everything that had happened the day before and during the night, was this really what I wanted to do? But in the end, I decided I wanted a physical reminder. After all, an object only has power if we give it power. Echoing Frank Herbert and his book **Dune**, I told myself, "I will not succumb to fear. Fear is the destroyer of minds, the harbinger of a swift and merciless end." This jar of water would serve as a reminder of that mantra.

As I rounded the corner and caught sight of the Grotto up ahead, my attention was immediately drawn to the River Gave. Without hesitation, I went to the river first and took some photos before turning towards the Grotto. I snapped a few pictures from a safe distance; there was no way I was going near that place again.

As I stood in that area, something didn't feel right. It felt almost dark and evil. The thought of collecting water from the River Gave crossed my mind, but a voice inside me told me the "holy water" from the fountains would be the lesser of two evils. Well, now. I reminded myself to stay away from the river and its banks. It was like a warning: look, but whatever you do, don't touch. So, there I was, standing between two forbidden zones and on top of a potentially dangerous one. Got it, I thought to myself as I collected water from one of the fountains. As I looked up, I noticed the sun moving behind the Upper Basilica. It would make for a beautiful photo, so I started taking pictures of the view from below with the sun crossing its path above and to my right. In the distance, Bearded Vultures of the Pyrénées soared high above the Basilica, adding an extra element of loftiness to my shots.

To clear my mind of the eerie feeling creeping over me, I continued walking into the town until I reached Château fort de Lourdes, the historical castle. While it has a history dating back to Roman times, the oldest standing structures are said to be from the 11th century. During Henri IV's reign (1589-1610), it served as a prison. The castle was strategically built and provides a stunning view of Lourdes and its surroundings. Intrigue led me towards the portion with the old prison cells. I could feel a sense of anguish lingering there, left behind by those who were once held in those cramped spaces. Just the same, this anguish was nothing compared to the intense heaviness I felt at the Grotto and the River Gave nearby.

I arrived just in time for lunch and joined the group for a walking tour of Lourdes afterwards. Our tour guide, Dave, led us around the Sanctuary, eventually entering through St. Michael's Gate. To the right of the gate is a small building with an exhibit containing miniature models displayed behind glass showcases. The models illustrate the experiences of Bernadette, providing a condensed version of her story. They also offer a glimpse into what the area looked like during the time of the apparitions. The River Gave was much wider and surrounded by swampland, making it difficult to reach the cave where Bernadette had her visions. Visitors either had to ford the river or navigate a steep rocky cliff and boulders. The cave itself was only half its current size, meaning those who wanted to witness Bernadette in her ecstatic state had to perch on the cliff or stand across the river, which was a dangerous proposition either way.

Dave led us through the various showcases, sharing tidbits of information along the way with his infectious enthusiasm. When we reached the display about the first apparition, he pointed out that it was rare for parents to allow children to visit Massabielle. According to him, the area was typically described as a dump or pigsty, a fact I had already learned from Ingo's chapter. But what caught my interest was when he said, in a clear deviation from his prepared script, the location was rumored to be haunted. Until then, I had only been half-listening, but now I was fully engaged, eager to learn more about this unexpected aspect. I made a mental note to get Dave to elaborate on the designated "haunted" status of the location.

Our next stop was Bernadette's childhood home, which had been turned into a "museum" for visitors to get a glimpse into the "lavish" lifestyle she once lived before her family fell into abject poverty and lived in a former prison cell. While we waited for the group ahead of us to clear out, I took the opportunity to chat with Dave and subtly extract, okay vampire, information about the haunted history of the Grotto, before it became known as "The Grotto."

I began, "Hey Dave," as I maneuvered my way as to stand next to him, "when you said 'haunted' earlier, what did you mean?"

His nonverbal cues were a dead giveaway; he was getting anxious. I could tell that in his excitement for the events, and especially for Bernadette, whom he was particularly fond of, he had crossed a line by mentioning the cave's haunted past to us. He probably hoped no one would notice, but now that I was clearly aware of it, there was no turning back. He was in it now. He didn't have a cover story prepared for his inadvertent revealing of the secret and awkwardly mentioned how the cave's dark history is never spoken of, except for two books, in French, that mentioned animal and human sacrifices taking place there. My internal reaction was "WHAT?!," miraculously, however, I was able to maintain a puzzled expression on my face. This went beyond just spooky stories told by villagers to scare their children from playing in the local dump. It had become much more absorbing.

"So, you're talking about historical interactions, like with the original inhabitants of this region, hundreds or maybe thousands of years ago?" I inquired.

The quiver in his voice revealed his nerves, almost trembling as he struggled to speak. "No," he stuttered, "I mean like back in the 1700s." Now completely unable to hold any semblance of composure together, my face must have betrayed my shock, for Dave's eyes widened in alarm. In a desperate attempt to steer me away from the topic of the Grotto's history of being anything but holy, he abruptly changed the subject and blurted out something even more scandalous: during the third apparition, dark, twisted figures, demons he actually said, had emerged from the murky depths of the River Gave, directly across from where the ethereal image had materialized.

My eyes widened further. It was the exact spot where I had been standing, feeling a dark presence and taking photos of the river and Grotto. And now I learned demons had risen from there.

But Dave continued, thinking he had quelled the matter, Our Lady raised her hand and lowered it, causing the demons to flee into the water. I was speechless. Before I could process this revelation, the crowds dispersed, and Dave quickly ushered us along. He had plunged into treacherous depths, and it was not hard for me to see he was eager to escape the gravity of his words.

As I walked through the "museum," a labyrinth of thoughts and theories began to form in my mind. This story just gets wilder and wilder, I thought. It began as a simple account of a strange and enigmatic land, its past shrouded in mystery.

But now, it had evolved into something far more complex – a deception hidden beneath a carefully crafted façade. The holy water Ingo said Bernadette had brought suddenly felt like a necessary weapon against the apparition she claimed to see, one that could only be explained as a demonic presence.

My mind raced back to Ingo's chapter; words that had once seemed meaningless[55] now took on a chilling significance. A creeping feeling of "I too was in it now," settled over me as I realized the true nature of what I may have become intertwined with.

I then recalled another thing Dave had told us back at the exhibit, how Bernadette's name for the image, "Aquero," translated from her local language, a variant of Occitan, the language of the region before French, as "that thing" – also often translated as "the one," as Ingo described in his chapter – and how it had been interpreted as the Holy Mother. I hadn't really paid attention to that but under these new circumstances, it pervaded my mind. I made note to investigate what Aquero meant in her language and time, not how it had been translated by those affiliated with the Church.

As Monday night drew to a close, I found myself diving deep into the vast expanse of the internet. With no service on my phone, I reluctantly succumbed to using the hotel's Wi-Fi. The humming, which had been growing increasingly intense throughout the evening, continued to pulse in the background. To drown it out, I put on my noise cancelling headphones and plunged into my search for answers about this place and

---

[55] If I had taken the time to fully absorb Ingo's chapter, I might have questioned why she brought holy water and sprinkled it on the Lady. But I didn't even consider it. In that moment, I quickly understood the importance of paying careful attention when reading.

what Bernadette had seen. It was a tedious process, sifting through endless web references of the accepted "holy" narrative of events at Lourdes. But I persisted, determined to find any hint of a different perspective. It wasn't until the early hours of the morning that by chance I came upon a few scattered references here and there. Jotting down notes, I made mental plans to investigate these sources further once I returned home.

Exhausted from hours of research and battling against the persistent humming, I finally made my way down to the front desk to inquire about changing rooms. A sign written in French greeted me, its meaning clear even without translation – if you need help, call and someone might answer...but probably not since this is France after all. I was on my own for the rest of the night. I returned to my room and hunkered down for what would surely be an arduous night ahead. The hours crept by slowly as I attempted to get some rest, tossing and turning with my headphones on. But by seven in the morning, I had reached my limit. In a sleep-deprived state, I approached a now live body at the front desk and requested a room change. As soon as I mentioned the low frequency noise emanating from the rock in my room, the woman's suspicious gaze fell upon me. In my delirium, I had foolishly thought honesty was the best approach. In hindsight, perhaps it wasn't the best approach; had I been in a clearer state of mind, I would have led with a more logical explanation – that the noise was coming from a machine at a nearby hotel, even though it wasn't entirely to blame. With her eyebrows now raised, I quickly amended my story to the one I should have led with. The noise was coming from the other hotel, I assured her.

"Where to, madam?" Her tone was impatient as she repeated the question several times. It was clear she just wanted me to leave her desk as soon as possible.

I muttered under my breath, "Anywhere but near that f***ing hellhole of a rock." But out loud, I said "Anywhere above and far from the back will do." She practically thrust the new key card into my hands and told me this room was on the sixth floor, with a view of the streets below. I hustled back to my first floor confines shoved everything into anything I had, hastily, and left, dragging my stuff to the nearest elevator and up and away from that godforsaken place. I collapsed onto one of two twin beds in the room; things were already improving.

After finally getting some much-needed sleep, my verdict on the matter was to avoid the Sanctuary. I had been set on my decision until I joined everyone at breakfast, where their excitement for the low stations of the cross event scheduled afterwards was infectious. Without a second thought, I abandoned my previous stance. I just needed to put my stuff back in my room first I told them. As I entered the lobby ten minutes before our scheduled departure time of 10:00am, I was surprised to find it completely empty. Confusion set in as I checked the itinerary posted nearby; I was in the right place, but where was everyone else? It wasn't until a pair from my group arrived – a son pushing his mother in a wheelchair – that I realized something was amiss. Without questioning it further, although I honestly should have, we left promptly at 10:00am and made our way to the main statue of Mary, where we assumed the rest of our group would be waiting. But they were nowhere to be found. I decided to wait while the son and his mother took off. After some time, I followed suit and found the group at the third station. As they turned to face me, I could feel their shock – "We thought you weren't going to show up," which really meant good job, now you're right back in it.

The low stations are situated in a secluded and shaded spot on the opposite side of the River Gave from the Baths. Our priest recited passages from the **Bible** and offered prayers at each station. The carvings, etched onto slabs of stone depict important events in the Passion of Christ. As I walked along and observed these scenes, I felt warmly introspective.

Afterward, driven perhaps by a reckless confidence, I gave in to the irresistible pull of scaling the treacherous rock hill to experience the high stations atop it by myself. With each step though, I regretted my decision to climb the hill more and more. By the time I reached station seven, the scene depicting Jesus being put into the Sepulchre, the regret turned into a deep gnawing at my bones, urging me to descend and leave. I quickened my pace and was down and off the hill in no time at all.

For the rest of the day, to play it safe, I acted tourist in the city.

On Wednesday morning, despite the events of the day before, I returned to the Sanctuary grounds to take some photographs. My goal was to have documentation of the place for future reference, but I made sure to avoid the Grotto entirely. Our afternoon though was filled with a planned tour of two nearby locations.

The first was Bétharram, specifically the Chapelle Notre-Dame located 25 minutes away to the west of Lourdes. This chapel, built in the 17th

century on the banks of River Gave, has a significant history. According to some sources, it stands where a group grazing their flocks saw a bright light and found either a statue or the Blessed Virgin herself. Even before this event, the location had been recognized as a holy Marian site by Christians since medieval times and was often visited by pilgrims.

Across the river from the chapel is a marker indicating another sighting, where a young girl fell into the river and was saved by the intervention of the Blessed Virgin holding out a branch to her. A small shrine called the Madonna Who Saves now marks this spot and gave the location its name – Bétharram, meaning "beautiful branch" in the local dialect. It was at this chapel that Bernadette and her family had visited just days before her first sighting at Massabielle.

Our group had the special privilege of holding mass in the reserved chapel at Bétharram during our pilgrimage. This was my second time attending mass on this journey, the first being at the Chapelle du Sacré-Cœur above the Chapelle Notre-Dame des Douleurs on my first day in Lourdes, not within the Sanctuary. As we waited to enter, I felt drawn towards the nearby River Gave. It was as if something in the water was calling out to me. I stepped away from the group to take photos of the river and a shrine marker. When I looked up, I realized everyone else had already been let inside.

In a hurry, I joined them. Although the outside of the chapel seemed run-down, the interior was quite grandiose, ostentatious almost. I sat towards the back and about halfway through the service, I sensed something with negative intentions behind me, slightly to my left. The feeling became so strong I discreetly took out my phone – which wasn't exactly allowed during mass – and snapped some photos. The first one seemed to capture something – there were multiple white orbs in the spot where I felt the presence. Nonetheless, all subsequent photos only showed the intricate artwork, stained glass windows, benches, and flooring near me.

After mass ended and we had some free time to explore and visit the small gift shop – which I did – I headed straight back to the River Gave. The atmosphere around that part of the river was awesomely seductive. Nearby, I found a set of old stone stairs leading down from the road towards the water, but they ended at a stone wall preventing anyone from reaching it. I stood there and took photo after photo of the river's reflections and nearby vegetation.

As I looked through them later while on the bus, they almost seemed like they were from a fairy tale with their mystical quality. But upon closer examination, I noticed some reflections extended further than they should and appeared more vibrant, like light dancing on the water's surface. In the last photo I took, I could sense something different. Looking back at me from a misty blue area above the water line was the face of a woman, with no trace of a smile. There was something strange going on with the water and River Gave in this specific region. I made a mental note to research it further.

Our second destination was Bartrès, a quaint village located north of Lourdes where Bernadette had spent significant time during her life. She was sent there twice: as an infant to a wet nurse and later in her teens to care for the same woman's flock. In this village stands the local parish church, St. John the Baptist, which holds a precious relic of St. Bernadette.

As soon as our bus arrived at the parking lot, the skies opened, and a heavy downpour began. Despite the rain, we made our way into the village and stopped briefly inside the church. While the rest of my group paid their respects to St. Bernadette's relic, I stayed back and observed from a distance. Two people in our group lit candles and placed them before a shrine dedicated to St. Bernadette on my left, after contributing coins to a collection box.

A sense of unease started to build within me, and I quickly made my way out of the church as soon as I could. When I reached the bus, I was soaking wet, but I felt relieved to be away from that place. Although I was incapable of pinpointing exactly why, I knew I did not want to be anywhere near that church. That night in my hotel room was one of the best sleeps I had on the entire trip, but two members of our group who had lit candles at the church told me the next morning they had had a terrible almost haunting night without any sleep. Something about that church just didn't feel right.

Thursday, other than lunch at noon and a final mass at two o'clock in the chapel we had had mass in before, I spent my time wandering aimlessly around town and exploring the Sanctuary's different gates that require special access. When we finally arrived at the airport, I noticed a beautiful rainbow off to the left. I stopped to take a photo, sardonically smiling at the thought of this being our sendoff and the irony of those two moments in time – stepping through this airport just days ago versus now.

Upon returning home, it was time for me to unravel the mysteries I had encountered on my trip. Twice during my journey, I stumbled upon pennies.[56] These small copper coins, a remnant of my time with Ingo, always seemed to be messages I was on the right path. The first time was on Tuesday, the day I had made the decision to avoid the Sanctuary. As I walked past St. Joseph's Gate and headed towards the tourist train, I noticed a one euro cent lying on the ground. It was a rare find, as most of the currency I had used in Lourdes ended in zero or five. The only exception was a handmade hat I purchased for a figure which ended in nine euros, but even then, I had used my credit card. As I pondered the events of the day and the commercialization of Lourdes that seemed to be taking over its true purpose as a pilgrimage site, cracks and signs of decay appeared before me – both literally in the streets and buildings, and metaphorically in my thoughts. Was this all just a façade to hide a deeper truth? And then, just like that, a single penny appeared at my feet, offering no answers but amplifying my questions.

The second penny appeared in Charlotte, stationed behind my car in the parking garage. Once again, as I reflected on faith and the buried truths that may lay beneath its surface, this small American one cent coin surfaced. As if teasing me with hints and clues, it begged me to uncover what was truly going on in Lourdes.

Therefore, as I sat in my office, I realized that to comprehend my experience, it was crucial I understand the true meaning behind the visions and Bernadette's experiences, looking through a different lens than the sanitized "official" account. To truly comprehend these events, I needed to uncover the dark context surrounding them: the pervasive supernatural superstitions that plagued 1858 France. And what about the mysterious rituals taking place at Massabielle? Were those sacrificial ceremonies real or mere folklore? And most hauntingly, what evil beings lurked beneath the surface of those murky waters?

I decided to start with the demons the apparition had dispelled, thinking it would be the easiest thing to unravel. Au contraire. I quickly realized it was not the case and that I would have to revisit this topic later.

---

[56] On lazy afternoons, during my early years at 357, Ingo and I would embark on penny explorations. He always claimed people couldn't be bothered with these discarded coins, leaving them to fend for themselves on the streets. But he saw treasure where others saw trash. And upon our return to 357, a silver dish on Ingo's desk would become their new home.

Instead, I turned my attention to the water where these demons had emerged from and returned to – the water in the River Gave itself. After some rooting around the internet, I discovered that the source of this river is believed to be on Cirque de Gavarnie Mountain located on the French side of the France-Spain border. Water also feeds into it from its neighboring mountain, Monte Perdido, situated in Spain. This revelation did not come as a surprise to me; it only confirmed my suspicions. It was almost too coincidental to ignore – the River Gave's water coming directly from an alleged human extraterrestrial collaboration base,[57] which could have been an interdimensional enclave before that. There are ongoing discussions on social media about trans-dimensional beings living and traveling underground or in bodies of water. Could it be that the river acts as a sort of interdimensional highway, with entry and exit points bringing these entities in contact with us? Given the extensive history of sightings and interactions in this area, dating back centuries, it seems like a plausible explanation.

With the new connection established, I approached the demon quelching alongside the apparition with renewed determination. I faced some initial obstacles, such as an interview with Stefano Mazzeo, the director, writer, and producer of a docudrama called **The Message of Lourdes**. He claims, without citing any evidence: "What I didn't know was that there were demonic attacks during the apparitions... No one has mentioned this. Our Lady silenced the demons with just one look." Intrigued by this idea of a "one look" intervention, I kept searching and eventually found a book from 1958 titled **The Challenge of Bernadette** by Hugh Ross Williamson. Although our guide didn't mention any specific titles for those two French books during his momentary lapse into "unholy" territory, I had a strong feeling this book was akin to them.

In it, there is an account of what happened during the third apparition when Bernadette reportedly heard "confused voices" resembling thousands of angry people screaming curses and threats behind her, originating from the water. One voice stood out as being named the Devil and screamed "Get out of here," not directed at Bernadette but at the vision she was seeing. With just a glance, the vision quelled the evil presence and made it disappear.

---

[57] See the note in Historical Tidbits titled "Exploring Otherworldly Possibilities."

This, however, did little to stop ongoing demonic encounters and attacks at Massabielle, as Williamson documents. Due to these frequent "diabolical manifestations" experienced by multiple individuals, doubts were cast on Bernadette's credibility, he exclaimed. Then Eureka! I discovered a second book.

This tome is brimming with what I would call scandalous revelations about the apparitions at Lourdes. Penned in 2003 by Thérèse Taylor, and boldly veering from a believer's perspective, the book bears the title of **Bernadette of Lourdes, Her Life, Death and Visions**. The book reveals harrowing accounts of supernatural occurrences at the Grotto, including sightings of unearthly lights attributed to malevolent nature spirits. These menacing encounters have been ongoing, with one priest from the 1960s, she wrote, describing the cave as a "lair" where terrifying stories seeped forth. He went further, she said, proclaiming the Grotto to be a gateway to another realm, from which any nightmare could materialize.

I was thus struck by the immense gravity and significance of the situation at hand. Williamson refers to it as a trifecta – the convergence of Catholic Dogma, Catholic Power, and Catholic Worship – all hanging in the balance. The truth behind the ongoing demonic happenings, if unearthed, would cast a looming shadow over the very foundation of the Church itself. It is like a dark cloud hovering over Lourdes, a place that has been "Christianized," its demonic nature covered up and its pagan history buried according to Williamson. In his closing thoughts on this matter, Williamson daringly proclaims that from the very beginning of Lourdes' story, there has been a river of deceit and distortion, still flowing strong today.

Captivated by these distortions, I set off on a voyage through the past of Massabielle and the beliefs in the region to better understand them.

The cave and the spring within it are stationed in a mountainous region of France, a land steeped in stories and secrets from prehistoric times. The land has seen the rise and fall of civilizations, starting with the Romans and continuing with the Muslims, Visigoths, Saracens, Franks, English, and Huguenots. Meaning centuries before Catholicism reigned supreme, this land was shaped and molded by diverse cultures and beliefs, creating a rich mix of religious practices which took hold in the region and evolved into various forms with each invading confederation, until the days of Catholicism.

The name Massabielle may in fact reveal hints about some of these beliefs and practices that occurred there. According to some accounts, it translates to "old rock," evoking images of weathered stones and ancient structures. Others suggest a more mystical origin, linking it to the "old mass" of pagan rituals and worship that once took place there. It is not surprising as the worship of natural forces can be found among ancient peoples all over the world, with water holding particular significance. This made Massabielle an important and sacred place, for its spring was well known even if it had become covered over by the time of Bernadette's day. In fact, it is believed the Romans held their festival of Fontinalia, a celebration of springs, in honor of the Roman god Fons within this very cave. Fons, son of Janus – the god of beginnings and endings – and Juturna – goddess of fountains, wells, and springs – was considered a deity closely tied to the source of water itself. Fons was also associated with expiatory sacrifices, often involving blood.

The celebration at the site may have gone in concert with the Roman's belief in nymphs. These deities, described as young girls, were associated with sources of fresh water, springs, grottos and especially with healing springs. Was this the beginning of animal and human sacrifices in the cave and its association with nymphs or fairies or were the Romans building on something older?

But as time moved on and the mid-19th century approached – during Bernadette's lifetime – it was common for those of humble means and limited education, like her family, to practice what is best described as folk-Catholicism. This meant merging elements of pagan and Catholic beliefs into one system. On the pagan side, there was a deeply ingrained acceptance of a variety of supernatural creatures, including nature spirits and white female fairies – the Roman nymphs – known as dames blanches or demoiselles in French, and demaiselas in Occitan – the dominant language during Bernadette's lifetime. These ethereal beings were described as tiny, youthful, captivating, and often mischievous if not downright evil. This made me wonder how her folk-Catholic beliefs and past experiences may have influenced her understanding of the occurrences in the cave, an understanding that has seemingly been altered over time.

To understand this in more detail, I turned to Ruth Harris' 1999 book about Lourdes, **Lourdes: Body and Spirit in the Secular Age**. Harris mentions during Bernadette's time, it was common for caves to be associated with witches, demons, and fairies. Similarly, Taylor's book discusses the popular belief in the area that grottos were home to fairies, wraiths, and sorcerers. The superstitions surrounding Massabielle itself were both sacred and demonic, according to Harris. While Taylor quotes French professor and historian Isaure Gratacos who called Massabielle "tuta deras hadas," which translates to "cave of the fairies."

It was at this juncture, I asked myself: What if their adherence to pagan beliefs was not a result of limited resources and education, but rather because they truly perceived and communicated with them? Regardless, these creatures were said to have made their homes in dense forests and deep caves.

Clearly, at least to me, it would seem the cave was no simple dwelling for the Aquero; it was a sacred place, imbued with an air of mystery and playfulness intertwined with darker energies all linked to the element of water. And so, as I finished my survey, I realized while the cave's origins remain an enigma, one thing was clear: Massabielle has been harboring hidden truths since ancient times.

I directed my thoughts next to Bernadette and the details of what she experienced during her "ecstasy." According to accounts, when Bernadette first witnessed her vision, her family's initial reaction was that of fear. Her sister even described her as "rigid and pale," adding to their dread and suspicion. As a result, her family attributed the ordeal to the malevolent power of demons.

Despite their probable blend of pagan and Catholic beliefs, their initial reaction was not unlike that of other cultures. In some circles, mysterious human experiences are often associated with possession by evil spirits. And for Bernadette, this was no exception. As she entered her second ecstasy, she felt a sense of unease. Such trances were unfamiliar and unsettling, especially considering what had happened during her first vision at the cave. To protect herself from any potential evil forces, she brought holy water with her and threw it upon her vision. But to her dismay, the image disappeared before she could properly discern its origin.

Immersed in her second vision, Bernadette was completely unaware of her surroundings. Those who accompanied her described her as being "unable to notice what was happening around her." It was as if she had been transported to another place entirely. Those watching her were powerless to shake her out of this state, so they picked her up and carried her to a nearby mill where she remained lost in her abstraction for some time. It seemed the enchantment had taken hold of her completely, causing some to question if she had gone mad.

Years later, as Sister Marie-Bernard, Bernadette recounted these events and how she had no memory of being carried to the mill or of any external events that took place that day. In contrast, as she neared the end of her life, various sources attest, feverish nightmares plagued her mind. She would often recall Massabielle and the evil spirits she believed she saw there. In one conversation with a fellow Sister, Taylor records, she even revealed she thought she had seen the Devil himself.

Therefore, the question lingers in my mind: what was it that Bernadette truly saw? This entity she described as Aquero, that thing or that one. Taylor's book explores this mystery and uncovers that Bernadette placed a special emphasis on the word "white" in her description, hinting at a being from another realm with unknown intentions. Despite pressure for more information, she only described a small, pale figure – never daring to utter the name of the Blessed Virgin herself. In early accounts, her description was even labeled as "dame blanche," a fairy.

And just like that, in an instant, the answer to a riddle I pondered countless times in relation to this – "if you've got me, you want to share me; if you share me, you haven't kept me" – clicked perfectly into place. Suddenly, everything made sense. The solution is a secret.

Unexpectedly too, I was hit by a tsunami of realization. I had unknowingly stepped into a convergence of powerful energies: a flowing river inhabited by transcendental beings, some benevolent and others malevolent, all playing their own roles in the grand scheme of things. The cave, with its history of ritual sacrifices and supernatural encounters, was pulsing with echoes of dark events.

And then there was the rock, like all the other sacred sites I had visited before, holding onto its own secrets. No wonder the warning words echoed in my mind – "leave, leave now." But why had I been directed to this place if it held such danger? Ingo's cryptic words from his chapter resurfaced in my mind, his unanswered question, not so rhetorical as it might seem, still persistent – "Who else could Aquero [the soft glow often experienced as orbs by many] be than the Holy Mother?" A feeling of utter clarity enveloped me, I had indeed found the answer for myself, in spades.

WHERE TROUBLE BREWS

May 26, 2024

Conjunctions

Mysterious Happenings

During my early days of browsing the internet for sites to visit, I stumbled upon a book by folklorist, cryptozoologist, and investigator Ronald L. Murphy, Jr. called **Unexplained World of the Chestnut Ridge: A Hike Through the Goblin Universe of Western Pennsylvania**. Intrigued, I purchased a copy. The book starts with a description of the Chestnut Ridge, a beautiful locale which is located on the western edge of the Allegheny Mountains in Pennsylvania and stretches all the way to Morgantown, West Virginia as "a hotbed for strange occurrences." But it was the table of contents that truly captured my attention. A quick glance revealed this area has had sightings of UFOs, Bigfoot, howlers, dogmen, thunderbirds, ghosts, tulpas, fairies, and gnomes. I flipped randomly through the next few pages and then to his conclusion. As Murphy speculates later in the book, many people may not realize that when they hike or drive through this area, they are entering the Goblin Universe – a paranormal world hidden behind a veil that intersects with our own. I was immediately drawn in when Murphy mentioned the Ridge is filled with limestone and sandstone due to its geologic formation. If there was one place I needed to visit, it was here.

I marked out several key locations in a section of the Ridge known as the Laurel Highlands, located south and east of Pittsburgh. With my focus narrowed to this specific area, I planned my journey. However, due to the vagueness of some of the locations mentioned in the book, I turned to YouTube and came across a documentary titled "Invasion on Chestnut Ridge - Full Documentary (2017 Bigfoot Sasquatch Paranormal Movie)." I quickly skipped through the footage, careful not to spoil the surprise for myself. Along with discovering the precise locations, I also learned about a reported UFO crash at Kecksburg and saw a map highlighting the Ridge and towns with reported activity. The video pointed out a path from Keystone State Park to Derry, Kecksburg, Blairsville, Latrobe, Connellsville, and Mount Pleasant. Satisfied with what I had gathered so far, I stopped watching so that I wouldn't feel too influenced one way or another.

I was uncertain about how close I wanted to be to the towns labeled as having "activity," so I chose a centrally located place to stay – the Log Cabin Lodge & Suites in Donegal, Pennsylvania. The website advertised a modern, clean, and affordable lodging experience in the heart of Pennsylvania mountain fun. As a bonus, the motel was attached to an interactive/petting zoo called Living Treasures Wild Animal Park – providing a sort of "safe buffer zone" for me. I had originally planned to spend two nights there, but last-minute changes extended my stay to three days. On Friday, May 24, 2024, I arrived at the Lodge around nine o'clock in the evening. Unfortunately, my car had decided to stop allowing me voice access to Google Maps after I left Virginia at the same time it made the executive decision to avoid toll roads. This meant I had to rely solely on visual directions through winding and hilly one-lane roads in the mountains for four hours – some during daylight and others at night with impatient drivers behind me. By the time I reached the Lodge, I was completely exhausted and less than amused with my car.

After checking in at the zoo's office, I received a key with a plastic attachment stating my room number in bold letters. The atmosphere felt like a college dorm room, but there was also a handwritten note on a pad of paper in the room, wishing me a pleasant stay with a big heart as an exclamation point. Overall, it was quite entertaining. But the highlight of my room was the large tub/jacuzzi situated between the bed and bathroom. Just looking at it brought joy back to my soul. Of course, before closing the curtains and settling in for the night, I couldn't help but glance out the window and throw a side glance at my car parked just beyond my room's window.

My plan for Saturday, the following day, was to explore nearby state parks. They seemed like logical first choices because they were in the center of my designated "hot zones," and I could access them legally. After a five-hour drive with a stop to have lunch with my son, followed by another five-hour drive, I fell into a deep sleep as soon as I crawled under the covers. In my dream, I saw a glowing statue of Mary inside a shell placed on some rocks near a train station. I had an inexplicable urge to touch it, but something told me not to. Was this like Lourdes? I wasn't quite sure what to make of it, other than feeling compelled to travel due north. When I checked my phone after waking up, it was 3:24 in the morning. Before falling asleep, I had been deciding between two different state parks – Keystone State Park to the north and Laurel Ridge State Park to the east. But after my dream, I knew I had to go to Keystone. It would take me through Latrobe, which had been identified as an area of activity. I promptly drifted back to sleep with thoughts of an interesting day ahead.

As the sun began to rise, I checked the details for Keystone. According to the internet, it would open at noon on Saturday. Still, I was confused as the park's Sunday hours were listed as 24 hours. How could a nonstop Sunday coincide with the condensed Saturday hours? I did look at my phone skeptically, however, eager to start my day, I searched for other nearby places I could visit before Keystone opened. After some more browsing, I found a hiking trail called West Penn Trail, just 15 minutes north of Keystone and under an hour from where I was staying at the Lodge. It had a parking lot which was all I needed to know. I decided to drive there, explore the area, and then head to Keystone when it opened at noon. My car still refused to let Google Maps speak, but at least it was daytime as I drove on the deserted back roads.

I must admit, the area is undeniably striking. Murphy was right about that. The landscape of rolling hills and verdant pastures in the Laurel Highlands stretched out before me as I drove, resembling something straight out of a storybook. The atmosphere was peaceful and tranquil, with only the gentle hum of farm life permeating the air; there was no sense of an electrified paranormal hotspot anywhere. That did seem odd.

Before I knew it, I had reached my destination. The dirt parking lot for the trail was easily visible and set among a grove of trees. As I pulled in, I noticed two crossover SUVs parked closely together next to a towering tree. I chose a spot in the expense between the car closest to the tree, but on the opposite side of it, and an older, worn-out brown pickup truck on my right. Beyond the truck was a gate serving as a barrier between the parking lot and an access road. It appeared wide enough for vehicles to use and most likely led to the actual walking trail.

I rolled down the car windows, not having much else to do in the empty parking lot. So, I called my son to pass the time. Midway through our conversation, I heard engines approaching. Turning to my left, I saw a large black SUV that looked like it belonged to the FBI speeding into the lot and then making a sharp right turn onto a small dirt road connected to the lot – something I had not noticed before since it all looked like forest around me. Following closely behind was a white pickup truck, also coming into the parking lot at high speed. Here we go, a white pickup truck, something was in play here. Sure enough, the white pickup truck made a quick right turn onto the same dirt road without even slowing down. A few moments later, the black SUV emerged from the dirt road and drove out of the lot, followed by the white pickup truck. All of this happened within minutes while I was on the phone with my son, giving him a play-by-play of the events as they unfolded.

Once everything had settled down and there were no more high-speed vehicles zooming around me, I turned my attention back to the area around the lot. Before this incident, I hadn't really paid much attention to my surroundings. However, now that there was a white pickup truck involved, I told my son I was going to explore the area and possibly check out the nearby trail. I promised to call him back after reaching Keystone before hanging up the phone.

Sitting in my car, I gazed out the car's windows at the trees and noticed two young women walking towards the gate from the path beyond it. They had short hair and wore trendy clothes that showed off their elaborate arm tattoos. As they entered the parking lot, I followed their movements with prying eyes. To my surprise, they got into the beat-up brown pickup truck and drove away. I had assumed they would go to one of the two sleek crossover SUVs parked on my left based on their appearance and the state of the pickup. But I was wrong.

As soon as the brown pickup pulled away, I stepped out of my car and my eyes were immediately drawn to a pair of small shoes practically touching the SUV crossover parked next to the tree. They were clearly meant for a toddler, with their tiny size and bright colors. Without hesitation, I snapped a photo of them, my mind racing with potential explanations for their presence. My rational mind kicked in, telling me they probably belonged to the child who had been with their guardian near the vehicle parked next to the tree.

Perhaps they were simply forgotten in the rush to get the child into another pair of shoes. Surely, they would notice and retrieve them upon their return. Still, a nagging thought of a potential abduction crept up, but I brushed it off as an overactive imagination. Lost in these thoughts, I suddenly heard voices behind me and turned to see an older couple – I shouldn't say older they were probably my age – approaching from the trail beyond the gate. Feeling a bit silly for my initial abduction fear, I headed towards them and passed by as they walked around the gate. As we passed each other on the paved pathway, we exchanged hellos.

I continued down the path which quickly turned and ended at another perpendicular road. Glancing left and right, I saw nothing but trees and vegetation lining the road. The only sign of life was the gentle rustle of leaves in the breeze. Deciding to turn left and explore further, I took a few steps before noticing something strange on the hill over which I had traversed thanks to the trail. There appeared to be a tiny stream flowing from what looked like a small rectangular shaped cavern, except the cavern was situated lower than the stream itself. Confused by this oddity, I reasoned that perhaps there was water bubbling up from beneath the ground. But as I stood there taking pictures of the strange sight, a growing sense of being watched welled up in me. The eerie sensation lingered, causing me to constantly glance over my shoulder. I couldn't tell if the source was behind me or hidden within the dark cavern. Undeterred, I continued to snap photos of the rectangular space, hoping to capture any hint of a non-human presence in my lens. But instead of glowing eyes or wispy orbs, the images revealed only a void. I was far from amused; it felt like something was just out of reach, teasing me with its presence but never fully revealing itself to be captured photographically. Then the heebie-jeebies kicked in. Part of me wanted to ignore the feeling and stay to explore further, hoping to find something inside the cavern. Be that as it may, a voice of caution tugged at my mind, warning me of potential danger lurking in the shadows. Who knows what could be hiding just beyond sight? It would be wise to make my way back. And so, I did.

Upon returning to the parking lot, I noticed the couple had taken the vehicle parked next to the tree, the one with a pair of shoes laying nearby. It caught me off guard; the whole situation seemed off-balance. You know that feeling when something just doesn't seem right? That's what I was experiencing. I walked closer to the tree to investigate. As I approached the area, my gaze fell upon a baffling sight. A large metal spoon was placed against the tree's trunk. This was no ordinary spoon – it was massive, like the ones used in school cafeterias. It had small circular dents all over and a strange yellow substance smeared on it. From its position, I knew instinctively hadn't been discarded or forgotten. Just beyond it lay the pair of shoes, except from my new vantage point, they appeared to have been abandoned mid-stride, as if their owner had simply vanished into thin air. It was clear something unusual had occurred here; something was definitely amiss.

The contrasting images of the worn-out shoes and a tarnished spoon, side by side, collided in my mind. The feeling of an offering saturated my thoughts. I snapped a photo and began to slowly back away, keeping a watchful eye on my surroundings. It felt like I had entered and was intruding upon a sacred area of some sort. I was mid-stride in backing up when the sound of an approaching vehicle caught my attention, and I turned to see the white pickup truck rumbling up the road towards me. Instinctively, I took a picture of it as it drew closer, making a mental note to remember this encounter. Sego Canyon had taught me to be attuned to white vehicles.

The truck turned down that side dirt road it had earlier in pursuit of the black SUV, piquing my interest even more. I walked closer to the road, and I found myself drawn to take a picture of the No Trespassing sign near it, as if I was summoned by the odd energy permeating the area. Moments later, the white pickup truck reemerged and drove off with me still standing there. Now well attuned to the white vehicle message, I read it loud and clear, it was time to go and leave this place behind. I jumped back into my car and was about to make my exit when another vehicle appeared – a newer version of the brown pickup truck that had left earlier. It parked in the exact same spot as its earlier incarnation had. This was followed by two stylishly dressed women stepping out of it and heading down the trail; again, with arms awash with tattoos. It was as if I was watching the earlier scene with the older brown pickup truck but in reverse.

There was something more than coincidence going on. I wondered given now two pairs of women attached to brown pickup trucks if I had entered a witch's or coven's territory. My inquiring mind outweighed, and frankly simply overtook, my idea of leaving. I rolled the windows down.

Well, if this was a coven's territory I would ask someone who might know. Sending a direct message via **X** to Worthless One/Medusan Witchery, @WKberzk (designated as WITCH), I attached a photo of the shoes and spoon and asked if they held any significance. It was now half past 11. He responded immediately; our conversation went as follows:

"Saw this today at an out of the way wooded trail. Do you think it means something?"

"Wow it certainly feels like it."

He then adds that I may be looking at a modern rendition of the Cottingley Fairies, something he tells me is a contrived scene of some sort.

I press on, wanting to know more. He says there is a trend these days of kids making gnome homes at the base of trees.

"Why base of trees?"

"Just for fun, to make people believe Gnomes and elves live there."

"Interesting. So they are faking an event?"

"It is a modern expression of an ancient event. Basically, they are honoring the 'Djinn' if you want to look at it as that. ... We see that and think 'abduction.' It is a way of spreading the 3 M's: Magick Mystery of Mayhem. ... If it was someone's Magickal mischief, IT WORKED :) Imagine if the perpetrator knew who was actually talking about their magick?! They would flip the f*** out!!!!! Elly Flippen and Worthless talking about my gnome home."

"Indeed. It just feels like an offering. I will definitely have to look more into this."

"I feel like you should print this out and stick it in an envelope and put it into one of the shoes!!!! Hahaha. ♥ Thank you so much for sharing this with me!!!!! I can't wait to tell Carol [his wife] about [this] she is going to be so happy to hear it."

I replied with a series of smiley and laughter emojis. Glancing at the time, I noticed it was almost noon, and I knew I had to leave soon to make my scheduled appearance at Keystone by noon. Yet, I reached Keystone at 12:02pm, following ironically in the footsteps of Judaculla. In contrast to the stillness of the ancient rock, this park was buzzing with activity. People sat in chairs and fished by the lake, kayaks and canoes dotted the water, hikers and bikers traversed the trails. It seemed like this park had been open for hours. As I drove along the park's roads, the atmosphere was completely ordinary, devoid of any eerie vibes. It was almost disappointing, as if this place had no secrets or mysteries to uncover.

I eventually found a parking spot near an information center and called my son to let him know I was alright. With now lots of time on my hands, I sat in my car trying to figure out the best route back to the Lodge using Google Maps. That accomplished, I zoomed in to see where I had been earlier. I noticed that part of the trail followed old sections of the Pennsylvania Railroad – which was interesting, considering my dream from the night before revolved around a railroad. Perhaps there was some deeper meaning hidden in it all, something to ponder and unravel later. I was curious though about where that dirt road marked by the "No Trespassing" sign led. I located it on the map and saw it led to a small private looking cemetery – Livermore Cemetery according to the map. Had I, in retrospect, truly read Murphy's book and scrutinized the table of contents in greater detail, I would have learned more about this cemetery, but I hadn't, so all I knew at that point looking at the map, was that it was there, and that a white pickup truck was hastily coming and going from it, possibly making sure I went nowhere near it.

My stomach growled, so I headed out to grab something to eat. I stopped by the local Sheetz near the Lodge and grabbed a hamburger before making my way back to my room. I figured the Lodge would be relatively empty during this in-between time of check-out and check-in. But when I arrived, I was surprised to see every single parking spot, even those outside of the Lodge's designated area, had been taken up. Confused, I looked around and saw families with young kids putting on sunscreen. Apparently, the petting zoo was a popular weekend destination; I hadn't seen that coming.

After some creative parking, I sat outside my room in one of the plastic chairs provided, enjoying my hamburger while watching the hectic scene at the zoo. It was quite entertaining to observe parents and grandparents struggling to navigate the crowded parking lot and wrangle overexcited children into sunscreen applications. Eventually, the person parked in front of my room left and I quickly moved my car into the now-vacant spot. Returning to my chair, I continued to watch as tired parents and grandparents dragged exhausted kids out of the zoo, many of whom put up quite a fight about leaving.

After I was worn out from all the excitement happening in the parking lot, I picked up my **X** conversation with The Worthless One. Among other things he had in the messages since I had signed off back at the trail's parking lot, talked about gnomes and then: "Carol has mixed feelings about the baby sneaker spoon mystery. My artist's eye says the placement seems to indicate a sense of proportionality and a deliberate choice of placement. It's too neat. It looks staged. But Carol's sense diminishes my confidence in that assessment. The ground is very open and clear and it seems to me that a legitimate villain would be hyper aware of leaving such glaring evidence at such an obvious place. Speaking as a someone raised by a self-identified gangster, I think have more confidence in my criminally minded assessment than any other." I laughed, to myself.

I responded by recalling how he had messaged me on **X** about a gnome image, and I remarked that there are no coincidences. Then, I added... "What does she think the sneaker/spoon situation is? It feels like it was an offering of some sort." I attached a photo of the cavern and stream I had discovered, making sure to mention that it was located off from the lot at the bottom of a hill from where the spoon and sneaker were placed.

He responded, "I think you're probably correct about the offering. The way I see it, the fairy door trend, or the staging of that kind of experience, is also very definitely an Offering in itself, and a powerful one. A cynical old shaman might say: it's 'Ritualized Litter' whether it's intended for fairies or algorithms, the tree doesn't want Chinese housewares, the tree wants tobacco!" He then comments on the appearance of the cave, calling it "crazy," and asks if it's located at an intersection. I confirm that it is, and he updated his assessment, now believing that a Santeria fertility spell may have been performed near the tree. He gave me specific details to look for, such as "knotted plastic bags tossed under a bush." After examining a photo of the cavern and stream, I spotted something that resembles what he described, although it's not exactly under a bush. We discussed this briefly before ending our conversation for the day.

The next morning, Sunday, I got right to my coven theory, I had been intentionally trying to ease into it: "Another question. When I arrived at the parking spot there was an old beat up brown pickup truck parked to my right. After a bit two women came from the trail and got in it and drove away. When I was preparing to go, a newer brown pickup truck parked where the old one had been. Two women got out of it and headed down the trail. Could this have been a coven's territory? I was looking at the map of the parking area and saw off the parking lot is another small dirt road leading to a cemetery very close by."

He tells me it's unlikely because there aren't many covens operating these days, and the litter aspect of the sneaker and shoe situation goes against their respect for nature. He adds he personally condemns animal abuse and littering, noting as he does, "In my estimation a real Witch uses poetic devices to demonstrate that those shortcuts are usually a terrible idea." He then moved on to the women in the brown truck, and started with the cemetery first, "Cemetery dirt, tombstone chunks, coffin nails (in the old days) and human remains are often called for in Santeria and Voodoun ceremonies. It's possible that these women are collecting materials to sell at the Botanica." Then added, "If you wanna get crazy here, find your local botanica and look for brown pickup trucks parked outside. Those ladies would adore you if they knew you were interested. They would wind up asking you to come and learn directly from them if they knew you were even thinking about it. They're probably a blast!! Laughing and running around in woods and cemeteries!!!!"

"Always an adventure," I countered, my face betraying a monkey-like grimace. My mind then started racing, making note of the possible connections between Santeria, Voodoo, cemeteries, and brown vehicles. As for my plans for the day, they would have to be altered. No, I wasn't suddenly heading to a botanica; instead, I would make a stop at the memorial for Flight 93 to the east before swinging by the Kesksburg UFO shop, a reminder of the bizarre occurrences in the area, on my way back to the Lodge.

I was working in downtown Washington, DC when the first plane crashed into the tower in New York City on 9.11. My colleagues and I were glued to the office TV for the rest of the morning as the city shut down around us. Eventually, a Metro train was permitted to pass through the Pentagon station without stopping, and I was on it. The smell of smoke filled my nostrils as we slowly traveled through the station. It was for me profound moment.

Years later, in 2016, I found myself staying at a hotel near Ground Zero while attending an exhibit at the Leslie Lohman Museum of Art that featured some of Ingo's artwork. On the morning before the opening, I decided to visit the World Trade Center site. It was a solemn experience as I walked around and observed the memorial grounds. But when I turned a corner and came upon a particular section, I was overcome with intense anguish. Quickly, I had to leave. I learned later this spot was where many individuals who were trapped in the towers had chosen to jump fell in their escape of the fire. It felt to me like the ground beneath me seemed to absorb the torment of their final moments.

Visiting the site where Flight 93 had crashed seemed like a necessary part of completing my understanding of the events of 9.11. But more so, I also hoped that my journey to this place would provide some insight into the strange happenings in Southwestern Pennsylvania, possibly caused by the land itself. It took me about 45 minutes to drive there from the Lodge. The area is now called The Flight 93 Memorial and is managed by the National Park Service, spanning over 1,000 acres. The atmosphere of the space was somber, tranquil, peaceful, and respectful. I didn't sense anything unusual or significant during my visit to the Memorial; it was just like any other place of solemn reverence. Strolling along the designated path, tracing the impact zone of Flight 93, it didn't feel like anyone had perished on the ground from the crash. Instead, it felt as if they were already gone before the plane even hit the ground. My gaze swept over the landscape, taking in the distant trees and surrounding nature. Nothing seemed out of the ordinary. The ground beneath my feet felt unaffected, but the air around me was thick with sadness.

I decided next to give the UFO Store in Kecksburg a chance, hoping it would provide some answers. Based on what I read, it was under the jurisdiction of the nearby fire department. When I arrived, I discovered it was connected to a recreational building owned by the fire department. It was almost comical how fitting this setup was as a parallel to the current state of Ufology: a prominent sign reading "UFO Store" with an arrow pointing to a door labeled "BAR." I parked my car and took in the deserted lot around me. The sound of a loud siren only added to the odd atmosphere. Realizing this place likely wouldn't have what I was looking for, I turned my car back on the road towards the Lodge instead of getting out and going inside. This time, I expected the lot to be full at the Lodge and wasn't surprised when it was.

On the morning of Memorial Day, I left the Lodge in the early hours and drove along deserted back roads. A thick fog covered the fields and roads. In the darkness, I stumbled upon a sign while driving up and down hills and through fields. Without any voice guidance from my car's link with Google Maps, I didn't see it until I was passing by. The sign warned the area was known for frequent crashes due to drunk driving. I laughed at the irony; we become so intoxicated by the concept of something, lost in its dogma and allure, all we end up doing is crashing and burning in pursuit of it. To me, it encapsulated my entire Chestnut Ridge experience. At least, that's what I believed, not knowing what was to come.

Once back, the first thing on my list was to investigate the paranormal aspects of the cemetery. Supposedly, per several sources on the web, it is a hot spot for ghost sightings, unearthly noises, and strange electrical malfunctions, I found. I did wonder if Murphy had written about this place, considering its location in "his" area of Chestnut Ridge and its supernatural reputation. I grabbed his book from my shelf and opened it to the table of contents. Sure enough, there was an entire chapter devoted to what he called the "Livermore Investigations."

Apparently, Livermore was once a town that now lies at the bottom of a lake after being flooded by a dam built to protect Pittsburgh. But during its time as a town, Murphy explained, it had its fair share of paranormal incidents. Now, the land has been reclaimed by nature with some hiking and biking trails running through it. However, Murphy warns that despite its serene appearance, this land is a potential gateway to the "Goblin Universe." And I had to imagine the cemetery, perched on a hill and spared from reclamation efforts, was connected to this Goblin's paradise.

I scanned the chapter and came across a mention of a private road leading to the cemetery, accessible from a parking lot and marked with a "No Trespassing" sign and wire fence. The image of the white pickup truck and the warning sign flashed in my mind. Murphy went on to share that young people often try sneaking in at night to use Ouija Boards there, but he warned against it, saying these devices can open doors that should remain shut, adding, spirits already have enough entry points without our help – something The Worthless One was touching upon while I sat in my car parked just feet away from the entrance of the cemetery road.

I flipped the pages, moving on to stage two of Murphy's investigation at Livermore. Apparently, it all began in the parking lot near Penn Trail, right next to the cemetery. It was like I had both a sixth sense and no sense at all; I had been there earlier but had no idea how significant that spot really was. In my dream, I was drawn to the railroad tracks further north, and now I understood why. As Murphy and his team were investigating in the parking lot, they encountered two young men who had just finished fishing at a nearby pond along the former train tracks. These men claimed to have been followed by some kind of creature. The team searched for evidence along the trail but found nothing and returned to the parking lot. As night fell, they began scanning the area with flashlights and soon their light was blocked by a large black mass, which Murphy described as "absorbing" the light before disappearing into the woods beyond the fence blocking the cemetery road. Now I knew why the white pickup truck kept coming and going; after my experience with Holy Cow and my other wanderings despite warnings from someone "watching over me," it was there to ensure that I did not enter the restricted area, the "look but do not touch" comment while in my dream now ringing through my head. And here I thought Keystone was where all the action was.

I moved on. During our conversation in the parking lot that day, The Worthless One brought up gnomes. I had a feeling now this could be significant, so I searched through Murphy's book knowing he had mentioned them. I found what I was looking for in another chapter.

Here Murphy briefly mentions the gnomes and their connection to legends from other countries and ancient times. He also explores the Iroquois' – the Indigenous peoples of the area – beliefs about "the little people" who inhabited the woods and wild areas of their region. He next connects these beings to Bigfoot but then poses a thought-provoking question: is it more likely that there is just one entity capable of shapeshifting into various forms, rather than a variety of different creatures?[58]

He calls this shapeshifting a form of projection, allowing these beings to control how they are perceived by us, like Ingo's Hologram Metaphor. In a way, he compares this to a theatrical performance playing out in our imagination. In an instant, in my mind, memories of shapeshifters from ancient legends and rock art all over the world collided with theories about extraterrestrial beings being demonic entities.

It is a clever manipulation tactic, a brilliant ploy, a deception designed to keep us tangled up and confused, always on the hunt for something that may not even exist in the form we perceive it to be. Because of this, we fail to connect the dots between past and present, between the various descriptions of creatures that defy categorization by witnesses. We continue to see these encounters as isolated incidents rather than part of the larger picture. It was all synthesizing for me. But one question remained, what about those brown pickup trucks and botanicas?

---

[58] Regarding this, one intriguing subject for contemplation is the evolution of cultural lexicology across time. According to legend, the Islamic Djinn were formed from fire, while other sources suggest that the early term used for fairies was "fire folk."

No matter how hard I looked, though, I came up empty. If I wanted to truly understand the relationship between the two, I would have to follow The Worthless One's advice and stake out these places. That being said, the scenarios that played out in my mind did not end well, so I abandoned the idea. Instead, I decided to take a step back and try to understand Santeria from a broad perspective.

From what I gathered, it focuses on tapping into a supernatural force through rituals, allowing for communication with and possession by this force. Basically, it's like kicking open Murphy's door. It was at that moment, the dream where Mary was engulfed in light finally made sense to me. It wasn't a divine glow, but a deceptive façade. Lourdes thus held a deeper meaning that stretched far beyond its mere geographical location. It symbolized the temptation of supposedly pure and divine beings who were sinister forces in disguise. By seeking their malevolent power or falling for their false offers of salvation, one essentially forms a binding contract with darkness, allowing its corrupt energy to seep in. The darkness becomes you and you become the darkness; there is no separation between the two. I finally understood the deep, inexplicable pull towards the Chestnut Ridge. I had thought it was for one reason and it turns out it was for another one altogether.

With the day coming to an end, I headed over to my apartment complex's gym to get in a quick workout. As I approached the door, I noticed it was closed and peered through the glass to see inside. Usually, the room was empty, but on this day, there was one guy lifting weights. The elliptical machines, my normal choice of equipment, were all unoccupied, which was a relief. Yet, as soon as I opened the door and stepped inside, a wave of negative energy hit me like a brick wall. I attributed it to the fact that the room wasn't empty like usual, but I pushed past it and made my way to one of the ellipticals.

As I started my workout, I began to feel something was off in the room. With one hand on the machine, I reached toward my phone with the other to start some music. In a split second, everything changed. A force lifted me off the machine, leaving me suspended in mid-air before slamming me down hard onto the ground. I guess I had my phone in my hand because it flew out of my hand as I landed while my earbud case in my pocket went flying in another direction. Dazed and in pain, I looked up to see I had landed dangerously close to where the man was using weights. But he didn't even flinch or pause his workout.

Slowly, I crawled around on the floor to retrieve my belongings, all while feeling a dark presence behind me. But I refused to let it break me. With a determined mindset, I got back on the elliptical and started exercising again, pushing through despite the growing pain in my body.

For 20 minutes, I persevered until finally leaving the gym and limping back to my apartment. The next morning, I checked myself for any serious injuries. Thankfully, despite a continued soreness in my back and legs, there was only a bruise on my arm from where I had fallen. After taking some painkillers, I managed to make it out of my apartment and into my car. As I drove away, I glanced back at the gym and noticed a majestic hawk perched on the railing outside, watching over the room as if guarding it. I stopped to take a picture, and even though I was close to it, the hawk didn't seem bothered by my presence. "Stay strong," I heard a voice say in my head as I continued driving away. The hawk's words continued to echo in my mind, reminding me I could not let the darkness of that day defeat me.

Shortly thereafter I had a dream, one that led me to take stock of everything. One more destination remained on my list: Beaver Dunes in Oklahoma. Without hesitation, I crossed it off and brought an end to my journey. There was no need for further searching; the truth had been right in front of me all along, but I had been too blind to see it.

The forests of his Mind, deep
and dark and endless, which had inexplicable
illuminations and in which strange thought-
animals meandered.

Ingo Swann, **Jimmy Wings**

THE WIND-UP

Conjunction.World

Resurrecting the Mysterious

Vis-à-vis my own self-knowlede-ing journey, I did, very early on, confirm for myself there is undoubtedly a presence in conjunction with us, one that coexists with us, operating at a frequency we can tap into through our own conscious or unconscious expansion of our inbuilt perceptional awareness systems. Alternatively, the land itself may act as a transducer or amplifier,[59] allowing us to pick up these vibrations within our bodies. It is akin to tuning in to a hidden radio station, unlocking a world of knowledge and understanding beyond our immediate perception. And in this obscured world, do malevolent forces lurk and manipulate us from just outside of our frequency? Is there a sinister entity steering these dark intentions, seeking to sow fear and disconnection amongst humanity? I believe so. Are we mere pawns in their twisted game, mere playthings for their amusement? It seems increasingly likely, not only on an individual level but also through the tumultuous events occurring in our world. What is their ultimate goal in their interactions with us? It's clear their actions

---

[59] I chose the different locations I visited in the US, excluding Mountain Lake Lodge, based on reported incidents and local legends. Interestingly, all these locations fell within a specific region known for frequent paranormal activity according to the indicator map. Judaculla Rock, where I experienced the most intense encounter with the supernatural, had the highest predicted level of paranormal activity.

have caused horrific outcomes, but could they be following an agenda or has something gone terribly wrong, beyond even their control now? They have had ample opportunity to destroy us if that was their intention, yet they haven't. So, what is their motivation?

Is there a higher power at play, working with what we would perceive as noble intentions? Maybe it is just our gut instinct guiding us, or maybe there is something even more powerful at work. As I traversed from one "adventure" to the next, this universe seemed to reveal its benevolence through strange and almost unbelievable coincidences. It was as if white vehicles, birds, a last minute change in hotels, a group who left me behind, people who may not have even been real, and even a cow were all placed in my path deliberately, guiding me towards my destination or away from hazardous ones. These serendipitous moments appeared suddenly and decisively, almost like flashing neon signs directing me on my journey. They could not be brushed off as mere luck or happenstance; instead, they seemed divinely orchestrated on my behalf. However, I am unsure if this benignity is driven by pure selflessness or if it serves a covert agenda.

Through my own personal encounters, I have observed that these opposing factions of "good" and "evil" employ vastly different tactics: one side relying on strategy and teamwork, utilizing carefully planned maneuvers, the other relying more on brute force and chaos.

And are there very powerful human actors working with forces we cannot see with personal gain on the line with good as much as with ill-intent aiding and abetting them? For me that is a resounding yes. I can see such "partnerships" as old practically as humanity itself.

But could there be more to this "situation" that I'm not seeing?

I was nearly done with my "project" when, after "the gym incident," I woke up in the middle of the night from a vivid dream. I tried to fall back asleep, but my mind refused to shut down. In the dream, everything was black and white, with shades of grey replacing white. It started with a choice between two paths, each leading to a different outcome. The first path led me straight into a shipping container floating on water. I was alone inside it. As I examined the interior of the container, I noticed old fist marks on the walls – the result of relentless attempts to break free. I knew I was doomed; it was only a matter of time. It seemed like anyone who had been trapped in this container had come to the same realization. Death was inevitable, slow and painful. What a terrible way to end up, I thought dismally.

Very quickly, I found myself walking along path number two and stumbled upon a ramshackle structure made of different types of wood, some wide, some narrow. It was surrounded by dark beings, but I felt hidden from their sight for the time being. Climbing to the top, I hid and tried to plan my next move. Eventually, I would have to descend and scavenge for supplies. Carefully plotting my path down, I thought I had outsmarted them, but it turns out they were playing with me all along. They found me, captured me, and before ending my life, I woke up.

Lying in bed I was fixated on the limited and forced decisions life presented. What was the purpose of it all? Was this some form of Hell or a simulation? It was then I recalled Ingo's theory about multiple non-human factions manipulating us like pawns in a grand game of chess. Maybe there are more facets to this than we are aware of. This could explain why Ingo felt the need to include the following in his book **Penetration**: "Well," I snarled, "whoever is in charge of these matters hasn't managed them very well as far as us ordinary public types are concerned." "I'll concede that, Ingo," Axel said. "Frankly, no one has known what to do, and many mistakes have been made." "Yes, and all in the name of what — privileged information in favor of the few, of the military, of scientists, or what?" "Sometimes. But the problems are more than you can imagine."

According to Ingo, our view of reality is limited by our own perceptions and beliefs. We are content with this narrow perspective, not realizing there may be other truths beyond our own perceived reality. And so, as I let my thoughts drift aimlessly between these two opposing perspectives, the classic dichotomy of good versus evil, a question began to spin in my mind. Is this truly the most accurate way to perceive things? Could it be we are only seeing it as they want us to? So perhaps the concept of good and evil is not as clear-cut as we believe; maybe it is not a simple binary, but rather a complex spectrum where shades of gray blend together in a tangled mess?

I then remembered a powerful example of this from Ingo's book, **The Great Apparitions of Mary**.

At the time, I was living at 357, and I often discussed the book with Ingo as he was writing it. One apparition that stood out to him was the one in 1896 at Tilly-sur-Seulles, France. In his book, Ingo emphasized how this apparition occurred during a time of peace and prosperity, before the chaos known as the Age of Anarchy (1903-1909), followed by World War

The Wind-Up

I. It was a fascinating occurrence for several reasons. First, Ingo observed that many people who witnessed the apparition also reported seeing other figures accompanying it – saints, angels, demons, devils, and other important figures. These additional beings seemed to surround the main apparition in a way reminiscent of what we might consider "special effects" today. Second were the physical reactions observed during these events. A young girl, Jeanne Bellanger, at only 13-years-old, would enter a trance and her body would become contorted in unusual ways. She would kneel in ecstasy, and her spine would curve back until her neck touched her heels. Many who witnessed this were disturbed by the sight and some even became physically ill. These visions and physical contortions continued to occur until 1899. Then nothing. However, 14 years after the events in Tilly-sur-Seulles, northern France was once again embroiled in war, this time World War I. The area around Tilly and the Normandy coastline became a hellish landscape of constant fighting, trenches, mud, lethal gas attacks, insanity, filth, sickness, and death.

Thousands of corpses lay rotting on the ground or were hastily buried in mass graves. Some bodies had even contorted into arches due to muscle contractions after death, mirroring the convulsions of some believers during the reported apparition years before. Thus, the world was left bewildered by the apparition, unable to fully understand its dark images and twisted forms in 1899, were only in hindsight able to grasp their meaning. Then and only then did they have a frame of reference, a new reality. With this an epiphany bloomed within me. Ingo had pondered the same concept, a frame of reference, in his book **Reality Boxes.**

Within the confines of human consciousness, there exist a multitude of reality boxes, each serving to restrict and shape our understanding of the world around us. But is this all that exists within the vast expanse of human consciousness? Or is there something more beyond these limited constructs? The only glimpse we have into this mystery is what individuals experience outside of these predetermined ideas – "which is a great deal, indeed."

His overarching question from the book was bouncing around rapidly in my brain: "Why do we feel like there is more to us than anyone could ever know?" Yet, the paradox became for me almost palpable when I observed society's attempts to answer this very question. In a world where technology and science are readily available for answers, we use it to be spoon-fed, eagerly accepting whatever nonsense the latest "influencer" spouts out. We hold onto the belief that one person or idea will save us, make things better, or prevent things from getting worse, instead of taking on the challenging task of figuring things out and making a change ourselves. And amid it all, we glorify and idolize these non-human beings who exist among us. In sum, it seems we seek knowledge and guidance from the scientific world, from sources of information, and even from entities outside ourselves, failing to realize everything we need has been within us all along.

The actor Terrence Howard was recently on the **Joe Rogan Experience**. He said something which struck me; well, he said a lot of things which struck me. In this case, this moment, it was something which resonated with my own newly budding understanding. He said in us is something divine.

I had crossed paths with Howard once. We didn't meet, I just watched him walk into a room, speak, and then leave. At the time he was starring on Fox's show **Empire** and his art pieces, geometric constructions of acetate and glass, were being exhibited as part of the AVAM's "The Visionary Experience: St. Francis to Finster" in 2014-2015. Howard spoke at a private luncheon for insiders attached to the exhibit, my mother and I included. The show was also the debut of Ingo's art at the museum; the launch of Ingo's art's permanent display. Replaying the show in my mind, I saw the symbolism present in the placement of Howard's art juxtaposed with Ingo's. As you walked into one of the exhibit rooms on the museum's second floor, Howard's constructs, ones he had created as a teenager, were located as you entered the room, Ingo's painting, **Universal Intelligence**, was where you exited. It was a living metaphor for my own journey – from the constructs of where I once stood to the universal knowledge implicit in where I now was headed.

What Howard was highlighting, his words ringing out with a powerful resonance, is the inner divinity and potential that resides within everyone. His message serves as a reminder to look inward for guidance and fulfillment, rather than seeking it in external sources. This idea is not new; it can be found in various established religions around the world.

- o One of Buddha's fundamental beliefs was that everything you need is within you. He taught, "You are a seeker. Delight in the mastery of your hands and your feet, of your words and your thoughts."

The Wind-Up

- o   The passage from Luke 17:21, as depicted in the New King James version of the **Bible**, proclaims: "Neither shall they say, Lo here! or, lo there! for, behold, the kingdom of God is within you."
- o   You are already complete and whole, a part of a greater Oneness, the Taoists explain.
- o   Imam Ali, the cousin and son-in-law of Islamic prophet Muhammad and one of the earliest followers of his teachings, is often credited with saying: "Your sickness is from you, but you do not perceive it, and your remedy is within you, but you do not sense it. You presume you are a small entity, but within you is enfolded the entire Universe. You are indeed the evident book, by whose alphabet the hidden becomes manifest. Therefore you have no need to look beyond yourself. What you seek is within you, if only you reflect."
- o   According to ancient Hindu Yogins, each person is a self-perfecting unit within whom exists the basic framework for enormous powers of the body and mind.
- o   As the ancient Egyptian proverbs etched on the walls of the Luxor temple remind us: "Know the world in yourself. Never look for yourself in the world, for this would be to project your illusion."

Ingo had been toying with the idea himself of starting a school, as evidenced by notes from 2000, along these very lines. But at the age of nearly 67, it was likely an overwhelming prospect for him. Instead, he focused on his writing and used his words to educate others about how they might do this instead, effectively creating his own "school."

If he had created the school, I believe it would have been based on his belief that we must understand these strange qualities of a perception and experiences beyond what we are taught to believe, are not exclusive to a select few individuals.

This misguided notion only serves to push others away from these attributes on a personal and human level. Instead, we must recognize these traits are prevalent among the larger population, saying in **Psychic Literacy**: It is difficult to determine the number of individuals who recognize the human organism's inherent abilities such as intuition, perception beyond the five senses, and attunement to past or future "wavelengths" or dimensions.

While many may have personal experiences that hint at these attributes, without a deep understanding of them, they can only be utilized minimally or sporadically.

Ingo urged us to expand our senses beyond the commonplace five we are taught to rely on, assuring us that what we may initially perceive as irrelevant will eventually reveal itself to be of great significance. As we open ourselves up to new perspectives, we become attuned to the presence of both monsters and saviors in our surroundings, though their true nature may intermingle at times. The key lies in unlocking the door, but even with the key in hand, there is still a bolt keeping the door firmly shut. This is where the "control theory" of Jacques Vallée, a renowned figure in the world of internet technology and venture capital, as well as being an author and Ufologist, becomes relevant: according to this theory these entities create guideposts and gaps in our perception of reality – Ingo's reality boxes. How can we overcome this obstacle caused by the guideposts and gaps and create a new frame of reference? Ingo said we must move past our desire to enter this quagmire in the first place.

In terms of this, I was reminded about something I learned while working as a transitional CFO for an international non-profit organization focused on human rights. It was during my last stay at 357 with Ingo. As part of my role, I traveled to various foreign offices, including one in the island nation of Timor-Leste, off the coast of Indonesia. The journey from Java, Indonesia was shared with United Nation workers, as the country was still in its early days of independence after enduring a brutal civil war and military occupation by Indonesia for 24 years.

The office I visited shared space with another international organization that helped locate mass graves scattered around the island. During my visit, I toured a former political prison where the island's people suffered under the occupation. The tour included a history of the trauma endured and showed us the small cells where prisoners were held. Although smaller than the box in my dream, these cells contained unimaginable suffering, evident from the carvings on the walls. The tour ended in a peaceful garden with scattered chairs.

On one of the walls surrounding the garden, there was a message asking what each person would do for human rights now that they were aware of this horrific reality.

In terms of this now being "aware," the memory of Ingo's book, **Master of Harmlessness**, flooded my mind. I turned to the last chapters,

The Wind-Up

the ones on demons, angels, and rapture. In the eighth chapter of the book, Ingo discussed demons. The ones we are familiar with – hate, intolerance, suspicion, and anger – were all easily recognizable because we could identify them within ourselves and others. These negative traits had formed from all the hatred, intolerance, suspicion, and anger we experience and encounter in life. But there were also what he called "mega-demons," created by catastrophic events like war, abomination, holocausts, and Armageddon. Ingo wrote, "ask yourself if your own demon of hatred – or any other demon – has a place in the realm of miracles that you yourself are a part of...war and other such atrocities are not miraculous or astounding. Therefore, these mega-demons can only be sustained by those who dwell in a non-miraculous state of thinking." He encouraged us to work on these negative traits within ourselves. But there were also unknown demons lurking about us – "very strange creations indeed" – with their true meanings shrouded in mystery. Ingo continued, "do not ask where or how these demons are formed, for then you will become lost in the complexities of demonology."[60] The following chapter details the arrival of angels, glorious light beings with wings and sprouting magnificent light in all directions. About them, a character in the book tells us what we need to know: "This is a part of me. It's always been there, but now it's free."

When I first edited **Master of Harmlessness**, none of the concepts above really resonated with me. I found the book to be profound and enlightening overall, but I didn't truly absorb the message at the time. Upon reading it again, however with my newfound self-awareness, everything snapped into place. It was like an Ingo truth hiding in plain sight: instead of wasting energy trying to understand the "others," you will just get lost in "demonology," focus on extinguishing that which holds you back i.e., the demons, and unleashing your own magnificence i.e., the angels. As Howard had alluded to, we need to reclaim our divine essence that has been lost. It is something Ingo spoke about at a conference in Edgar Cayce's A.R.E. in 2003, saying our society is a constant force, suppressing the natural goodness within us as both a species and as

---

[60] Once embarked upon this path, there is no easy escape. The only way to break free is to either succumb to the all-consuming desire or demand that led you down this treacherous road, which could ultimately prove destructive, or to renounce it entirely in a manner reminiscent of the fervor with which you first stepped foot on this perilous journey.

individuals. The fear of too much good threatens to topple the carefully constructed power structures in place. As a result, we are bombarded with messages that highlight our flaws and weaknesses, keeping us distracted and ignorant of our potential for greatness. We are taught to focus on the negative, constantly seeking out what is wrong with us and fixating on our shortcomings, never fully realizing the immense goodness that resides within each and every one of us.

But how do we overcome something greater than ourselves that seems determined to keep us from realizing our potential?

In this, I was reminded of my last night at the Wildflower Cabin, high atop the La Sal Mountains in Utah. I woke up early, around four o'clock in the morning. Looking out the window, all I could see were low-lying clouds obscuring the sky. I had hoped to catch a glimpse of the almost-full Moon as it set, but it was concealed behind the thick clouds. My main desire for this trip, even more than seeing a UFO, was to witness the stars sparkling in the dark sky at night. With no light pollution and a location high above the valley, I expected my two nights there to be filled with stargazing. But instead, the only thing filling the sky was an endless sea of clouds. Even in these early morning hours before dawn, just like the past two nights on the mountain. The sun still had a few more hours before it would rise and I knew the Moon was hanging low and would soon set, but I saw nothing but the clouds. So, I sat and read on my phone; too awake to do anything else but wait for daylight.

The situation changed. The space around me suddenly grew lighter, as if a switch had been flipped and the room was now flooded with light streaming in from a west-facing window. I looked up, drawn to the source of this sudden brightness. A small break in the clouds had allowed the Moon to peek through, casting its glow into the room. Without hesitation, I grabbed my phone and headed outside, eager to capture this moment before it disappeared. The night air enveloped me, it was cool and crisp and reminded me of one of Ingo's childhood stories. I could almost hear his voice repeating the words captured on film: "The nighttime skies in Telluride were fabulously beautiful because there was no light, light degradation of the stars and the heavens, it was cold and clear and you could see the Milky Way, the stars and everything against this wonderful black backdrop." As I stood there, although it was cold it was anything but clear, and certainly no black backdrop. Disappointed but still grateful for the glimpse of the Moon, I headed back inside as the clouds quickly

The Wind-Up

reclaimed their territory, continuing their journey westward with the Moon in tow.

I settled back into a different spot on the sofa, choosing a window seat facing south with the hope of catching a glimpse of the stars through the clouds. In that moment, I didn't purposefully force my thoughts to converge, but they coalesced nonetheless into a sharp focus. I yearned for the stars, even if only glimpsed fleetingly as I sat there. But time continued to slip away, the seconds ticking by as I stared out the window at a dark cloud filled sky.

As I continued to wait for dawn, I scrolled through my phone, trying to pass the time. But then, something caught my attention outside the window. Had my instinct sensed an animal nearby? I looked around, nothing there. Next, my eyes were drawn upward to a sky completely devoid of any clouds. It was breathtaking and I could understand why Ingo often spoke of his childhood fascination with the stars. Stepping outside, I gazed up at the endless expanse and cried. I had been to dark sky zones and planetariums before, but nothing compared to this. As much as I tried to capture the moment on my phone, I knew no photo could do it justice. The experience only lasted ten minutes before the clouds rolled back in, but in that brief time, I grasped how disconnected we have become from our own existence and of the things Ingo said we have lost.[61]

Exactly four weeks after being body slammed, with all my pain gone, I entered the workout room again and was surprised to find two pennies placed in a specific way near where my phone had landed during the attack. One was dated 2016 and placed heads up, while the other looked dirty but seemed to be from 1980. I wasn't sure what this meant or how to interpret it, but I kept the pennies as part of my collection of found coins.

As the week went on, I took some time to contemplate the strange occurrences that seemed to be tailor-made for my benefit. While it's commonly believed finding a penny with its head facing up is lucky, finding one with its tail facing up is not. But Ingo had taught me that metals were gifts and would bring good luck regardless of their orientation. So, whenever I come across a lost penny, I consider it a lucky

---

[61] Ingo's chapter from **Resurrecting the Mysterious** titled "Investigating the Psychic Ruin" spelling this out in detail. The full chapter has been copied and is included in the Appendix.

find. Even if it's just one cent, it's still more than what I had before. And so, I always bring found pennies home with me as a sign that something has been added to my life.

This concept of good versus bad luck reminded me of the greater battle between good and evil in our world. I pondered this while examining the tails-up penny from 1980 (or so I thought). I wondered if 1980 pennies were still in circulation and turned to the internet for answers. My search led me to a video claiming that 1980 pennies with double letter imprinting of the word "Liberty" were valuable.

Excitedly, I cleaned off the penny to see if mine had this rare imprinting only to discover it was from 2005.

Disappointed but still intrigued by the narrative aspect, I searched what significant events happened in 2005. The first result mentioned that "Me at the zoo" was the first-ever video uploaded to YouTube – one small event in a vast list of events from that year according to Wikipedia. Thereupon, a flurry of quotes collided and merged in my mind:

1) During a confidential discussion, I was told, Hal Puthoff[62] shared a thought that stayed with me when it was passed on to me: "We are living in someone else's zoo."
2) In an interview, paranormal research funder William Henry Belk claimed "they" control the planet from a dimension beyond our perception.
3) During a radio show interview in the year 2000, Ingo revealed to the show's host Art Bell, the president works for those who hold dominion over the planet.
4) The rest of Fort's quote from **The Book of the Damned**: "I suspect that, after all, we're useful – that among contesting claimants, adjustment has occurred, or that something now has a legal right to us, by force, or by having paid out analogues of beads for us to former, more primitive, owners of us – all others warned off – that all this has been known, perhaps for ages, to certain ones upon this earth, a cult or order, members of which function like bellwethers to the rest of us, or as superior slaves or overseers, directing us in accordance with instructions received – from Somewhere else – in our mysterious usefulness."

---

[62] For additional information on him, refer to the various notes in Historical Tidbits.

The Wind-Up

Observing the state of our world and witnessing the way we mistreat one another, I do wonder. The disturbing concept of being owned by "higher intelligences" and kept in line through human actors, whom Fort referred to as "the cult," caused me to consider the destructive nature of war. It's been ingrained in our history for thousands of years; the first recorded war dating back to 2700 BCE in Mesopotamia. But who knows how far back it truly goes? We seem to excel at destroying each other, and despite advances in technology and society, not much has changed. The war rages on, as does the constant power struggle between factions vying for control. And amid it all, humanity sinks deeper into chaos and suffering.

So back to the question from that former prison garden: If you carefully peel back the layers of this seemingly perfect façade and discover it was all a lie, what then? What if you reach the end of the yellow brick road and find yourself face-to-face with a puppet master, manipulating us like farm animals for their own agenda? What would you do in that situation? Would you rebel against the strings controlling your every move, or succumb to being just another pawn in their game? I think this is the message implied in the penny from 2005.

As for 2016 and its head-up orientation, I began by sorting through my emails from that year, specifically ones I had sent. I was searching for any important or meaningful messages. In my search, I stumbled upon an email I had written to Cook while we were collaborating on Ingo's biography. This was before my mother, Cook, and I all agreed to publish **Resurrecting the Mysterious** instead.

After combing through my emails, I found one dated October 26, 2016, with the subject "energies and forces." In this email, I wrote about our psychic abilities, believing that Ingo's ideas in both **Psychic Literacy** and **Your Nostradamus Factor** about "Psychic Sensing Systems" were onto something. He suggests that humans have the capability to understand and interpret the various energies and forces surrounding us, thanks to a mind-body connection. I added that ancient cultures recognized this as a natural part of their environment, but science dismissed it as nonexistent. However, I made sure to note, there is a stark difference between claiming something doesn't exist and it actually not existing.

The pennies were symbols; it was clear to me. They were set there to remind me I have a choice: to focus on the bleak narrative of the zoo and lose myself in it, like humanity seems to do over and over again, or to focus on the blessings we possess and find things that bring me closer to my true self. I could in this way create my own world, one without limitations or boundaries, an unlimited blank space, free from any color or definition. I possessed the ability to make my wildest dreams come true, whether they were positive or negative, extraordinary or ordinary. The glittering expanse of stars those pre-dawn hours confirmed this truth to me.

I believe in practice, though, the journey from a state of despairing decisions to one manifesting my true purpose required a crucial step: a transformation. For believing I was awake didn't necessarily mean I was outside of the reality prison; I was still carrying some of my "delusions."

As I have previously mentioned in a footnote, once you embark upon a particular path – be it seeking answers, unraveling mysteries, or fighting for a cause – the path itself can consume your every thought and action, overshadowing the very goal you set out to achieve. It is all too easy to find oneself trapped in an endless loop with no means of escape. No wonder Keel said a mild curiosity can become a destructive obsession.

The only option I found was to either surrender completely to the intense drive that led me down this treacherous road, possibly resulting in my utter destruction, Keel's warning, or to renounce it entirely with the same fervency and zeal with which I initially pursued it. Then and only then, I think, could I illuminate the path forward. It is not, as I have found, an easy or effortless process, but rather one that demands dedicated effort and perseverance. But then what?

During a recorded conversation in **Penetration**, Ingo and Axelrod hint at the existence of something beyond telepathy. Ingo struggles to articulate this concept, describing it as a cross-dimensional presence that can be felt but not seen. Axelrod suggests that telepathy combined with something else could explain this phenomenon, but Ingo clarifies that it's actually something else combined with telepathy. He explains that nothing happens in isolation and there are always processes involved. Axelrod questions why mind-to-mind communication is limited to three dimensions, but Ingo points out that the physical universe is three-dimensional while the mental universe may operate differently. Ingo admits he struggles to put this into words and only gained a better understanding when studying CHI GONG in 1989, shedding light on what this something else might entail.

The Wind-Up

The concept of Qi, originating from ancient Chinese philosophy, encompasses a wide range of meanings. It is often described as vital energy, believed to flow through the body and sustain life. However, some interpret it as universal energy, encompassing all forms of energy such as heat, light, and electromagnetic waves. The relationship between matter, energy, and spirit is also a central aspect of its definition. In traditional Chinese medicine and martial arts, Qi serves as the fundamental principle that underlies these practices. Gong (or kung) is another important term often associated with Qi. Its translations include cultivation, work, practice, skill, mastery, achievement, service, or accomplishment.

To me, this means that by putting in dedicated effort and hard work, to activate what Ingo said was our perceptual awareness systems, we can tap into our full potential and reach great heights.

In this, he intends to redirect our focus towards the true purpose of awareness and direct perception. He argues that we have been conditioned away from the original understanding of "aware," which has two primary functions: detecting danger and recognizing opportunities. While the processes of direct perception originate from our senses, operating with their own set of rules and logic. They are capable of perceiving and conveying information without the interference of our consciousness.

So, I began to contemplate my body, or as Ingo called it, my bio-body. We are not simply beings made up of flesh and bone; we are intricate creatures composed of water and energy. Our bodies act as conduits for electromagnetic currents that flow through and around us, constantly shaping and impacting our surroundings. In simpler terms, we could say that sensing this energy or emitting it is like giving off good or bad vibes. Whether knowingly or unknowingly, we have the power to manipulate this energy by placing our attention onto something.

One striking example is when Ingo was tasked with affecting a well-shielded magnetometer at Stanford in 1972, which ultimately launched SRI's "anomalous phenomena" covert funding.

He achieved this feat through his psychic probing and focused attention on the device. This sheds light on the subtle ways in which we acquire, utilize, and even take energy from others. We can focus our attention on something, draw attention, crave attention, attract unwanted attention, steal someone's attention, give someone our undivided attention, or divide someone's attention.

In all these instances, it boils down to the exchange of energy between individuals. Whatever we pay attention to, we give our energy to, and it grows stronger.

So why not focus on manifesting something amazing, even if "others" try their best to stop me? After being body slammed by some unknown force and putting up a psychic barrier to protect myself from further attacks, the next day I noticed the presence of a hawk. Did my call for positivity attract it from another realm?

A few days later, still recovering, I returned to the workout room and remembered the incident that occurred there. I wondered if whatever had attacked me was still loitering in the room. As I gazed out the window during my workout, I saw the same hawk perched on a nearby telephone pole while a mockingbird tried relentlessly to pester it. The hawk remained calm and didn't retaliate or show any reaction towards the mockingbird's actions. When the mockingbird finally flew away, I stopped my workout and took photos of the hawk. The hawk's eyes, dark and intelligent, turned to meet mine. It seemed to convey a silent message, "Pay it no attention."

So, I started reducing my time on social media and limiting the content I consumed. I cut out scary, violent, and negative media that only served to amplify the very things they depicted.

Time and time again, even during serious documentary interviews, I noticed people repeating the phrase "I just had a gut-feeling" or "deep down in my gut I knew," so I got to work on my gut health. I added prebiotics/probiotics while cutting out caffeine, processed foods, cane sugar and corn syrup, table salt, gluten, dairy, soy, and seed oils from my day-to-day diet. I've essentially adopted a paleo diet, although I sometimes still give in to the temptation of fast food. But the longer I stay away from it, the worse I feel when I do indulge in it.

I made sure to incorporate stretching and basic strength exercises into my daily routine, as well as some form of cardio like walking. I also prioritized spending time in nature and bonding with others in a community.

Inspired by Ingo's words, I ordered one of the bioelectric books he spoke about during his speech to the United Nations I mentioned earlier. I devoured its contents cover to cover. It dawned on me this could be why "they" were so interested in us – our bodies are truly miraculous machines, operating on complex levels I am still trying to comprehend and unlock.

The Wind-Up

With a renewed sense of purpose, I began to pay close attention to the subtle cues that surrounded me. These signals were in plain sight but easily ignored, guiding and speaking to me in whispers and nudges that seemed to always be there, waiting for me to open my "eyes" and "ears" and "listen."

The more I turned to these things, the more I found the kind of resurrection Ingo was speaking about. It was as if my mind and body were weaving together in a powerful connection.

I stepped out into the world with a different lens, truly observing my surroundings and noticed the abundance of light and love present in the world, if we are open to receiving it. During this time, I had a dream that stuck with me so much that I recreated it using an AI image generator. The finished product of a heart with wings as a beacon of light in a tower surrounded by a tumultuous sea of darkness, serving as the last thing I see before going to bed and the first thing I see when I wake up.

As I look at it, in the back of my mind, I recall Ingo's words from the documentary: "What the world does with anything is up to the world."

And it's true – as I learned firsthand – it's our choice. We can waste our days trying to participate in or unravel or even resign ourselves to the chaotic world around us, adrift in thoughts of what is wrong with us, or we can use that time to find what is good within us, resurrect the mysteries within ourselves. Either way, despite whatever they are trying to do, just like the hawk and the mockingbird, I have come to understand, thanks to my own journey, power, at least some semblance of it, I believe, has always been in our hands.

As for the incident I mentioned on the first page of this book, well, in that particular moment, it was evident the entity, with its oblong head and ethereal black cap for a body held power over some type of device. My mind went blank, and the only words I could muster were Ingo's, which I boldly projected telepathically towards it: "Earth's psychics are your only enemies." Surprisingly, this apparently did not go over well. Suddenly, a sickening electric shock coursed through my body, as if I was being tasered by some inter-dimensional force – although I have no idea what being tasered actually feels like. There I remained being tasered and there it remained tasering me until clarity crept into the moment, "Pay it no attention." Immediately I stopped doing just that; I said, "You're not the boss of me," "left," got up, and poured myself a glass of water, feeling surprisingly unscathed. And so, as Ingo would often proclaim, end of story.

Or perhaps it was only just beginning? In his book, **Resurrecting the Mysterious,** Ingo wrote that our current era is rife with accusations of decadence, corruption, immorality, and depravity. Pseudo-prophets are emerging, predicting the imminent end of the world. Our established hierarchies and codes are crumbling before our eyes. But beneath it all lies a desperate search for purpose that is fueling a renewed interest in spirituality. New sects and cults are springing up, along with beliefs in esoteric practices and a confusing array of ideologies. We are consumed by fear and uncertainty about what lies ahead. These qualities of our times may seem unique to us, but if you were a scholar, you would recognize them as existing in the Holy Land during the time of Jesus as well. This suggests that despite a two-thousand-year intervention since the last "end times," humanoid consciousness has not fundamentally changed at all.

But within this expanse of existence, Ingo said, there are three distinct states that embody their own unique qualities and enigmas. The first state reflects the introverted nature of the soul, a realm of consciousness where self-awareness can bind one in an endless cycle of introspection. In this solitary state, the mind is like a labyrinthine maze, with each turn leading to deeper levels of thought and contemplation. The second state represents humanity's outward potential, where immense power awaits to be harnessed and wielded to its fullest extent. But with such great power comes the risk of catastrophic consequences for the world. And lastly, there exists a third state that remains a mystical dream for most, shrouded in mystery and sought after by only the most daring souls who believe in its existence. It is a realm of wonder and possibility, with secrets waiting to be unlocked and revelations waiting to be discovered.

It was in this way, amidst my own journey of self-discovery of just that, I turned to Ingo's collection of essays in his **Superpowers of the Human Biomind** database. Once in, I discovered a jumble of interwoven concepts to unravel and found myself editing and reworking sections. And in doing so, I had a sudden realization: why not compile my own selection of these profound musings? And thus, my collection was born – **Why Do We Feel There is More to Us Than We, or Anyone, Knows About?: A Collection of Ingo Swann's Superpowers of the Human Biomind Essays Excerpted and Edited by his Niece Elly Flippen**. In publishing it along with this book, I hope it serves as a launching pad for the testament to our limitless potential as human beings.

HISTORICAL TIDBITS

EXPLORING OTHERWORLDLY POSSIBILITIES
A Brief Dive into the Extraterrestrial and
Interdimensional Concepts
(182)

AH. YES!
The Technology Side
(198)

INGO SWANN
A Brief Biography | Timeline of Remote Viewing
(216)

EXPLORING THE LINK
Remote Viewing | UFO Bases | Non-Human Entities
(226)

Exploring Otherworldly Possibilities
A Brief Dive into the Extraterrestrial and Interdimensional Concepts

Physicist Enrico Fermi posed a question to his colleagues during a lunch break at Los Alamos National Laboratory in New Mexico in the 1950s. He pondered the contradiction between the absence of concrete proof of advanced extraterrestrial life and the seemingly high probability of its existence. Obviously, with just a modest amount of rocket technology and a strong desire for expansion, any civilization could rapidly colonize the entire galaxy. Yet, as we look around our own galaxy, there is no clear evidence of any thriving galactic empire or United Federation of Planets. This realization prompted Fermi to pose an obvious question – "where is everybody?" In a universe presumed to be filled with intelligent beings, why do we see no signs of them? This perplexing contrast became known as the Fermi Paradox.

An unidentified object in flight, commonly known as a UFO or UAP (unidentified anomalous phenomenon), is any perceived event that occurs in the air, water, or other mediums and cannot be immediately identified or explained. These objects have become increasingly intriguing as there is no definitive explanation for them. Some speculate these vessels may be manned by beings from other worlds or dimensions, while others believe they are unmanned probes sent by extraterrestrial civilizations. There is even the possibility that these entities are time travelers or part of a simulated reality we are living in. These are the "realities" we have created to account for them.

But as Ingo often said, we often assume we have complete control over our own realities. He proposed that if we gather enough information and put it together, we may discover a startling truth: they may not be who we have come to believe they are.

Because of this, it struck me that the elusive beings attached to the UFO/UAP phenomenon may in fact be the ones fabricating false identities to conceal their true selves.

Therefore, I do think it is beneficial to explore the evolution of our modern concepts and compartmentalizations of them.

The mere notion of time travel alone is enough to make one's head spin, especially when coupled with the countless "forms" and interpretations that accompany "them." It's like trying to solve a Rubik's Cube with some of its colored squares missing. And while there is much speculation surrounding the eternal battle between good and evil, intertwined with biblical prophecies and theories about the very fabric of our reality being a simulation, I will focus on the narrower scope of just the extraterrestrial and trans-dimensional possibilities.

We'll begin with the story of the extraterrestrial premise, or rather its cousin, the ancient astronaut theory.

Published in England in 1968, Raymond Drake's book **Spacemen in the Ancient East** was the second in a series attempting to popularize the ancient astronaut theory. This idea suggests that ancient civilizations were either colonies of extraterrestrial beings or were heavily influenced by contact with aliens. Drake had written another book on this topic in 1964, titled **Gods or Spacemen?**, and would go on to write over a dozen more.

However, he was not the first to bring up this theory, nor did he receive recognition for it. Throughout recorded history, legends, myths, and even cave drawings and archaeological evidence have depicted gods, angels, and star people visiting our world using fantastical means of transportation like flying chariots or celestial ships.

The idea of ancient astronauts, also known as paleocontact,[63] first emerged in the world of science fiction at the turn of the 20th century most

---

[63] The concept that advanced beings from other planets, also known as ancient astronauts, may have visited Earth long ago and had an impact on human development, including culture, technology, and religion.

recognizable through the writings of Howard Phillips (H.P.) Lovecraft. As the "Father of Cosmic Horror," Lovecraft used his stories to explore themes of cosmic terror and otherworldly revulsions – things that are beyond human understanding and comprehension. His narratives often depicted monstrous beings with unimaginable powers, capable of driving people mad just by their mere existence.

These ideas were heavily influenced by Lovecraft's own experiences as a child, where he would have terrifying night terrors filled with demon-like creatures: faceless humanoid figures with black, rubbery skin, bat-like wings, and barbed tails. But could these experiences have been more than just products of his subconscious mind? Could they have been manifestations of a deeper, pervasive reality?

Despite receiving little recognition during his lifetime, Lovecraft's writings have had a monumental impact on contemporary culture. Today, we can see his influence in countless successful novels, films, video games, and even music. But how exactly can we trace the idea of ancient aliens back to Lovecraft? The answer lies within his 1926 short story "The Call of Cthulhu," where he takes myths of ancient gods and transforms them into a race of extraterrestrial beings who descended to Earth in the distant past.

This concept was somewhat inspired by Charles Fort's[64] books, particularly **The Book of the Damned**[65] and **New Lands.** One of Fort's most famous quotes from **The Book of the Damned** reads: "I think we're property. I should say we belong to something: That once upon a time, this earth was No-man's Land, that other worlds explored and colonized here, and fought among themselves for possession, but that now it's owned by something: That something owns this earth – all others warned off."[66]

---

[64] An investigator and researcher of strange air ships, mysterious creatures, and unexplained powers, today's anomalous phenomena, during the turn of the 20th century, considered a trailblazer in this field.

[65] According to Fort, being "damned" meant being excluded from scientific study. He listed things like telekinesis, teleportation, the Bermuda Triangle, animal cryptids, mysterious disappearances, and strange colors in the sky as examples of these excluded phenomena.

[66] Ingo and his friend UFO/paranormal researcher John Keel were both members of the Fortean community, often espousing the beliefs and theories put forth by Fort.

Historical Tidbits

Throughout the latter half of the 20th century, Lovecraft's ancient gods are ancient aliens existed primarily within the realm of horror science fiction. The concept remained there until it suddenly burst forth into the world of pseudohistory.[67] This leap occurred during one of humanity's greatest technological feats – the Space Race – thanks to Erich von Däniken's now-famous 1968 book, **Chariots of the Gods?**. Yet, von Däniken was not the first to bring this idea to mainstream non-fiction; he simply became the most well-known, and titillatingly, the words did not even come from him, but rather from his ghost writer.

Von Däniken, a Swiss hotel manager and former Catholic, had always been fascinated by flying saucers and turned away from his religious beliefs at a young age. He was likely inspired by astronomers like Carl Sagan and Joseph Shklovskii, who had discussed the possibility of extraterrestrial visitation in their book **Intelligent Life in the Universe**.

Von Däniken's initial book, in any event, was rejected by numerous publishers until a German publishing company ultimately decided to release it. Their decision came with a catch though: the book had to be completely rewritten by Wilhelm "Utz" Utermann, a former Nazi and bestselling author who also served as editor for Völkischer Beobachter, the propaganda newspaper of the Nazi Party.

Initially founded as an anti-Semitic tabloid, the newspaper was eventually taken over by the Thule Society[68] – a German/Nazi occult group that merged Tibetan black magic with Nordic mythology – before Adolf Hitler "bought" it from them.

In its revamped and published form, the resulting book, **Chariots of the Gods?**, having been ghost-written or restructured by a former propaganda editor, embodies the idea that extraterrestrial beings came to Earth, interbred with humans, and played a role in the development of ancient cultures and technologies. Its narrative draws heavily from French science fiction writer Robert Charroux's 1963 publication, **One Hundred Thousand Years of Man's Unknown History**.

According to Charroux, human civilization thrived thousands or even millions of years ago with powerful technologies far beyond our current capabilities. Charroux supports his theories by citing passages from

---

[67] Presents myths, legends, sagas, and other similar literature as historical fact.
[68] The "Ah, Yes!" note that follows is filled with chilling details of the Thule Society, the hidden backbone behind the Nazi regime.

ancient texts such as the **Bible**,[69] **Talmud**,[70] and **Vedas**,[71] as well as various sacred writings and folk tales. More importantly, Charroux's work may have been influenced by another French book published just three years prior in 1960: **The Morning of the Magicians: Secret Societies, Conspiracies, and Vanished Civilizations** by Louis Pauwels and Jacques Bergier.

Regardless, the publication of **Chariots of the Gods?** in 1968 catapulted it to bestseller status, paving the way for numerous subsequent books, documentaries, podcasts, TV shows, and more. The enduring popularity of this topic among ancient astronaut theorists around the world can be traced back to this influential book.

But the actual origins of ancient alien ideologies can be traced back to a deep and mysterious river, the source from which this pool of beliefs sprung. Even influential horror writer Lovecraft was influenced by this powerful current. The true backbone of these ideologies can be found in the Thule Society's beliefs, which were strongly rooted in Western Esotericism. This path of knowledge and spiritual enlightenment was championed by figures such as occultist Helena Blavatsky and the Magick[72] practitioner Aleister Crowley. As their teachings and practices have greatly shaped our modern understanding of anomalous happenings with these beings, it is essential to make a pit stop and take a closer look at them.

During the last few decades of the 1800s, a period known as the "mystical revival," Blavatsky rose to prominence. She was at the forefront of the "new spiritual movement" called Spiritualism, a belief that departed souls can interact with the living. Blavatsky claimed to channel a group of

---

[69] These holy scriptures, revered in Christianity, Judaism, Samaritanism, Islam, the Baha'i Faith, and other Abrahamic religions, contain religious teachings and stories considered sacred.

[70] Considered a holy text, this compilation of ancient teachings is central to Rabbinic Judaism and serves as the main foundation for Jewish religious law and theology.

[71] **The Rigveda**, also called the **Rig Veda**, is a collection of Vedic Sanskrit hymns from ancient India. It is one of the four sacred texts in Hinduism and is collectively known as the Vedas.

[72] Often misconstrued, Magick is the science and art of causing change to occur in conformity with the Will. The color designations of Magick, black, white, gray, green, is simply meant to designate intention.

entities known as the Great White Brotherhood, also referred to as the Great Brotherhood of Light or the Spiritual Hierarchy of Earth. These immortal beings, classified as Ascended Masters or Masters of Ancient Wisdom, were said to closely watch over Earth. Her influential volume, **The Book of Dzyan**, was believed to have been channeled[73] from this group and became the foundation for her tome, **The Secret Doctrine**. Blavatsky's work was heavily influenced by Eastern religious philosophy, which some argue she blended, or even stole, for her esoteric ideology. It is speculated that much of **The Book of Dzyan** may have been derived from the Vedas.

Organized into a cohesive concept, her teachings gave rise to a new religion called Theosophy. After her passing, her followers went in various directions. In the United States, some became famous channelers like Alice Bailey who also established the Arcane School in New York. Ingo himself attended this school in the early 1960s and described Bailey as the "intellectual heir" to Blavatsky. In fact, the "New Age," as a term is credited to her, with Ingo noting that Bailey's school aimed to spread a "Great Universal Plan" dictated by a hierarchy of spiritual masters. In Germany, thanks to clairvoyant and channeler Rudolf Steiner, Theosophy evolved into Anthroposophy – a belief system centered on the idea that humans can use their intellect to contact spiritual worlds. Ingo also studied at Steiner's center in New York during his quest for spiritual enlightenment in the early 1960s.

Around the same time, there was a surge of interest in magical and occult ideas in Great Britain known as the "magical revival." This movement saw the creation of new societies, including the Theosophical Society – mentioned earlier – and the Hermetic Order of the Golden Dawn, commonly referred to as just the "Golden Dawn." This group focused on studying and practicing occult and metaphysics, with an emphasis on spiritual growth and theurgy.

Also referred to as divine magic, theurgy is one of the two key areas of study in the magical realm. The other being practical magic, or thaumaturgy. Theurgy revolves around performing specific rituals and ceremonies intended to invoke the presence of one or more deities, to

---

[73] The process of channeling involves allowing a spirit to temporarily inhabit your body to communicate, achieved through meditative or trance-like states. This allows for messages to be transmitted from entities that may not be of this world or human in nature.

attain henosis – a state of union with the divine. It is thought that through this discipline, one can attain a deeper level of comprehension and connection with the divine by perfecting themselves. Many modern beliefs and customs in traditions such as Wicca – an earth-centered pagan religion – can be traced back to rituals and magic practiced by the Golden Dawn, making it one of the most influential groups in Western occultism during the 20th century.

And it was Crowley who stood out as a prominent figure in the English "magical revival" movement. He was originally a member of the Golden Dawn, but eventually built his own set of occult principles and ideologies, which he called Thelema – the concept of discovering and following one's True Will, a way for one to align their actions with their truest spiritual calling. Many of these concepts can be seen reflected in modern "Psi" practices. In his writings, such as the **Book of the Law**, which he claimed was dictated to him by a Holy Guardian Angel named Aiwass in 1904, Crowley laid the foundations for Thelma. In another book, titled **Magick, Liber ABA, Book 4**, Crowley refers to Aiwass as "The Devil," "Satan," and "Lucifer."

And so, in getting back now to the ancient astronaut theory, to truly grasp its essence, we must turn to Blavatsky's **The Secret Doctrine**. Here lies the cosmology of Theosophy – a belief in seven root races that have inhabited Earth. Humanity is currently on its fifth race, having originated from the ancient land of Lemuria, now lost beneath the depths of the Pacific Ocean. Blavatsky referred to this root race as the Aryan race. According to Theosophy, two more races will appear in the future. The third root race was known as the Lemurians, believed to be giants capable of great feats. The fourth root race, the Atlanteans, were also thought to possess immense strength and power. Other Theosophists expanded upon this notion, including Steiner in his 1904 book **Atlantis and Lemuria** and William Scott-Elliot, a devoted follower of Blavatsky's root race theory, in his 1896 book **The Story of Atlantis** and later in his 1904 book **The Lost Lemuria**. Combining Blavatsky's ideas with those of Steiner and Scott-Elliot, the story goes something like this: 16 million years ago, beings from a parallel universe residing on the planet Venus came to Earth through a metaphysical connection and took control over the inhabitants of Lemuria. These otherworldly beings within the Lemurians were responsible for great cultural advancements and technological progress.

They eventually spread throughout Lemuria, evolving into the Atlanteans before ultimately meeting their demise

Using this as our perspective, the concept of ancient astronauts is a recurring theme. Lovecraft also drew from **The Book of Dzyan** and other works by Scott-Elliot in crafting "The Call of Cthulhu." Some suggest that Lovecraft's ideas in the story may align with those of Crowley, while Kenneth Grant, Crowley's personal secretary and intellectual successor, believed there was an unconscious connection between Lovecraft and Crowley. He believed that both authors drew inspiration from the same "mystical forces," i.e. entity, for their writings, even though Lovecraft himself was unaware of this supposed otherworldly influence on his literary works.

In Lovecraft's tale, Venusians arrived on Earth in spacecraft. Pauwels and Bergier expanded upon this idea, accepting **The Book of Dzyan** as historical truth. Charroux referenced spiritualists and occultists and briefly explored legends from ancient India and Afghanistan about spaceships arriving from Venus millions of years ago. Similarly, Drake's **Spacemen in the Ancient East** relied upon the narrative found in **The Book of Dzyan**, while his book **Gods or Spacemen?** plunged into various ancient myths and legends about divine beings from space. He also gave credibility to Blavatsky's concept of root races, specifically the Atlanteans who he believed were giants based on evidence such as giant fossils and weapons found.

Though, they are not the only ones making connections between Venus and Earth's past. In 1960, an East German film called **The Silent Star** (later in English **First Spaceship on Venus**) premiered in cinemas behind the Iron Curtain. The storyline followed a group of scientists who discover a magnetic device at the site of an explosion in Siberia. After decoding it, they learn that it came from Venus. A planned mission to Mars is redirected to Venus to solve this mystery. Upon arrival, the astronauts find a planet destroyed by atomic war and evidence that the Venusians were planning to invade Earth before their demise. This is intriguing because during the same time, there was also speculation about Mars being linked to ancient astronauts. Sagan and Shklovsky mention the Martian moons Phobos and Deimos as possibly being manmade structures left behind by advanced Martians. This theory is further explored in Drake's **Spacemen in the Ancient East** and von Däniken's **Chariots of the Gods?**, both authors proposing that Mars may have once been home to intelligent life that was wiped out by a catastrophic event. Their ideas they said were supported by a Mariner photo revealing a quadrangular structure on Mars, as referenced by Drake, and von Däniken connecting ancient cultures and their myths with the red planet while ruling out Venus as a potential origin for extraterrestrial life.

The movie, in its plotline, highlights the shift of attention from Mars to Venus, which I find significant. It signifies the splitting of our focus, from a concept originating with Blavatsky and the idea of a parallel dimension existing on the planet Venus, to extraterrestrials. But, if one dug deeper into the source material for von Däniken's work, they would have found a tour through European history influenced by occult beliefs and secret societies, particularly those linked to Nazi ideology and interdimensional beings.

This leads to the revelation that these supposed extraterrestrial beings may not be from space at all. Instead, their origin could be attributed to other dimensions or vibrational forces. Yet, this information was overshadowed by Theosophists' belief in ancient astronauts coming from Venus and becoming gods to humanity. As the narrative evolved and the possibility of Venus being inhabited seemed unlikely, the focus shifted to Mars – misconstruing the possible actual truth to that.[74] Overall, this idea of invaders gained traction from science fiction literature like H.G. Wells' **War of the Worlds** where alien invasion from other planets became a popular concept.

Thus, the concept of extraterrestrial invaders had been swirling around in the public's consciousness for decades, gaining a secure foothold when unidentified objects flying began to be reported in droves after the end of World War II.

By the 1950s, under the phenomenon's new moniker, UFO, mania had reached a fevered pitch, and the first UFO Convention was introduced and sponsored by Flying Saucers International.

Held in Hollywood, California in August of 1953, the event revolved around an occult, now rebranded as the "New Age," experience of UFOs thanks to the burgeoning popularity of "abductee" and writer George Adamski and his best-selling book **Flying Saucers Have Landed** that same year. Adamski, one of the most well-known of several self-

---

[74] For additional details on Ingo and other individuals' psychic journeys to Mars, visit the Planetary Exploration section of the website ingoswann.com.

proclaimed UFO contactees in the 1950s, claimed to have had an encounter with a humanoid being from Venus. This otherworldly being supposedly warned of the dangers of nuclear war and left Adamski with a feeling of love and wisdom beyond human comprehension.

It is worth noting here that in the 1930s, Adamski was known as a small-time player in the world of California occultism, preaching his own blend of Christianity and Eastern spiritual practices under the names "Universal Progressive Christianity" and "Universal Law." He had studied Neo-Theosophy in the 1920s, a practice commonly associated with Bailey, who I mentioned earlier popularized the term "New Age." Other influential figures in the Neo-Theosophical movement also influenced – and were influenced by – the leading edge of this ideology. Their ideas went on to shape various the belief systems we see in modern New Age and New Thought concepts and organizations.

This is all to say, together, the convention and Adamski, acted as ground zero for the now splintered from the ancient astronaut concept and rapidly spreading New Age-Extraterrestrial-Cosmic Love – with claims that aliens were here to guide and help us – theme.

The theme of cosmic love bearing extraterrestrial narrative is evident even in the highly advanced training targets assigned to Star Gate Remote Viewers, including one task focused on a mysterious organization known as the Galactic Federation.[75]

After combing through declassified documents, news articles, and online sources, the phrase Galactic Federation appears in some intriguing contexts. For example, it is mentioned in a now declassified report titled **Uncertainty in Estimating the Number of Extraterrestrial Civilizations**. Written in March 1980, it explores the idea of "Galactic Colonization." The paper suggests a factor to consider when devising a search strategy for such a civilization engaging in such colonization is whether a Galactic Federation exists.

During the 1990s, a new UFO religion emerged called the Ground Crew Project. It later split into two factions: the Ground Crew and the Planetary Activation Organization. Members of these groups claimed their purpose was to prepare humanity for an imminent first contact between

---

[75] For further details, please see the note labeled "Exploring the Link" in Historical Tidbits. It also seems to coincide with Scientology's extraterrestrial narrative of a Galactic Confederacy, although there were no known Scientologists in the RV program at that time.

Earth and the Galactic Federation, an extraterrestrial organization dedicated to helping humanity evolve.

In early 2020, articles began to circulate about claims made by Haim Eshed, former head of Israeli space security. He stated that not only do extraterrestrials exist, but that President Trump is aware of their existence and that a "galactic federation" has been waiting for humanity to reach a certain level of understanding before making contact. Today, the concept of the Galactic Federation has become popular among various subgroups on social media who claim to have had higher intelligence contact or experiences with UFOs. This federation is often portrayed as a protectorate with its own leaders who possess greater knowledge and seek to elevate humanity's consciousness.

Continuing to the next topic: the trans-dimensional theory. This concept, encompassing the existence of beings in other realms parallel to our own, can be traced back to ancient civilizations and is even mentioned in various religious texts – such as the Christian belief in angels and demons residing in their respective kingdoms.

What I find interesting, however, is that this explanation for the origin of UFOs emerged around the same time as the extraterrestrial theory and can also be linked back to early occultists. These esotericists spoke of other planes of existence known as the etheric planes, where higher intelligences resided – including the same entities said to bring us privileged wisdom and guide humanity towards a higher level of consciousness, as described by Blavatsky's Ascended Masters. But it was a college English professor, Ufologist, and paranormal researcher by the name of Meade Lane who brought the connection between UFOs and interdimensional beings to the forefront.

Layne's concept was based on information channeled from a group called The Inner Circle by psychic medium Mark Probert in the mid-20th century. According to Probert, this group of Ascended Masters were beings from another plane of existence who had knowledge of UFO occupants known as the Ethereans. These ethereal beings could change their vibrational rate to become tangible to our senses, existing in a realm that overlaps with our own. The information obtained via these channeling sessions also made references to Theosophic ideas such as originating from Venus and connections to occult concepts and civilizations like Atlantis and Lemuria. Layne compiled this information into a book titled **The Coming of the Guardians** which introduced the term "interdimensional hypostasis" as an explanation for the presence of these beings.

My next clue about "this situation" came from Edith Nicolaisen, the founder of Parthenon, a Swedish publishing house known for UFO-related books. In the 1950s to 1970s, she was the go-to person for Sweden's UFO contactee movement. She was deeply devoted to occultist Steiner and considered him the greatest adept of the 20th century. She also studied materials from Heindel's Rosicrucian Society (see footnote #77 regarding Allen Hynek).

Initially, Nicolaisen believed that the space visitors people were seeing and interacting with came from different planets. But by 1958, her perspective shifted. She now believed that these interplanetary spacecrafts belonged to the so-called "etheric realm" and could not be seen by our physical eyes unless they wanted to draw attention or make contact. In those instances, their ships' vibratory rates would slow down enough for us to perceive them with our eyes. But she was not the only one making this change.

While reading Drake's 1968 book **Spacemen in the Ancient East**, I came across his theory on the sudden appearance and disappearance of UFOs. He believed that these sightings were manifestations from invisible worlds, able to change their frequencies and enter our physical realm. Drake reasoned that just as there are frequencies of matter beyond our perception, there may be co-existing dimensions within our own Earth. This could explain the phenomenon of seeing apparitions or even humans disappearing into other dimensions by "mischance."

The phrase "by mischance" caught my attention, its implications reminiscent of something I had read in Probert's channeling about the Ethereans. These light beings were said to be benevolent and kind but do have a penchant for taking people, large groups of them even, for reasons unknown, and sometimes leaving them on other planets aka disappearing them permanently. They were also known to conduct experiments on humans, and will continue to do so, but there was no need to fear them as they are our "space siblings," filled with love and compassion for us. I must ask here, do friends willingly let you get snatched and experimented on by other friends and taken permanently to parts unknown?

But then things changed or perhaps got added to.

John Keel, a well-known Ufologist and paranormal researcher, shared similar ideas to those of Drake. Keel was primarily interested in unexplained phenomena, especially UFOs. But shortly, by 1967, certainly, he began to theorize that these strange objects and apparitions were not extraterrestrial in origin. In his 1970 book **UFOs: Operation Trojan Horse**, he proposed the idea that perhaps a non-human or spiritual intelligence was manipulating these events as a means of enforcing certain belief systems.

After investigating numerous encounters with entities, he noticed striking similarities between the descriptions of extraterrestrials and mythical beings such as demons and fairies. In his 1971 book **Our Haunted Planet**, Keel coined the term "ultraterrestrials" for these entities, stating they could take on any form they desired. Except there is a slight nuance to his definition which I discovered after reading his book – so let's take a step back and investigate what Keel meant by this term.

As a species, Homo sapiens appeared suddenly in the history of Earth. Depending on which source you refer to, we are either the last surviving species or the most recent addition. An article in **The Guardian**, titled "Where did they all go? How Homo sapiens became the last human species left," highlights this debate among paleoanthropologists. There is no conclusive evidence as to who our immediate ancestors were, and there is also no single origin for our species.

In his writing, Keel explores three theories about how humanity came to be: 1) a divine or supernatural being created us; 2) extraterrestrial beings interbred with early humans; and 3) evolution over time. He suggests it may be a combination of all three. Keel draws upon a concept in Brinsley Le Poer Trench's books, **The Sky People** and **Men Among Mankind**: there were intelligent life forms existing here before our appearance on Earth. These beings operated at a different frequency and could coexist with physical life forms such as animals. Keel refers to them as "ultraterrestrials," while animals are "terrestrials."

To these ultraterrestrials, Earth was their playground and possession. Conversely, another group of ultraterrestrials from an elevated plane or operating at a higher frequency, known as the Alpha Group, sent humans to Earth as their new playthings. Humans are ultaterrestrial beings, now living in physical bodies similar to animals, but still connected to a higher source of energy. This was seen as an invasion by the Omega Group, leading to a war between the two groups where humans became hostages in their battle.

Keel believed both groups can manipulate and influence humans for their own purposes because we are essentially made of energy connected to a larger source. Although he has been labeled as someone who believed in demonic shape-shifting intelligences inhabiting a parallel dimension, his ideas are more complex. He suggested there have always been opposing forces, the Alpha Group and Omega Group, at play on this planet.

The Alpha Group is associated with morality and ethics, while the Omega Group seeks to spread greed, racism, and violence. Over time, though, it has become difficult to distinguish between these two groups as their tactics distort the lines between good and evil.

UFO researcher Jacques Vallée's book, **Passport to Magonia: On UFOS, Folklore and Parallel Worlds**, published a year before Keel's 1970 book, presented a similar idea to Keel's overall concept. He described a parallel universe existing alongside our own, where events such as encounters with an "aerial" race are possible. These beings can take on the form of humans, monsters, or other mystical creatures and have been documented throughout history in ways that reflect the beliefs and culture of that time and place. In **The Edge of Reality** – co-authored with his mentor Allen Hynek[76] in 1975 – Vallée further explored the idea of overlapping universes as the possible home base of these phenomena.

Thus, currently, it seems, we find ourselves in a familiar environment that has been given a fresh look. As I mentioned before, there are multiple variations of identities present. Names have changed, titles have been rearranged, and new faces have joined the fray. Among them, there are groups of followers devoted to certain individuals, cliques formed by like-minded individuals, and accepted beliefs and theories that may not hold much weight.

---

[76] Despite being known for his work as an astronomer and Air Force advisor on UFOs, Hynek's life was intertwined with the occult from a young age, according to Vallée. At just 16-years-old, Hynek purchased **Manly Hall's Secret Teachings of All Ages**, an exploration of Masonic, Hermetic, Qabbalistic, and Rosicrucian philosophies. Notably, Hynek acquired this book while a member of Heindel's Rosicrucian Society. Perhaps due to its association with secret societies or because it was considered a term used by Rosicrucians, when collaborating with fellow scientists on UFOs, Hynek adopted the name "The Invisible College" for his group. In recognition of this, Vallée titled one of his books published in 1975 with the same name.

In this way I am reminded of something Ingo wrote in **Penetration** regarding said such supposedly higher intelligences: To successfully cover up who they are and their agenda, there must be a complex web of confusion surrounding them and what they are up to. The confusion should not stem from the facts themselves, but from how they are perceived by us, humanity, and how we can be influenced to think about them. We tend to process information that is already "packaged" and given meaning, rather than randomly processing data without any context or significance.

This means "packaged" information is essentially controlled and manipulated for a specific purpose: to create intellectual alignment among individuals.

In simpler terms, if groups of us can be convinced to agree on the meaning of something, our thought processes will align with each other. This leads to Groupthink and can result in mindsets forming within a community. Ultimately, this creates a kind of collective consciousness.

Upon further examination, it becomes clear the main objective of this is not simply to deny certain information despite evidence supporting it. Instead, it is a deliberate effort to serve two main purposes: 1) to intensify confusion surrounding them and their activities in order to disseminate disinformation "packages" more effectively; and 2) to establish and reinforce a planet-wide intellectual alignment that lacks understanding of them and their affairs, rather than focusing on what is actually happening to us and around us.

It is evident to me this can be achieved through a variety of mediums, including movies, TV shows, video games, and social media. As an illustration, in 1993, Ingo was responsible for overseeing and coordinating a team of Remote Viewers privately investigating the alleged 1947 UFO crash in Roswell, New Mexico. While team members did sense there had been a crash of some kind, their ability to accurately identify the object was hindered, Ingo noted they said, by mental images influenced by fictionalized portrayals in popular culture, such as alien-themed movies and other media sources.

As I contemplate these ideas and align associations as Ingo had suggested, I can see that both the idea of extraterrestrial beings and interdimensional entities originate from channeled messages received from them. To rephrase, who and what they are, and even their agenda with us, I find has been and continues to be literally dictated to us.

Conjunction.World

Ah, Yes!
The Technology Side

In contemplating the idea of strange vessels moving swiftly through both the air and the water, a line from Ingo's **FATE Magazine** article, "The UFO Extraterrestrial Problem" comes to mind: "It goes far beyond the exciting technological possibilities hinted at by UFO hardware and the allegedly 'advanced intelligence' of beings who create and fly it." It is the disclosure or potential disclosure of UFOs/UAPs as "hardware," or "technology" – since these objects are viewed elementally as something created which is then flown – I think, which keeps us running, thanks to our science-backed world mindset, the most fervently on a hamster wheel. Lots of spinning but ultimately going nowhere.

In his 1992 piece "Can Remote-Viewing Penetrate the UFO-ET Enigmas," Ingo stated, "I believe that qualified remote-viewers can perceive and recreate visible forms of the UFO-ET 'hardware' – some of which has already been achieved."[77] With Ingo's words of "nothing just happens" echoing in my mind, the possibility loomed large that these lofty anomalies, crafted and flown by beings – noting Ingo did not say entities, just supposedly advanced intelligence of beings, humans, bio humans, perhaps? – must have an origin. After all, if we have already recreated such

---

[77] To read more about this and a decoding of Ingo's role with "speculative technology" from his book **Penetration**, visit the UFOs/UAPs section on the website ingoswann.com.

technology, it would have to have to exist and if it exists it must have a starting point.

This realization was intriguing to say the least and so I turned to historical evidence to piece together a story, for me anyway, of the origins of this said advanced technology.

My focus was on events during and after World War II when this technology seemingly emerged out of thin air. But let's begin at the very start: where all great stories do.

Nearly a thousand years prior to the birth of Jesus, King Solomon ruled as the third and final king of a unified Kingdom of Israel. Son of biblical David, he was renowned for his wealth and wisdom, and even considered an inspirational leader in Islamic tradition. Despite this legacy, his life was also marked by significant faults and transgressions. It could be said that he embodied both light and darkness.

During this period, the Jews believed God resided in the Ark of the Covenant, a wooden chest containing the Ten Commandments given to Moses. This sacred object was housed in their place of worship, which at the time was nothing more than a tent. Solomon, inspired by his father's desire for a grander and more permanent structure to hold the Ark, decided to build a magnificent temple on Mount Moriah in Jerusalem. This temple, known as the First Temple of Jerusalem or the Temple of Solomon, was not meant to be large in size but rather extraordinary in its design and decoration. Made entirely of gold inside, it symbolized an everlasting throne for God.

Alas, after 470 years, six months, and ten days, it was destroyed by fire. Later, a Second Temple was built over it, though it was not as elaborate as the first. In the decades leading up to the new millennium, a Roman, Herod the Great, oversaw a refurbishment of this Second Temple during his rule over Judea – the Roman name for Israel. The temple became the center of Jewish life, and its contents grew to include riches, religious artifacts, and esoteric texts.

This version of the temple stood for nearly 600 years before being destroyed.

But the story I was tracing was not of the building but rather who exactly built it and what it ultimately contained.

Long before humans on Earth,[78] perhaps millions of years, there existed a race of beings made from what can only be best described as smokeless fire; we would probably call it plasma today.

The **Bible**, or rather a hypothesis formed from ideas found in the **Bible**, refers to these beings as a pre-Adamic race often seen as "Gods Other People," existing before the biblical Adam on the original Earth before it became "dark and void." Legend claims they lived freely on the planet possessing great knowledge and power, before a cataclysm fell upon Earth, and they were banished from our physical universe, exiled one might say, leaving only their spirits to roam the Earth disembodied while humans occupy it.

Today, some refer to them as trans-dimensional entities having built upon the concept of an advanced "terrestrial" civilization from another order of existence, what we might call the people of the Serpent by way of innumerable ancient cultures or in our more modern tongue, demons. Known as Yōkai in Japanese lore, these creatures are described as fearsome monsters and tricksters. In Chinese legends, they are referred to as Yaoguai: supernatural beings that possess both evil and strange powers. In Islamic texts, they are known as the Djinn. It is said they can transform into physical forms in our dimension and can bring us incredible pleasures, but also equal amounts of misfortune, despair, torture, and even death.

God had also blessed Solomon with immense knowledge of our natural world and all its complexities, as well as an equal understanding of the hidden realm of magic and the existence of benevolent and malevolent spirits. It is possible this wisdom was not directly bestowed upon Solomon by God, but rather acquired through his study of ancient texts and artifacts. These could have been stone tablets or scrolls passed down from the first known civilization or even unknown civilizations before that.[79]

---

[78] See John Keel's theory in the "Exploring Otherworldly Possibilities" note.

[79] There is actual much we do not know about our history leaving our understanding of it full of gaps and uncertainties. Many peoples who conquered others deliberately destroyed any written records or texts that could have shed light on the past. This was the case when Spain invaded Central and South America, destroying all sacred books belonging to the Aztecs. In other instances, resistance from those in power has prevented alternative narratives from being heard. For example, in 2003 a library containing ancient texts and scrolls was

Historical Tidbits

This recorded esoteric and occult knowledge may have survived the great flood and made its way from Sumer to Egypt with Abraham, eventually reaching David and then Solomon. But the true source of his power may have been his ring. Legend has it that it was this ring, crafted from copper and iron, etched with the markings of a pentagram, bestowed upon him by the archangel Michael, which granted him authority over the beings from the invisible realm.

When Solomon put out a call for labor to build his Temple, he received thousands of slaves specifically for this purpose. But the human slaves, although incredible in number, and however forced their labor, some to the brink of death, were simply not enough. And thus, Solomon used his ring's power to command an army of demons, from this unseen world, beings that possessed powerful skills and tools to cut through stone and unearth precious metals and jewels, conscripting them into building the Temple as well.

It would be these demons who cut and moved the stone and dug for unending caches of gold, silver, and gems. One of these demons was Asmodeus, often referred to in texts as the keeper of secrets or the one who hides and conceals, and other times referred to as the king of demons. Forced into hard labor, the demons grew increasingly angry, vengeful, and deceptive. They had already been driven out of their own world by humans, but now they were also enslaved by them.

Bitterness festered and thoughts of revenge consumed them. Asmodeus himself promised Solomon that their time as puppets would be short-lived, and soon their powerful abilities would allow them to rule over humanity with ease. They could possess any human they desired, transform into any shape or form, and manipulate events to their advantage. Eventually, humans would worship them like gods without ever knowing the truth.

---

found hidden behind a massive wall in a Tibetan monastery. Initial reports suggested these writings dated back 10,000 years, maybe even longer – potentially up to 60,000 years. Some though quickly refuted this possibility on social media without even examining the texts. Despite this, only five percent of this newly discovered library has been digitized and translated thus far. Further, scholars argue that writing was invented by the Sumerians in Mesopotamia in the fourth millennium BCE, while there is still no definitive answer as to when Egyptian hieroglyphics were created.

When the Temple was done, and the Ark enshrined, and the demons relinquished, Solomon filled the Temple with the wealth the demons had unearthed together with garments from the priests and those said to have been from the Garden of Eden, along with scrolls and tablets containing vast esoteric knowledge. But after Solomon died, his ring of power simply slipped from his finger and disappeared, and knowledge about these beings tumbled first into admonitory tales, then folklore, then mythos, and in time into fringe occult accounts of the unknown.

Centuries later, just after the start of the first millennium, and agitation swirled in Jerusalem; a Jewish revolt was underway. The Roman Empire, dominion over the land now, moved to put down the rising insurgency and in doing so took the opportunity to sack the city. In tearing down all that had been built so carefully and magnificently, Herod's, former Solomon's, Temple with it, they uncovered a portion of the Temple's material treasure, that is the gold, silver, and jewels, which had been buried hastily throughout the city just before the Roman Army unleashed their devastating siege. But even a portion was beyond calculation and considered an immense booty, and with such riches, the Romans found then no need to look further.

And so, it remained that way until the fall of Rome at the hands of Germanic tribes like the Visigoths, when the Roman portion of the treasure was unearthed it was taken to a fortress in Gothic territory located in the mountainous region of southern France. Amongst these spoils was a map leading to the remaining portion of the Temple's riches scattered throughout Jerusalem. Along with the Ark of the Covenant and other treasures from ancient times, this included items accumulated during Solomon's reign until the destruction of Herod's Temple. The map also held secrets and esoteric knowledge passed down through generations.

The secret was well-kept in the mountainous region, passed down from the Visigoths to the Franks and then to the remaining inhabitants. This area was a melting pot of cultures, with people from Persia and Northern Africa merging with soothsayers and druids from different parts of Europe. This resulted in a blend of different religious beliefs, as elements of eastern mysticism, ancient druidism, and early Christianity came together.

This led to the formation of Catharism, a purer form of Christianity centered around two opposing forces: good and evil. In the following millennium, it would be the people of this region who would rise to prominence in the courts of France. These descendants, who considered the map a crucial part of their heritage, embarked on the Crusades under the guise of religious duty. To them, it was simply a means to an end: capturing land in order to conduct a secret search for hidden treasures.

Following the Crusades' religious objective and the successful capture of Jerusalem, a French leader was appointed to oversee the newly acquired land. From this region in southern France, a group of nine knights, also known as treasure hunters, formed an organization called the Poor Fellow Soldiers of Christ and of the Temple Solomon, which later became known as the Knights Templar or simply the Templars. In secrecy, they dug according to their map's directions and unearthed a remarkable cache of riches and esoteric knowledge beyond imagination.

As they searched, they discovered ancient Christian artifacts such as the Spear of Destiny, believed to have pierced Jesus' side on the cross, and texts that revealed new information about his life and teachings. These texts were obtained from the Essenes and their library, including what we now refer to as the Dead Sea Scrolls, as well as the Gnostics who possessed secret knowledge – hidden understandings – of God. Under their banner, the entire hoard was smuggled out of Jerusalem and joined with the Visigoth loot acquired during their Roman siege. The spoils were then divided; the tangible wealth was transported to the Templars' headquarters in Paris, while the hidden wisdom contained within the texts remained concealed in the caverns of southern France.

But then Destiny had other plans.

The Roman Catholic Church soon turned against the Cathars, labeling them as heretics. They were hunted down and burned at the stake, and it was only a matter of time before the fate of the Templars would follow suit. Some managed to escape, others vanished without a trace, and eventually reemerged as what we call today, Freemasons, carrying with them the arcane knowledge found in the seized texts. The material wealth however was divided and scattered across the globe with the bulk, though, being returned to the caves in mountains of southern France. There the treasure remained, secured, buried deep. At least that is what everyone thought.

They could never have imagined a mere few centuries later a Nazi wildfire spreading over the world, let alone one which at its core was fueled with a deep and dark agenda, and certainly not one which would leave the treasure woefully exploited.

The Nazi's dark agenda was rooted in Germany's long-standing fascination with Spiritualism and the occult, dating back to the onset of World War I. Austria and Germany, in particular, were hotbeds of mystical beliefs and practices during the early 1900s. The Thule Society, which played a significant role in the formation of the German Worker's Party – later transformed into the Nazi party by Hitler – solidified this connection between occultism and Nazi ideology. It was not difficult for the Nazis to promote this belief system, as even key German philosopher Alfred Rosenberg acknowledged many Germans were drawn to Nazism because of their interest in romanticism, mysticism, and the occult.

After Hitler's rise to power and the establishment of the Nazi party in Germany, Heinrich Himmler, leader of the infamous SS division and member of the Thule Society, founded a paranormal research group in 1935. Known as the Ahnenerbe or "Inheritance of the Forefathers," this group was dedicated to finding religious relics like the Ark of the Covenant and the Spear of Destiny, which they believed would grant them incredible powers. They were also on a quest to locate evidence of an ancient Aryan race from a mystical land called Thule – their version of Atlantis.

This theory was heavily influenced by the beliefs of early occultists who were convinced of the existence of the lost civilization of Atlantis. They believed it to be the source of divine perfection for all races, tracing back to prehistoric times. According to the occultists, Atlantis was destroyed by a global flood and the few surviving inhabitants migrated to the mythical Tibetan city of Shambhala.

Here, they founded a secret society known as Agarthi, described as a kingdom of demi-gods residing in underground caves in Tibet. This idea also drew inspiration from various sources including World Ice Theorists who believed ice played a central role in cosmic, geological, and evolutionary processes on Earth. Ultimately, this theory proposed Aryans were once considered gods of ice who ruled over other racial groups. Accordingly, these Aryans possessed supernatural abilities such as telepathy and flight, which could be harnessed by humans if their genetic code was unlocked.

This idea was readily adopted by Nazi leaders including Himmler and Hitler's second-in-command, Rudolph Hess, who sought to resurrect these lost abilities through selective breeding. A few years later, in 1940, the Ahnenerbe, with its extensive cache of scientists, researchers, treasure hunters, psychics, and astrologers, was folded into the SS, and known thereafter as the Ahnenerbe-SS.

The Nazis, who harbored a strong hatred towards Freemasonry, had been systematically destroying and looting Masonic Temples – Freemasonry meeting places – in their conquered territories. In addition, the Ahnenerbe-SS were actively searching for treasures around the world. Their travels took them to various corners of the globe, from Iceland and Tibet to present day Afghanistan and North Africa. They also ventured to Russia, the Far East, Egypt, South America, and even the Arctic. By 1943, thanks to their Masonic Temple looting and various treasure hunting expeditions, they had gathered enough clues to piece together the possible location of the Templar's treasure.

Under orders from Himmler, an expedition team from the Ahnenerbe-SS was quickly sent to southern France, near the border with Spain. The team focused their efforts on Château de Montségur, a former stronghold of the Cathars. Despite months of excavation, they found nothing of value.

Undeterred, Himmler assigned SS-colonel Otto Skorzeny to lead a second expedition. Skorzeny, renowned for his intelligence background and daring tactics, dismissed the previous expedition's location as strategically unsound for burying treasure. He turned his focus to a sharp rocky cliff on the side of the area. Scaling the seemingly vertical surface, he discovered a path leading away from the base of the mountain and into a nearby valley. Following this path, he came upon a walled-up cave. After ordering his team to break through the artificial wall, they made their way deeper into the mountain and eventually stumbled upon the treasure.

The haul, some sources claim, included gold bars, stolen artifacts from Solomon's Temple such as fragments of the Ark, a golden urn, a staff, a harp, a sword, countless golden plates and vessels, numerous small bells made of gold, stone tablets with ancient inscriptions, an abundance of precious gems, and a vast collection of religious relics dating back to the time of Solomon and beyond. The cave was emptied, it was said, and all items were transported to salt mines in Merkers, Germany.

During the latter days of the Third Reich, as the Nazis watched their empire crumble, they quickly melted down and dispersed their gold to secret locations across the globe. When General George Patton and the Allies took control of the area in Germany where these salt mines were located, they found much of the treasure had already been scattered. They did manage, nonetheless, to recover over 8,000 bars of gold bullion, 55 boxes of crated gold bullion, hundreds of bags filled with gold items, nearly 2,000 bags of foreign currency, and various other valuables in paper form. Despite this seemingly significant haul, it was only a small portion of what had originally been stored there. Even as Germany fell, the dispersed wealth ensured Nazi ideology, now heavily influenced by occult beliefs, would continue to thrive.

In this, what I find interesting is that this fascination of the Nazis with the occult and their attempts to create their own superhuman race would have likely remained a mere obsession if not for their pursuit of scientific advancement in the creation of Wunderwaffe, or wonder weapons. For this we must return to the height of World War II.

There is no doubt that the Nazis possessed highly advanced and often referred to as exotic technology. The list is extensive and unbelievable: flying saucers, lethal sound waves, air-made bullets – just to name a few. What was baffling was how they managed to make such remarkable leaps from being technologically behind their neighbors to producing machinery more fitting in a sci-fi novel. This equipment was shrouded in such mystery that even today, its existence remains classified. And this turn to such Wunderwaffe may never have happened if not for a set of its own interlacing circumstances.

In the early years of the Second World War, or the "good war" as it's often referred to, Hitler was determined to dominate Europe. Despite his overconfidence, Hitler had a hidden fear: that fighting on two fronts, one with Britain and one with Soviet Russia, would ultimately lead to Germany's downfall. To avoid this outcome, Hitler schemed to form an alliance with one country and overthrow the other, believing it was necessary for the Third Reich to achieve its ultimate destiny. This is where the thorny story of Rudolph Hess begins.

In 1941, on May 10th, Hess climbed into a German fighter plane and flew himself to Scotland undetected. His mission was to discuss peace and alliances with high-level British operatives who wanted to overthrow their Prime Minister, Winston Churchill, and ally with Germany. This plan had been in the works for months and everything had been carefully arranged. But, as Hess reached Scotland, he missed his landing spot and ran out of fuel, causing him to crash and be captured by a farmer before being thrown into prison. He was quickly disavowed and became a social outcast in Germany.

Historical Tidbits

The story, however, takes an intriguing turn about a year later. The King of England's brother, George, the Duke of Kent, who was suspected of being a Nazi sympathizer, met his end in what is known as the Dunbeath air crash.

This tragic and mysterious plane accident occurred in Scotland, not far from where Hess was imprisoned. All but one of the 15 passengers on board died in the crash. Witnesses noted there was another passenger who perished, but this person was not listed on the flight log. Some speculated it could have been Hess himself, secretly transported for unknown reasons. But if this conspiracy were true, it would be an insurmountable public relations nightmare.

Further there were whispers the crash may have been machinated by Winston Churchill himself. We will never really know though as coincidentally, all records of the flight and crash disappeared without explanation. After the war, a man by the name of Rudolph Hess was turned over to the Nuremberg Trials during which he proclaimed no memories of the events of his ill-fated flight at all.

So, with the ally/peace mission resulting in failure, the story continues, Hitler's fear of a war on two fronts became a reality. In a state of panic, the Nazi hierarchy turned to science to save themselves, but perhaps science was just the excuse.

It was in late 1941, it is said, when Hitler commanded the Ahnenerbe-SS to use the paranormal for tactical purposes and engage in occult warfare. And that is exactly what they did it seems. The Ahnenerbe-SS, under Himmler's leadership, I believe, went back to the origins of the Nazi party and their ties to the occult and communicating with otherworldly entities, the demons with their unrivaled technology Solomon had commanded.

Behind closed doors, it is rumored, their attention was solely directed towards harnessing the ways and means of the occult and transmissions with "enlightened beings" for their own gain.

Did they boldly communicate with these entities, feeling a sense of equality and fearlessness in their presence? Did some startling revelation found during their treasure hunting and raids on Masonic Temples give them a false sense of power over these sinister creatures? Maybe they used **The Lesser Key of Solomon**, a mysterious book of spells shrouded in sorcery and steeped in the lore of the **Testament of Solomon,** a purported chronicle of the powerful king's supernatural dealings with demons. Perhaps they had even stumbled upon evidence of Solomon's legendary ring itself, fueling the rumors and boasting of their dominance over a race with a technology far beyond our own? Whatever their methods, the Wunderwaffe program flourished, and soon highly advanced weapons began appearing. Allied pilots reported encountering strange aerial phenomena known as "foo fighters." Sometimes these were balls of light, other times flying discs or even ghost rockets.

As World War II was coming to a close, the US Government began to obtain intelligence on the Nazi super-weapons. The shocking reality began to sink in – they were lightyears behind in terms of technology. The capabilities of these weapons were beyond anything imaginable outside of Germany.

After the war ended and Nazi "reparations" of this technology, and the scientists who worked on it, were divided between the East and West,[80] it became clear, I think, that both sides would have to bear the weight of this advanced technology and its repercussions. It was a dangerous game, I believe, they had inherited, one with no doubt unfathomable consequences.

Was this the reason for the US Navy's surreptitious "invasion" of Antarctica in the continent's summer of 1946-1947? The covert operation, codenamed Highjump and led by Admiral Richard Byrd, was cloaked in mystery and terminated abruptly. Yet, rumors and conjecture still circulate about the true events that unfolded during Highjump, thanks to whispers of a covert Nazi stronghold concealed in the icy terrain. Some believe Byrd and his forces encountered extraterrestrial beings, as evidenced by Byrd's own report in March 1947, describing a new enemy capable of flying from pole to pole in an instant.

And then there is this, a declassified document, dated January 1973, titled "Extra Sensory Perception and Telekinesis: The COMSEC Threat – A Brief," which made a shocking claim. Amid discussions of scientific research on ESP and telekinesis, there was a sudden and unexpected inclusion of historical information. The document stated Adolf Hitler, known for his pursuit of harnessing extrasensory abilities, was also responsible for unleashing unspeakable horrors upon the earth.

---

[80] A post-World War II internal US Government program known as Operation Paperclip was established to absorb roughly 1,600 German (former? Nazi) scientists, engineers, and technicians who had migrated from Germany to the US and put them to work.

This revelation was followed by a unexplained conclusion, without any context, and seemingly not tied to anything:[81]

> **Uncareful use of** either offensive or defensive **psychic powers is exceedingly dangerous**. The Fanatical Hitler experience, where **a society of criminal leadership**[82] **thrust open an occult horror chamber which <u>cost</u> over 50 million dead**[83] should be more than a casual reminder that opening the Pandora's box of **deep human power can unlock more than beneficial effects,** but the lid is lifted and <u>will not be closed.</u>

After the lid was lifted on this concealed "occult horror chamber," the United States, having secretly brought over a multitude of Nazi scientists – and I suspect members of groups like the Ahnenerbe-SS and Thule Society – under Operation Paperclip, saw a strange wave of UFO sightings begin to sweep over the country. These sightings followed Kenneth Arnold's claim of seeing nine shiny objects in the sky while flying near Mt. Rainier in Washington state on June 24, 1947 – only three months after Byrd's perplexing statement – not surprising given how the report above states, to me anyway, that whatever was released was not going to be contained.

This in turn could potentially suggest a dual scenario involving not only the objects and technology, the UAPs, retrieved or derived from what some in the world of MKULTRA,[84] the CIA's horrific mind control program,

---

[81] In my opinion, given its enigmatic inclusion, it is important to read between the lines in this passage. Therefore, I have added my own emphasis in bold and underlining.

[82] Was it The Thule Society, the roots of the Ahnenerbe-SS, or simply the Abnenerbe-SS? Or perhaps it was some combination of the two?

[83] Between 50 and 85 million people were killed during World War II, with the majority consisting of civilians who were victims of genocide and mass murder perpetrated by their own governments in countries like the Soviet Union and China. Is the author implying this "occult honor" was responsible for all these deaths? Or perhaps they wanted all these deaths in exchange for unlocking the "beneficial effects," i.e. the cost?

[84] The MKULTRA program was an unethical series of human experiments conducted by the CIA. This program aimed to manipulate mental states using various techniques such as administering strong doses of psychoactive drugs. In addition to chemical methods, other forms of torture were utilized, including

referred to as Nichola Tesla's innovative space[85] but also the potential containment of otherworldly creatures and UFOs by this "box."

After all the paper's final words were, "And unless the man is firmly rooted in the foundation of the Spirit of Life [faith in Christ] he will not survive this great adventure into the World of Being [from Plato who believed the essence of reality lies in abstract and perfect entities called Forms, which are separate from our perception of reality, i.e., what we experience is a distorted shadow of the true reality]." In other words, if you want to survive in the actual reality we live in, you better be well-equipped with some heavy-duty light protection.

In 1952, the Pentagon responded by allocating funds to research in parapsychology, explicitly focusing on mediums that claimed the ability to connect with otherworldly beings. Soon after this contact program, the Pentagon ordered the Air Force to investigate and debunk UFOs.

One year later, the powerful Robertson Panel[86] advised the CIA to become involved in manipulating public opinion about UFOs by employing mass psychology and directed messages through the media.

The Panel's strategy involved disseminating specific propaganda to discredit any theories or evidence supporting the existence of UFOs. They warned that while the ongoing fascination with these incidents may seem innocuous, it could have serious implications as it holds the power to unravel everything we think we know about our existence. Shortly afterward, the CIA's director, Allen Dulles, launched MKULTRA.[87]

---

electroshock therapy, hypnosis, sensory deprivation, isolation, and even verbal and sexual abuse. The scope of MKULTRA was far-reaching, with research being conducted at nearly 100 institutions, including colleges, universities, hospitals, prisons, and pharmaceutical companies under the guise of legitimate scientific research. More on MKULTRA can be found on the conjunction.world website.

[85] Regarding Ingo's experience with this, refer the document "Ingo Channeling Transcript" on conjunction.world.

[86] Among the five-member panel were Lloyd Berkner and Luis Alvarez, both renowned physicists and suspected members of Majic-12. Majestic 12 (also known as Majic-12 or MJ-12) was an alleged covert group comprised of scientists, military leaders, and government officials. Their mission? Retrieve and analyze "extraterrestrial" spacecrafts. See the website conjunction.world for more details. To learn more about Alvarez's connection to Ingo, namely in relation to Egypt, see the Planetary Explorations page of the website ingoswann.com.

[87] Dulles was not the only influential figure in his family. His brother, John Foster Dulles, held just as much power and influence. He had served as President

Historical Tidbits

In Dulles' words, the goal of "brain warfare" was to target individuals and, thus, collective thought by conditioning people to react to external impulses rather than rational thinking and free will.

However, misdirection and mind conditioning are just two of the many tools in a large tool shed. To make use of these tools, one must actively employ them; otherwise, they're simply taking up space in the tool shed without serving any purpose. Regarding this, through my reading of Ingo's serialized memoir **Remote Viewing: The Real Story** (**RVRS**), I unearthed a hidden hint. It is revealed in the form of a dialogue with one of his mentor figures, Dr. Shafica Karagulla, a medical doctor, psychiatrist, and founder of the Higher Sense Perception Research Foundation.

Ingo described Karagulla in **RVRS** as one who "knew about how almost all of the world's intelligence agencies operated – those agencies known to exist, AND those which exist but are not known or even admitted to by anyone and don't even have names." About that conversation, he said, "Karagulla asked me: 'What do you think of conspiracies?' 'Oh,' I said, 'they're everywhere, aren't they?' 'WELL! Shall we compare some notes?' 'Yeah!'...A voice in the dark, Karagulla's: 'What about occult conspiracies?'"

Today, in our everyday conversations, the term "occult" is often used as a noun to describe a specific concept. It can refer to anything related to the esoteric or supernatural, including beliefs in magic, mysticism, and even extrasensory perception and parapsychology. This usage traces back to the word's 15th century origins when it evolved from the Latin word for secrecy or concealment. Though, the original root of the noun was actually a verb. This verb was derived from the Latin word "celare," meaning "to hide." Therefore, I suspect that there may have been a deeper and far more sinister ulterior motive behind their actions.

In a letter dated May 1973,[88] Ingo revealed that money was being funneled into "various effective mass mind control systems" as part of utterly disturbing motives of "quite invisible benefactors" working toward economic control of the planet. He warned this mass mind control, implying via and under the direction of human actors, will be used to create an uneducated, unproductive majority; a zombie population which will just go along with anything they are fed.

Eisenhower's Secretary of State while Dulles was running the CIA and had also been a trustee for the Rockefeller Foundation from 1935 to 1952.

[88] In "The Run-Up," I unveil another one of his findings he shared in this letter.

The timing of Ingo's announcement is intriguing. Roughly eight months later, in January 1974, a confrontational and controversial organization known for its extreme leftist views, before turning to the hard right, the National Caucus of Labor Committees (NCLC), created and led by the polarizing political activist Lindon LaRouche – **The New York Times** described LaRouche as a "quixotic, apocalyptic leader of a cult-like political organization" – released a document titled "STOP ROCKEFELLER'S NAZI DOCTORS."

This document outlines what I believe to be the underlying agenda at play; one carefully masterminded by Ingo's unseen benefactors.

These shadowy figures are utilizing human tokens – potentially former? Nazis brought to the US through Operation Paperclip – to carry out Karagulla's occult conspiracy. It states that the NCLC has evidence of extensive and inhumane CIA operations involving brainwashing and torture under the guise of "behavior modification" taking place in prisons, college campuses, hospitals, and other locations throughout the US and around the world. This would be MKULTRA.[89]

The objective is clear: to mold a compliant and mindless society – Ingo's uneducated, unproductive majority.

As for the occult conspiracy itself, this brings us to an article published in NCLC's newsletter **New Solidarity** around the same time. The article is titled "Uncover CIA-Police Plot to Take Over U.S.," based on a speech given by LaRouche under the name Lyn Marcus. In this article, which I have highlighted in bold and underlined for emphasis, is the following:

> But imagine the torture **you, a human being**, one day **you find yourself after extreme torture and degradation, sitting inside your own head like a conscious corpse sitting inside a tomb. There is no real connection between your conscious sense of self and your outer body. Your body is under the control of <u>an alien monster</u>**. [Ingo's quite invisible benefactors?]

---

[89] The origins of MKULTRA are rumored to have come from barbaric experiments in Nazi concentration camps, not to mention the potential influence of Dulles' brother's ties to the Rockefeller Foundation. Per author David Talbot, the Dulles brothers were deeply connected to many high-ranking Nazis during and after World War II, both eager, he says, to align themselves with "people who epitomize the worst evils of the 20th century."

Historical Tidbits

He makes sure to note that when you grasp the gravity of the situation, the truth is going to hit you like a sledgehammer and then "you'll understand what's important right now."

With respect to The Robertson Panel, they had one last trick up their proverbial "sleeves." They suggested infiltrating organizations focused on UFOs by using tactics that could be considered "subversive" to cause conflict and disrupt these groups' objectives. "Subversion" refers to a purposeful attempt to undermine and overthrow a system or group from the inside. Surely, modern intelligence personnel wouldn't still engage in this behavior? Would they?

And overall, could it be they are willing to go to such extreme lengths just to safeguard their twisted narrative, their veiled connection to its origins, and their controlling role in it all? Would they truly be willing to stop at nothing to protect their secrets? But then again, it's just a story.

Moving on now to what set this story in motion in the first place, Ingo's statement, "some of which has already been achieved,": the success of certain Remote Viewers in unlocking hypothetical technology. Let us start with his book **The Wisdom Category**. There he wrote that the establishment is NOT interested in the nature and scope of so-called "advanced civilizations" from other planets. Instead, he continued, they are fixated solely on their "advanced technology." Their narrow focus, he relayed, is on such beings "sharing" their knowledge and advancements with us or if not, then obtaining some of their technology through means of "reverse engineering" for what he called "venal and power-mongering purposes." It is something I believe he was quite entangled with.

It was with this entanglement in mind, I spoke on the **UAP Studies Podcast** at the end of February and beginning of March 2024. During the interviews, I walked through Ingo's "disclosure" of his involvement with such projects through his cryptic messages disguised in his recounting of stories in **Penetration**.

In the book, he described encounters with three distinct types of UFOs: one that appears as an illusion and likes to abduct animals and individuals, treating Earth like a supermarket; a drone operated from someplace else; and a massive diamond-shaped revolutionary machine resembling the now commonly reported black triangle UFOs.

For the latter two, to support my findings, the unpuzzling of his secret messages, I gathered a collection of documents, correspondences, and videos, things I call the dots that link the pieces together.

The dots for the "revolutionary machine" connect Ingo, a secretive Remote Viewing project funded by real estate billionaire Trammel Crow at SRI managed by Ingo, which took place just weeks after Crow hosted Ufologist Jacques Vallée for a talk on speculative technology given to several wealthy individuals, CEOs, and corporate representatives. It also involves the undisclosed training of a group of engineers in Remote Viewing by Ingo, and the believed UFO research being conducted by aerospace company tycoon James McDonnell and his company McDonnell Douglas, which Vallée believed was being done for the CIA under the guise of aeronautical research.

For the drone operated from someplace else, some of the dots include top-secret research at the Air Force's premier communications laboratory done under MKULTRA aimed at doing whatever it took to create a dissociative state in participants in order to force ESP, a NASA funded project at a joint NASA/Naval research facility focused on getting pilots to operate equipment in space through ESP, and NASA's funding of SRI's very first psychokinesis experiments with Ingo and Uri Geller to see if selected individuals could use their minds to interact with and influence sensitive electronic equipment.

I meticulously documented each step and connections I made, creating pages on the ingoswann.com website to contain all my findings. I also shared this information on the **X** platform. Yet, a thunderous silence so far had been the only reaction.

Since then, I stumbled upon something quite intriguing.

In 1975, the CIA, instead of consulting with Soviet researchers, parapsychologists, or even perception academics to review literature on the Eastern Bloc's advancements with psi phenomena, they turned to a seemingly unlikely source: Garrett AiResearch. This respected machine manufacturer was known for their pioneering work in aerospace technologies, and had even worked closely with NASA and McDonnell Douglas. The idea of exploring the biophysical aspects of psi through physical mechanisms, rather than solely through the lens of consciousness, appeared to be of great interest to the CIA. And the CIA's entrusted team at Garrett AiResearch's deep understanding of what they labeled as "Novel Biophysical Information Transfer" was evident in the comprehensive report they produced in 1976. Within its pages were recommendations that showcased, what I can best describe as, their advanced knowledge on the matter.

Ingo Swann
A Brief Biography | Timeline of Remote Viewing

Known in the bohemian circles of Greenwich Village, as "the psychic artist," Ingo was a free spirit deeply immersed in all things esoteric. His extensive studies covered a vast range of ancient texts, from Chinese and Hindu writings to early spiritualist beliefs, from ancient Yogis to George Gurdjieff's Fourth Way, even delving into early Christian Gnosticism and the teachings of L. Ron Hubbard's Scientology.

But who was this enigmatic figure? Born under the astrological signs of western Virgo, Celtic Swan, and Chinese Rooster on September 14, 1933, in his maternal grandmother's upstairs bedroom in Telluride, Colorado, Ingo embodied the traits of his zodiac signs: a logical and practical mind with a keen eye for detail, yet also highly critical; intense and secretive like the graceful swan; and bold and dramatic like the rooster. From a young age, Ingo experienced extraordinary occurrences such as seeing auras, having life-saving premonitions, out-of-body experiences, and an immediate connection with animals. These were just glimpses of the supranormal adventures that would shape his unique perspective on life.

In the fall of 1951, he enrolled at Westminster College in Salt Lake City, Utah. After four years, he graduated in the spring of 1955 and soon after joined the Army where he worked as a typist/clerk in Korea. Once he was honorably discharged, he relocated to New York City in 1958. He landed a job as a secretary at the United Nations and spent most of the 1960s going to parties and establishing himself as an artist. Although his paintings didn't sell well, he wrote racy novels to earn some extra cash, which he sold to the mob.

In the summer of 1967, fate brought Ingo into the company of two extraordinary women: Zelda Suplee and Buell Mullen.

Suplee, a former actress and magazine editor with a passion for all things New Age, was also the director of the Erickson Foundation. This organization supported groundbreaking research on gender and transsexuality, as well as explorations into psychic phenomena.

Mullen, on the other hand, was a renowned artist whose connections reached high into the echelons of society. Ingo affectionately named them Buell-Central and Zelda-Central. Both were known for hosting lavish dinner parties and Ingo was a regular guest at their gatherings, as they shared a deep fascination with all things psychic.

Through the guidance of Mullen and Suplee, Ingo was welcomed into a diverse circle of individuals who played crucial roles in his immersion into the world of parapsychology. Among them were Ruth Hagy Brod, a distinguished journalist and filmmaker; Dr. John Wingate, a renowned professor at New York University and prominent member of the American Society of Psychical Research (ASPR) board; and former actress Lucille Kahn, a powerful figure with strong ties to the "sleeping prophet," Edgar Cayce's A.R.E.

Despite his fascination with the esoteric, Ingo never considered himself to possess any profound abilities. All of that changed in the summer of 1971. During a dinner party at Suplee's place, an infrared camera was brought out and everyone followed suit into a dark room. They were all instructed to concentrate their energies. After the film was developed and to the surprise of everyone who saw it, Ingo's picture was taken with a luminous orb floating above his head. "You're psychic!" they all said.

Determined to integrate extrasensory perception (ESP) into the strict confines of the scientific world, Ingo turned his attention to demonstrating such abilities could be tested with utmost precision and repeatability. He persisted through long hours of monotonous trials, driven by a desire to prove the existence of psychic phenomena.

This dedication would eventually lead him from one set of experiments to the next and then to SRI and the development of Remote Viewing, the details of that development go like this:

1970

According to US intelligence, the USSR was investing millions of rubles each year into a secretive and classified field known as "psychotronics," After drawing an analogy to other fields such as electronics, bionics, and nucleonics, a French journalist coined the term psychotronics. The Czechs embraced this term to replace parapsychology, while the Soviets also used it briefly before developing their own term – psychoenergetics. These names were chosen in an attempt to give the field a more scientific or technological appearance. The funding and control of this research were primarily held by the Ministry of Defense, with some involvement from the KGB. It is also suspected that the Soviets were utilizing parapsychology for intelligence operations.[90]

1971

Dr. Harold (Hal) Puthoff, a laser physicist and researcher in quantum electronics, joins SRI to explore new fields of study. At a "Virgo Party" hosted by Suplee, Ingo meets Cleve Backster, a former polygraph expert for the FBI/CIA who is now focused on consciousness and plants. It's quite an eclectic group as Ingo also meets Robert Monroe at the event. Later, Ingo visits Backster's lab in New York City, where he "interacts" with plants that are hooked up to polygraphs. The plants seem to sense his intention to harm them, causing the polygraphs to react. In addition, Ingo tests his abilities in psychokinesis (also known as PK, the ability to move or disturb objects with the mind) on graphite in Backster's lab. Backster predicts that CIA agents will be very interested in Ingo's abilities.

Ingo begins experiments with eminent parapsychologist Dr. Gertrude Schmeidler. Schmeidler had heard of Ingo's successes with Backster and

---

[90] In 1975, the CIA hired a group of physicists and psychologists through a contract with AiResearch Manufacturing Company of California, also known as Garret AiResearch, a company well-versed in aerospace technologies. Their goal was to analyze Soviet research on the biophysical aspects of parapsychology. The report is available on the website conjunction.world.

set up an experiment at City College in NYC to psychokinetically alter the temperature of sealed thermistors. This is successful. Schmeidler is also VP of the ASPR. At this same time, Ingo begins to surround himself with mentors, Schmeidler being one, the others being Dr. Martin Ebon, paranormal expert, especially on Soviet psychic activity, which is deemed to be an increasingly serious threat, and Dr. Jan Ehrenwald, a noted psychiatrist and ESP researcher. The media gets ahold of the draft results of Schmeidler's tests and speculates that the psychic detonation of a nuclear weapon may be possible. Ingo was featured in **Time Magazine** and briefly became "the most famous person in America." Behind the scenes, the "psychic Cold War" between East and West ramped up.

Ingo and Backster continue their work on PK, specifically focusing on perturbing blood cells. Their efforts prove successful, leading Backster to exclaim, "You've accomplished something the Soviets have been attempting for years – the ability to invade a person's body using only their thoughts."

Dr. John Wingate, a trustee of the ASPR and a professor at New York University, suggests to Ingo he should undergo further testing at the facility. Despite believing he has been set up, Ingo ultimately accepts the challenge. Little did he know that by entering the doors of the ASPR, he was stepping into the world of international espionage. His main point of contact at the facility is Dr. Karlis Osis, Director of Research at the ASPR.

At the ASPR, Ingo and Osis began conducting out-of-body (OBE) experiments with guidance from Janet Mitchell, who was Osis' research assistant. The goal of these experiments was to identify "target objects" on a suspended tray near the ceiling. Instead of describing his impressions verbally, Ingo successfully sketches them, providing a crucial connection to Remote Viewing (RV). Drawing his perception of the "targets" instead of speaking about them would prove to be essential in accurately conveying target data during remote viewing sessions. The first successful rendering of objects on the tray through drawing occurred on November 24th.

At the ASPR, under Mitchell's watchful eye, Ingo conducts a remote viewing of weather conditions in Phoenix, AZ. The term Remote Viewing is invented by him and Mitchell and formally adopted.

1972

At the ASPR, Ingo conducts his first experiment involving an "outbound beacon." His subject, Vera Feldman, is sent to a secret location in New York City while Ingo attempts to "see" what she sees. To his amazement, he succeeds. This event coincides with a major upheaval at the ASPR. The chaos was sparked by ASPR discovering Ingo's ties to Scientology, which they had previously been unaware of.

Ingo returns to Backster's lab and brings up the concept of "psi signaling" and its instantaneous speed. Backster then tells him about Puthoff, who has a keen interest in tachyons – particles that can move faster than light. Ingo is initially hesitant to reach out to Puthoff, as he is also a Scientologist, but eventually decides to read his research papers. One particular paper catches Ingo's attention, as it discusses Soviet research on quantum theory and how it relates to the inner workings of human beings as a system.

Ingo sends a letter to Puthoff; he suspects Puthoff had called Backster to discuss Ingo and his experiences. He knows Puthoff contacted Osis, Schmeidler, and Ehrenwald about him, as he has copies of the letters. Ingo ultimately decides to leave the ASPR and focus on writing "sex novels" under pen names. Puthoff urges Ingo to visit SRI in California.

Ingo is pleasantly surprised when the reception held in his honor at the ASPR turns out to be a great success. The main purpose of the reception was to showcase seven of Ingo's paintings.

Following the party, rumors circulate about Ingo's sexuality and promiscuity. At the time same-sex sexual activity was illegal. He confides in Puthoff, concerned that his reputation may tarnish Puthoff's work and SRI. Nevertheless, this does not prevent him from later obtaining highly classified clearances from the CIA. Despite his alleged sexual tendencies, Ingo is still deemed trustworthy enough to handle top-secret information by the government agency.

The ASPR Publishing Committee shocks everyone with their abrupt decision not to publish the result of the successful Ingo/Osis/Mitchell OOB experiments. They also prohibit any further studies on Remote Viewing. Ingo is fed up and declares a lifelong grudge against the parapsychology community, particularly ASPR. He immediately contacts Puthoff and announces that he will be leaving for California to work at SRI.

Ingo arrives in California. As Ingo had previously shown an ability to affect thermometers, Puthoff wants to witness this ability firsthand. He takes Ingo to a highly-protected magnetometer used for scientific experiments located underground at Stanford. Ingo disturbs the normal functioning of the magnetometer and then accurately draws the internal design of the machine, which has never been publicly shared before. Dr. Russell Targ, a laser physicist who had always been fascinated by parapsychology, officially joins SRI.

Puthoff and Targ began their rigorous testing on "psychics," with Ingo as their primary subject. Countless experiments were conducted, each one exploring the limits of ESP, until finally a breakthrough was made – Remote Viewing using geographical coordinates.

The DIA starts providing financial support to SRI in order to investigate the existence of anomalous mental abilities like extrasensory perception and psychokinesis, and their potential usefulness for national concerns.

1973

Ingo suggests the first of what will go on to be several clandestine-supported psychic projects using Remote Viewing to view targets at geographical locations. Ingo calls RV an intellectual process of gathering data from sites. Sponsored by the CIA, SCANATE, the name having been derived from the process of scanning by coordinates, begins. "Project SCANATE: Exploratory Research in Remote Viewing," CIA-RDP79-00999A000400050002-4, a 2002 CIA declassified document, provides insight into Ingo's early work on this and incorporates some of his RV sketches.

Together, Ingo and psychic Harold Sherman conduct psychic probes of different planets, including Jupiter. During a session, Ingo "sees" a ring surrounding the planet and describes it to the others. At first, however, the scientific community disregards his findings. It was not until data from NASA's Mariner probes confirmed the existence of the ring that his "psychic probe" results were validated.

Pat Price, a fellow Scientologist, becomes a part of the program. The following year, Price is tasked with psychically probing a Soviet nuclear facility known as "URDF-3" located near Semipalatinsk. However, after questioning the validity of Price and analyzing his sessions, the CIA begins to suspect he could potentially be working for the Soviets.

1975

After Price's death, the CIA decides to end its contract with SRI. The US Air Force's Foreign Technology Division (FTD), which specializes in studying and gathering intelligence on foreign air, space, and ballistic missile systems, takes over the role of primary sponsor for Remote Viewing research. Dale Graff, an aerospace engineer and physicist, takes the lead under the guidance of DIA's intelligence operations.

1977

Under the codename "Gondola Wish," the US Army enlists the help of Robert Monroe and his Monroe Institute to conduct Remote Viewing experiments. Monroe's method, Extended Remote Viewing, ERV, utilizes altered states of consciousness, specifically out-of-body experiences. Some of Ingo's work on this project can be found in the CIA declassified document: CIA-RDP96-00788R001800060001-7.

1978

Under the Army's Intelligence and Security Command (INSCOM), Gondola Wish is renamed and goes operational as "Grill Flame" at Fort Meade, MD.

1979

The initial Remote Viewing mission for the Army is conducted in cooperation with Graff at FTD. SRI becomes an official part of the Army program. The Air Force discontinues its own Remote Viewing program run by FTD. The Defense Intelligence Agency (DIA) takes over the operation, led by Jack Vorona.

Historical Tidbits

1982

Ingo trains the first two Army students in his intellectual process protocol, known as Controlled Remote Viewing (CRV): Thomas M. McNear, a retired lieutenant colonel who was previously a captain in the US Army, and Robert (Rob) Cowart, whose specific Army designation is unknown.

1983

Grill Flame is sunsetted, then re-designated by INSCOM as Project "Center Lane," continuing to use psychoenergetics, namely Remote Viewing, to gather intelligence.

1984

After syndicated columnist Jack Anderson reveals the top-secret aspects of the Remote Viewing program in **The Washington Post**, the National Academy of Sciences' National Research Council conducts a closed-door discussion and delivers an unfavorable review of the program.

Ingo trains William (Bill) Ray, CPT, US Army (Retired as a Major), Paul H. Smith, CPT, US Army (Retired as a Major), Edward Dames, CPT, US Army (Retired as a Major), and Charlene Mettee Cavanaugh (Shufelt), DAC, US Army as operational Remote Viewers under a direct contract with the US Army and setting up an office in New York to do so. However, the Army cuts off funding for RV, resulting in all Army Remote Viewers transferring to the DIA the following year.

1985

Puthoff departs from SRI and initiates the Institute of Advanced Studies in Austin, TX. The program head role at SRI is taken over by nuclear physicist Edwin (Ed) May.

1986

Remote Viewing is now referred to as "Sun Streak." Ingo begins his retirement; his official end with the program is in 1988.

1990

At Fort Meade, Graff takes the reins of the operational RV unit and changes the project name to "Star Gate."

1991

May transfers RV scientific research from SRI to the defense contractor Science Applications International Corp (SAIC). The security classification changes from an "SAP" (special access program) to a "LIMDIS" (limited dissemination) program.

1994

The responsibility of budget management for the RV program shifts from the DIA back to the CIA.

1995

Under the direction of Congress, the CIA is tasked with officially researching Remote Viewing as a potential intelligence tool, despite having used it covertly for years. In a report commissioned by the CIA and conducted by the American Institutes for Research (AIR), the program is discredited and deemed no longer effective.[91] This leads to Remote Viewing being publicly disclosed for the first time. As a result, the CIA terminates the Star Gate program. The popular TV show **Nightline** airs an investigative report on the government's use of Remote Viewing technology.

---

[91] Prior to the public disclosure and discrediting of Remote Viewing, there were classified briefings from individuals who were "in the know" about non-human entities. A confidential memo from SAIC in March 1995 detailed a meeting between Ingo, a retired member of the RV program, and influential members of the intelligence community to discuss these entities. For further information on this topic, refer to the note titled "Exploring the Link."

Exploring the Link
Remote Viewing | UFO Bases | Non-Human Entities

Back in March of 2000, renowned **Coast to Coast AM** radio host Art Bell conducted an interview with Ingo, who by this time was known as the "Father of Remote Viewing." One of Bell's goals during this conversation was to make sense of various pieces of information, such as why the covert program of Remote Viewing, which had been active for almost 20 years, suddenly disappeared.

Ingo Swann: The CIA has only volunteered to go public on something three times in their history and the discrediting of Remote Viewing [aka psychic spying] was one time and it was completely unexpected at that.

Art Bell: They do everything for a reason.

Ingo Swann: Yes, but you have to really look into what those reasons might be you know and, in my mind, anyway one of those reasons was that they didn't want to ever have Remote Viewing connected with anything extraterrestrial because you put those two things together and you have a developing situation that these chains of command don't exactly know how to manage from the get-go.

Art Bell: You're telling me that at some point the program, and maybe you would like to tell me at what point in the program, the people involved became aware of more than just terrestrial information.

Ingo Swann: Well, actually, I think it was Pat Price, you've heard of him, haven't you?

Art Bell: I've heard the name.

Ingo Swann: He was one of the early people that worked with Hal and sometimes me and I think it was him who first enunciated the location of a [nervous laughter] I will put it, a human extraterrestrial[92] cooperation base.

Art Bell: Oh my!

Ingo Swann: Oh my, YES! And you can imagine the bells that started going off.

Art Bell: Oh, absolutely a human extraterrestrial cooperation BASE!, the location thereof.

Ingo Swann: I told Pat Price: Gosh I don't think you should tell anybody about this. ... But he was stubborn and went ahead and talked about it, even unofficially.

Ingo was cautious and deliberate during their conversation, carefully selecting his words to avoid straying from a narrow path with Bell. They did discuss Ingo's harnessing, but he skillfully danced around the topic by stating those who refused to work with the powers that be didn't have long to live historically. When the topic of the president came up, Ingo clarified he meant a generic president or presidents and stated they work for the real powers that rule the world, not the ones who run it, but rule it. Under this guise, it's clear why he put such emphasis on Price.

In 1972, the intelligence community began funding research at Stanford Research Institute (SRI) led by laser physicists Drs. Harold (Hal) Puthoff and Russell Targ. Their focus was on exploring areas such as extrasensory perception (ESP) and psychokinesis. The goal of this research though was not simply to prove the existence of these "anomalous mental phenomena," but rather to harness them as tools for espionage and

---

[92] Throughout his life, Ingo consistently refers to non-human entities or different vibrational entities as extraterrestrials (ETs). Despite this, his understanding of them aligns more closely with his friend John Keel's concept of non-human entities or NHEs, beings of a different vibrational frequency. When he speaks negatively about these entities, he is referring to what we now identify as demons.

national security purposes. This resulted in the creation of Remote Viewing (RV), a method used to gather information about distant or unseen places, people, or objects. Over the next 20 years, RV was utilized by several top-secret US intelligence programs collectively known as Star Gate.[93] The RV program lasted until 1995, when operations under it were visibly drifting from mission objectives and garnering some very unwanted attention thereof.

In 1995, the same year Remote Viewing became public and was subsequently discredited, an article written by Jim Schnabel titled "Tinker Tailor Soldier Psi" was published in a British newspaper. The article discussed the program's advanced training targets, which Schnabel also mentioned in his 1997 book **Remote Viewers: The Secret History of America's Psychic Spies**. These advanced targets included viewing the Loch Ness Monster, Marian apparitions, and angels and demons using the methods developed by Robert Monroe. Schnabel noted the Remote Viewers were fascinated by UFOs and often had strange experiences when attempting to view them. He specifically mentioned Ed Dames, a former student of Ingo's as being involved in these sessions, but also stated other members of the program were officially tasked with UFO-related targets. Schnabel also discussed how Pat Price had been involved in psychic spying on UFOs before the program began at SRI and how Ingo downplayed his involvement in such activities as he feared the beings attached to the UFOs could invade his mind and possess his soul. Nonetheless, documents show Ingo himself was given official targets related to UFOs. This suggests he may have encountered similar experiences when trying to psychically penetrate them.

From the moment Ingo walked through the doors at SRI, it was clear he was involved in some shadowy endeavors. The air buzzed with secrecy and the scent of covert agendas. There were two reasons for this. The first could be traced back to a letter written by Ingo to L. Ron Hubbard, the founder of the Church of Scientology, on May 3, 1973. At the time, both Ingo and Puthoff were affiliated with Church. In the letter, Ingo hinted at furtive projects associated with the fact we are not alone on this planet and how "mind control" was being employed against the population. These revelations coincided with the sudden appearance of Price, another Scientologist, at SRI later that month. The second reason was revealed in

---

[93] Please refer to the note on Ingo Swann and the RV timeline for a more details.

a conversation between Jacques Vallée[94] and Puthoff in the fall of 1973, as documented in Vallée's book **Forbidden Science Volume 2**.

Vallée, a well-known UFO researcher, asked Puthoff if there was a secret government project actively investigating UFOs. To this, Puthoff confirmed there was indeed such a project, and they often utilized his "psychics" – presumably referring to Ingo and Price – to psychically penetrate locations where they suspected UFO bases existed. This further fueled Vallée's questioning about the true extent of their work and wondered if those running this secret project understood the gravity of the situation. But Puthoff reassured him, stating they were well aware of what was at stake. And just in case there was any doubt left, Puthoff emphasized they were officially sanctioned by government authorities.

This is likely the group Ingo identified as "whoever you guys are" in his book **Penetration: The Question of Extraterrestrial and Human Telepathy**.[95] A group Ingo described as constantly struggling with a persistent problem, relentlessly pursuing UFOs – especially the ones known for taking objects and even people – and noting how these UFOs hold some kind of sway, if not control, over humanity, leaving him to conclude that "Earth is under some kind of siege." More specifically, he revealed this group is attempting to make sense of these mysterious objects by enlisting the help of psychics – including Ingo himself.

In February of 1974, Puthoff and Vallée's UFO paths crossed once again. In his book, Vallée recalled how Puthoff introduced him to his intelligence contact, Christopher "Kit" Green. At the time, Green served as

---

[94] During this time Vallée was focused on developing the precursor to the internet at SRI. But he also gained recognition as a respected Ufologist on the side. Being friends with Puthoff, he occasionally served as a consultant for SRI's RV projects and assisted Ingo in refining the geographic aspects of what would eventually become CRV. Additionally, he received CRV training directly from Ingo.

[95] The book is divided into three distinct sections. The first section follows Ingo and his experiences with UFOs, extraterrestrials, and the mysterious activities and structures on the Moon. He is accompanied by Mr. Axelrod and the twins, who represent researcher John Keel's "Men in Black" – agents dressed in black suits who either intimidate UFO witnesses or protect secrets about UFOs. In the second section Ingo explains his theories about the Moon being a hollow, artificial satellite and explains various observed anomalies on its surface. In the third part, Ingo emphasizes the importance of developing our perception awareness systems as he believes that "advanced" beings, referred to as ETs, possess a heightened form of telepathy (telepathy+) and see us as pushovers to manipulate.

an analyst and intelligence officer with the CIA, but it wouldn't be long before he became the CIA's first program manager for Remote Viewing. Eventually, he would hold prestigious titles such as Branch Chief, Deputy Division Director, and Assistant National Intelligence Officer for the CIA's Science and Technology division.

According to Schnabel's account, Green[96] was a critical figure in Puthoff and Targ's work from the very beginning and was deeply involved in their experiments with Price and Ingo. The first thing Green did when they met at Puthoff's house was discuss a recent UFO sighting and reported abduction case. Vallée was astounded by Green's detailed knowledge of the case, even surpassing that of the investigators themselves. It was through this conversation Vallée learned of Green's vast network of contacts within the executive branch who shared similar interests and information about these unusual phenomena.

As Schnabel was probing the Remote Viewing story, investigative journalist Jim Marrs was also pursuing the same topic from the angle of a UFO cover-up. His book on the subject was supposed to be published at the same time as Schnabel's, but it was pulled at the last minute. Years later, a watered-down version called **Psi Spies** was released. In the intervening years, Marrs wrote **Alien Agenda** where he connected the RV program with targets related to UFO bases, extraterrestrial beings, and alternate dimensions. But both Marrs and Schnabel, however, had only scratched the surface of a much deeper story.

To truly understand this deeper story, we must travel back to the autumn of 1973. In October of that year, Price arrived at Puthoff's office with a file in hand, the same time as the pivotal Puthoff-Vallée conversation. The file contained detailed notes and intricate sketches, revealing the existence of extraterrestrial beings who had established four underground bases here on Earth: one in Spain at Monte Perdido in the Pyrénées; another in Zimbabwe, East Africa at Mount Nyangani; a third in Alaska at Mount Hayes; and finally, one in Australia at Mount Zeil.

Price asserted that he had telepathically accessed these bases and was familiar with their operations. He also revealed that four of the bases were connected to a central hub located on Mars, serving as their home port. While each base had its own specific purpose – the primary base at Monte Perdido served as a main maintenance and technology center, while

---

[96] In his book, Schnabel referred to him as "Richard Kennett."

Mount Nyangani housed a weather and geological control center, and Mount Hayes functioned as a personnel center – they all shared a common goal: to reinforce B.T.L. implants and transport new recruits, "manned," so to speak, by a sort that looks like us but is not us.

But what exactly are these B.T.L.s? According to Price, they stood for "between life implants" and appear, per sources in the public domain, to be part of Scientology's extraterrestrial narrative.

As a devout Scientologist himself, Price was well-versed in the concept of between life implants as part of the process of going clear[97] within the religion. After eradicating their "reactive mind" and achieving the state of "Clear," individuals can advance to the OT (Operating Thetan – a thetan is a spiritual being aka the soul) levels, which are higher spiritual states with secreted insights.

The third level of OT is where individuals are introduced to some of the veiled teachings. This is when they learn about Xenu, a powerful ruler from an extraterrestrial "Galactic Confederacy."[98] Price was an OT Level IV, so OT Level III would have been very present in his mindset, I would think.

Another aspect of Scientology's narrative is the belief that after you finish your physical life on Earth, your spirit leaves your body but is unconsciously drawn back to an implant station. Here, your memories of your previous life are wiped by powerful electronic beams, and you are programmed to return to Earth for another life. In a sense you could draw a parallel between an implant and a hypnotic suggestion. These implants use electronic fields, akin to electric shock therapy, to capture and zap the individual, programming them with commands and projecting lifelike

---

[97] **In Remote Viewing: The Real Story (RVRS)**, Ingo explains the process of becoming clear as proposed by LRH. According to LRH, one's reactive mind (equivalent to the unconscious) could be cleared by identifying and erasing traumatic experiences from past lives as well as in this current one through re-experiencing them in the present moment. This would result in becoming a "clear," as referred to in Scientology. The steps towards achieving the state of clear requires strict processes administered by a trained Scientology auditor, each step coming with a price tag.

[98] According to this teaching, 75 million years ago Xenu brought billions of his people to Earth in spacecraft that resembled DC-8 airplanes. Xenu then stacked these people around volcanoes and killed them with hydrogen bombs. In the eyes of official Scientology scriptures, the spirits of these aliens, known as thetans, still inhabit and negatively impact humans spiritually. Part of going clear revolves around ridding oneself of these alien spirits.

images to create false memories. This cycle continues for millions of years, with each lifetime leading back to the implant station.

Thus, Price's notes and sketches about underground UFO bases appear to me to have very strong similarities to Scientology's beliefs but also to the type of experiments done under MKULTRA.[99]

As context, and so momentarily taking a pit stop, let's start with something Ingo wrote in his **RVRS** about neuropsychiatrist and psi researcher Shafica Karagulla. "Open evidence of her brilliance consisted of the invitation to join the famous brain researcher, Dr. Wilder Penfield. And it was this woman, with all her impressive credentials, that had decided to focus on higher sense perception -- and to hell with what the rest of the world thought of it one way or another."

It all seems very straight-forward, without a doubt. But operating subterraneously, Ingo implies much more was going on. I say that because if you want to unearth some, what I call really big, clues, **RVRS** is unquestionably full of them, but you got to be willing to dig.

Let's go with the clues Ingo gave us here and starting with the renowned brain researcher Dr. Wilder Penfield, who Karagulla had the opportunity to study with. She wrote of this time, "After completing my work in England, I immediately went to Canada to work alongside Dr. Wilder Penfield for three and a half years. As the psychiatrist on his team, I assessed patients with conditions such as temporal lobe epilepsy and other neurological and mental disorders."

Penfield's primary interest at the time was in using electric stimulation on the temporal lobe. This method had a surprising impact on dream recollection, as well as causing sensations such as déjà vu, fear, loneliness, unfamiliarity, and detachment from one's own body.

As it turns out, she wasn't the only one Penfield invited. A decade earlier, another invitation was extended to a well-known psychiatrist and researcher who had also studied in Scotland, specifically at the Glasgow Royal Mental Hospital. His name was Donald Ewen Cameron. With Penfield's help, and some hefty outside funding facilitated by Penfield, the McGill University Allan Memorial Institute for Psychiatry was established and would serve as a home base for Cameron's research.

This is the Cameron who would go on to become the lead researcher for MKULTRA's Subproject 68 (1957-1964), after Karagulla's departure.

---

[99] For more on MKULTRA see the note "Ah, Yes!"

The official purpose of this subproject was to study the effects of verbal signals on human behavior. For this, participants were given chemical agents to break down their patterns of behavior. The preliminary funding request shows the largest appeal other than for salaries is for a soundproof room needed to keep participants in sensory isolation then continuous sleep for seven to ten days. That is language from the declassified documents. It sounds fairly innocuous. However, according to David Talbot's book **The Devil's Chessboard: Allen Dulles, the CIA, and the Rise of America's Secret Government**, these experiments, which took place in a soundproof room at the Allan Institute known as the "Sleep Room," actually involved inducing "electric dream" states through insulin overdoses, massive amounts of hallucinogens like LSD, and electroshock therapy. Cameron referred to this process as "de-patterning," aimed at erasing negative thoughts and replacing them with positive ones through constant exposure to, that would be a blasting of, taped messages while patients were in a nearly comatose state, thanks to the drugs and electric shocking, for weeks on end. In one extreme case, a patient underwent this reprogramming for 101 days. Essentially, this project involved illegal human experimentation in an attempt to develop mind control or brainwashing techniques or just how to enforce thoughts using drugs and psychological methods.

Cameron's experiments, which were authorized by Penfield on behalf of CIA Director Allen Dulles and funded through the Society for the Investigation of Human Ecology to McGill under MKULTRA, had been in progress long before MKULTRA since around 1948. These early experiments played a significant role in the CIA's pursuit of mind control as a weapon. Karagulla arrived at McGill in 1952, at a time when Cameron's early barbaric experimentations together with Penfield's own on out-of-body trials were well on the way. These experiments were in line with Karagulla's own research, which focused on the temporal lobes and their connection to hallucinations during abnormal mental states. She later named this phenomenon ESP, according to a 1972 article by the **Wichita Eagle** newspaper describing her research.

But back to our story, in terms of Scientology, rephrasing Hubbard's 1952 book **A History of Man**, not all preclears choose to disclose their experiences; being implanted once can cause a restimulation upon death, erasing memories of past lives. Some preclears have had one implant, while others have had five or even more. Many report having been implanted on Mars, but there are also cases of reports from stations located throughout the Solar System. On rare occasions, there have been incidents involving Earth-based report stations, which are always protected by screens or shields. The most recent Martian report station on Earth was set up in the Pyrénées Mountains.

In mid-1974, as per declassified documents, the CIA began to express concerns about Price's possible ties to the KGB and potential role as a disinformation agent. These suspicions were based on his frequently inconsistent information, which was at times either surprisingly accurate or outdated. By late summer, Price, no longer under the auspices of SRI, was tasked with working under a new handler and within a different unit in the CIA.

He relocated to West Virginia, taking on the role of President at the Princess Coal Company while also, it appears, continuing his work for the agency. Meanwhile, the program at SRI came to a halt and Ingo returned to New York City.

In an article about Price's coal mining company appointment, Price stated the recruitment process focused on his distinct talent for evaluating the company's potential for exploration without needing to physically leave the office. As for his exploration achievements, he claimed the ultimate evidence will reflect in the company's financial performance.

Thus, Ingo, Price, and Puthoff were in a literary sense, leaves scattered in the wind. However, Hubbard wrote a letter to Ingo in December of that year. Their project at SRI may have been on hold, but they were still connected through their shared purpose. Hubbard congratulated Ingo on his "continuing success" and mentioned how he, along with Puthoff and Price, were laying the groundwork for something important. It seemed like there was more going on – perhaps involving those secret bases Puthoff had told Vallée about where "his psychics" were aiding with their psychic abilities. Was this groundwork for some sort of disclosure initiative?

By the beginning of 1975, it appears Price's coal mining opportunity wasn't going as smoothly as anticipated. As a result, Price was ramping up work with his new unit.

His new covert employers though are quite fascinating, to say the least. A declassified memo from November of 1978 reviewing how **Gondola Wish** was designed to merge Soviet and East European parapsychology intelligence gathering with all-source OPSEC support[100] as part of a recommendation for its continued funding, provided background information on various US intelligence agencies' recent interests in this area of parapsychology. One assemblage listed stood out among the rest.

Before his unfortunate passing, Price, this document records, had been collaborating with a mysterious unit that was rumored to be involved in assassinations. However, these activities were said to have ceased in 1963.[101] The document also reveals details about a program related to psychic abilities and offensive intelligence collection that had been operational since the 1970s under this set, for which Price was their main source.

In October of 1975, the **New York Times** ran a story about this group entitled, "C.I.A. Assassination Unit Described." The article detailed how the first public acknowledgment of this group's existence came via a recent speech by then Minnesota Senator, and intelligence committee member, Walter F. Mondale at Denison University in Ohio.

In this speech, Mondale stated that Richard Helms, the CIA's former director, and Richard Bissell, the former head of the CIA's clandestine operations, created and operated what they claimed was an authorized and institutionalized assassination team within the agency, which the two CIA men referred to as "executive action."

It was ultimately someone from within this unit supposedly tied to "removing unfriendly foreign? leaders" and engaged in operational intelligence gathering using "paranormal" means who met with Price at the Key Bridge Marriott Hotel in Arlington, VA just across the Potomac from Washington, DC on April 26, 1975.

A separate declassified memo documenting this meeting noted that Price mentioned an upcoming article in the **National Enquirer**, a tabloid known for its insatiable headlines, for which he had given an interview.

---

[100] OPSEC (operations security) is a strategy used to determine if sensitive information could be accessed by enemy intelligence and if it would benefit them. The process involves identifying any potential threats, evaluating vulnerabilities, and implementing measures to prevent the exploitation of crucial information by the enemy. In the realm of parapsychology, this cycle included proposing methods for gathering intelligence using "paranormal" means.

[101] Records of this department were destroyed, like the fate of MKULTRA, under the direction of then-director Richard Helms.

The article was going to focus on topics such as psychokinesis, Remote Viewing, and their connection to Scientology, Price is said to have relayed. It is important to note here that during this meeting, again recorded in the memo, Price emphasized the need for more than just coordinates – just coordinates were the standard protocol of SRI's research endeavors – when asked if those would suffice. He mentioned that photos and detailed descriptions would be much more valuable. It appears that he was given locations and people to "psychically" investigate as he promised to send sketches and a bill.

Several months following his meeting with his new CIA employers, the supposed nonexistent CIA group responsible for assassinations, Price was found dead from a mysterious heart attack in a Las Vegas hotel room.

Just about two years after Price's death, and after more than a year of surveillance, the FBI conducted a massive raid on several locations belonging to Scientology's intelligence wing, known as the Guardian's Office (GO). The outcome of this raid, as reported in a **Washington Post** article from the same year titled "Scientology Raid Yielded Alleged Burglary Tools," was an immense number – possibly hundreds of thousands – of files that had been secretly obtained from governmental agencies and businesses in the US and abroad via infiltration tactics.

As stated in a **St. Petersburg Times** article from 1979 titled "Old-time religion? Forget it," it seemed that no individual or organization was immune to the schemes of this secretive group. Armed with miniature transmitters, lock picks, secret codes, forged credentials, and any other devices they deemed necessary for their operations under a program known as Operation Snow White, the members of Scientology's Guardian's Office stop at nothing to carry out their conspiratorial plans.

According to Vallée, based on seized materials, "the FBI reported in 1977 after a raid on the Church of Scientology office in Los Angeles, Price had served as a spy infiltrating CIA operations on behalf of Scientology."[102]

---

[102] It was speculated that Price had connections to Scientology's Guardian's Office and may have been involved in Operation Snow White. According to sources, a prominent member of the GO delivered the eulogy at Price's funeral, which was held at Scientology's Celebrity Centre. The only published article about Price's death can be found on rense.com and was written by Terry Milner. Milner was once the Deputy Guardian for Intelligence United States (DGIUS) in the Church of Scientology.

Historical Tidbits

At this point, one might question a few things, but two stand out: 1) Was the CIA manipulating Price to monitor his interactions with possible co-conspirators, as concerns about his potential role as a KGB informant were raised? And if so, did they find such co-conspirators and/or uncover any evidence linking Price to the GO's office, or possibly even a hypothetical connection between the GO and the KBG? And what exactly was in those files that led the FBI to suspect Price of theoretically being a spy against the CIA? Did the FBI serendipitously unearth the files while sorting through their massive trove of seized documents and materials and in doing so immediately grasp the significance of what they had found, or did they deliberately discover them? And intriguingly, how did Vallée come to know about it? Were the possible files connected to his work with the supposedly defunct assassination team, or were they exchanges between Hubbard and Price through the GO's office when Price was "sent," I believe, to SRI to assist Ingo and Puthoff with their efforts to penetrate and, I suspect, ultimately reveal what was going on at those bases? Regardless, these base files do, I think, provide evidence of ongoing mass mind control operations orchestrated by beings that look like us but are not us, as evident in Price's use of terms from Scientology describing implants and thought transfers.

But I digress, back to the second stand out question.

Or, 2) maybe, given Price's declining business prospects and the sensational reputation of the **National Enquirer**, that is their willingness imaginably to pay top dollar for salacious stories, was the interview possibly not solely focused on psychic abilities and such abilities' connection to Scientology? Could Price have ventured into the land of UFO/mind control bases here on Earth and his work as one of Puthoff's psychics with "someone" within the US intelligence wing to psychically penetrate them? Might this have been his downfall, as those bases held the most vital secrets to be kept from the public? By chance, is the reason behind Ingo's comment to Bell: "But he was stubborn and went ahead and talked about it."?

In any case, after Price's death, in the mid-1970s it appears, Puthoff began supporting groups critical of Scientology, which Schnabel notes in his book as being a way for him to distance himself from the Church and undermine its credibility.

Given all the aforementioned information, one might assume that Puthoff would want to destroy or hide any files given to him by Price, who was possibly connected to an infiltration operation that resulted in several Scientologists being imprisoned, including Hubbard's wife, not to mention Price using Remote Viewing as operational intelligence support for a "supposed" assassination group from within the CIA and a tinge of KGB disinformation agent-ness lingering around him. And then of course, there is his very suspicious death.

Yet, despite his anti-Scientology stance, and any misgivings, Puthoff kept the files – to me burning them seems like the more logical course of action, especially if: 1) he was quite adverse to Scientology; 2) he wanted to protect the Remote Viewing program from potential damage caused by any suspected "spying" and "assassination" revelations; and 3) did want to end up heart-attacked.

It was around this time too, SRI obtained financial support from the Navy, specifically from its NAVELEX unit – a command focused on creating electronic warfare systems and devices – for a twelve-month venture in "remote-sensing." With this new direction in play, it seems to me various internal RV components were being strategically placed on a game board.

Nonetheless, by 1977 the SRI Remote Viewing program was running out of money, ironically at a time when it was achieving demonstrable successes. Former Astronaut Edgar Mitchell, a friend of the SRI program from its early days, flew to Washington on behalf of SRI to meet with his close friend, CIA Director George H.W. Bush, per Annie Jacobsen's **Phenomena: The Secret History of the U.S. Government's Investigations into Extrasensory Perception and Psychokinesis**.

Bush couldn't approve CIA funds as the Agency was now under too much scrutiny from Congress. Instead, Bush tells Mitchell, according to Jacobsen, to urge SRI to find a military sponsor if Remote Viewing is to survive. SRI follows through on this and seeks support from various military agencies all very interested in advanced technologies and electronic communications:

1) **The Missile Intelligence Agency**. At the time of its funding, it was the team responsible for enhancing weapons development both offensively and defensively, which included directed energy weapons.
2) **Army Materials Systems Analysis Agency**. At the time of its funding, it was conducting systems and engineering analysis to support technical designing and acquisitions.

3) **The Air Force's Foreign Technology Division**. At the time of its funding, its objective was to acquire, collect, analyze, produce, and disseminate foreign aerospace scientific and technical intelligence.
4) **Air Force's Technical Applications Center**. At the time of its funding, it was engaged in a wide variety of detection/monitoring techniques, including seismic, debris collection, air sampling, geophysical diagnostics, electromagnetic pulse, magnetic, acoustic, hydroacoustic, satellite systems, very low frequency phases, high frequency radio waves, and atmospheric florescence.

Based on the above funding, especially when coupled with the NAVELEX project, it seems the RV program, in the mid- to late 1970s, may have become deeply entangled in the development of psychotronic weapons, means and ways, which use electronic, electromagnetic, and gravitational fields to manipulate thoughts and behavior.

In a brain and behavior lecture, renowned researcher Michael Persinger, whom Ingo worked with extensively in the late 1980s and early 1990s, proposed his famous hypothesis that the temporal lobes of the human brain are at the core of mystical experiences. He explained that subtle electromagnetic forces can have a profound impact on brain activity and alter consciousness if they are pulsed at specific frequencies. But this concept extends beyond just scientific research – it also has political implications regarding control over individuals' brains. So, no torture, drugs, sleep deprivation needed, just low frequency waves.

In searching on the internet for how one might apply psychic powers to in this way, the highest result I found was for video games, where players can create, shape, and manipulate "psychic gravity." This action allows one player to ground another player's thoughts and actions into a reality of the first player's choosing. Once that second player is securely in the first player's reality construct, the first player can use remote energy manipulation to interact with and even destroy the second player.

Is it possible this concept applies to more than just video games? Could this be something that happens in our everyday lives, all around us? Maybe video games are a metaphor for real events and influences shaping our existence?

A clue to this theory perhaps can be found in Ingo's speech at a 1977 Harold Sherman ESP workshop titled "Psychic Warfare," which he also presented at the United Nations.

In his speech, Ingo addresses humanity's obsession with war and highlights the fact this preoccupation isn't confined to physical battlefields alone. A psychic war is brewing, he exclaimed, one in which those who wish to use psychic means to attack are countered by those using psychic means to defend.

He referenced the movie **Star Wars**, calling it an allegory for what is happening to us today, all around us, we are all under psychic attack and have no idea. He said forces are at work externally manipulating us. Calling to mind brainwashing where suggestions are enforced, no doubt as he himself had witnessed, through what he called "vicious and violent physical trauma," – MKULTRA? at the bases he and Price had psychically penetrated? – he went on to say these external manipulations were subtler than that. He said all around us subliminal persuasion was being used against us, an ongoing covert psychotronic mind control game. Because of that he said, "I am preparing a book on psychic warfare and psychic peace. My research has led me to understand that forms of mind control behavior modification are a multimillion dollar a year business."

In his book **Penetration**, Ingo wrote about the confirmed use of subliminal messages to manipulate public responses. These submerged messages could be used to either activate or deaden a person's reaction to any given issue. As he explained during an interview with radio show host Art Bell, one effective way to downplay the existence of UFOs, and other than human beings, is by creating social conditions that discourage people from even thinking about it. It's a subtle yet powerful tactic, he wrote, one that can effectively control the beliefs and behaviors of a large population without them even realizing it.

In my interpretation, his "disclosure" – possibly the continuation of the groundwork efforts that began in 1973 – via this speech means that a crucial part of his work at SRI involved manipulating the physical and cognitive environments of others. I firmly believe he was heavily involved in psychotronic weapons experiments, ones that could penetrate living organisms and solid structures alike. This is likely the true motivation behind his 1978 "science fiction" novel, **Star Fire**.

In fact, I believe Ingo used **Star Fire** to reveal numerous secrets. He touched on topics such as government mind control programs, secret computer databases used to store the consciousness of individuals for transfer into bioengineered beings in underground labs, organ, sex, and exotic weapons trafficking linked to a world-wide conglomerate, sadists intertwined within the US government, and most importantly, how his abilities – which exist in the inner realm or what could be called the quantum realm – were utilized for more than just Remote Viewing. The book was removed from shelves, deemed too revealing of the truth. But which parts were considered dangerously accurate? Or was all of it?

Knowing all of this, the question that occupied my mind was why the intelligence community was so focused on electronic, telepathic, and psychokinetic connections, namely in how such a connection might link with mass mind control; what were they truly trying to conceal? Possibly a hint to that lies in Puthoff's next action, something I find completely surprising.

In the early 1980s, Puthoff made the decision to give the Price files to Lt. Frederick "Skip" Atwater, who oversaw Grill Flame for the Army, to test them out. This baffling revelation begs the question – why would Puthoff, a highly respected physicist and a known skeptic of Scientology, willingly hand over materials related to alleged UFO bases the contents of which not only border on science fiction but also contain terms and references from the Church and quite potentially hold a significant piece of the religion's ideology?

As to a clue, we must deviate for a moment. It is interesting to note the company founded in 2017 by Puthoff, Blink-182 member Tom DeLonge, and retired CIA officer Jim Semivan shares the same name as Hubbard's 1950 sci-fi story, **To the Stars**.[103]

The name correlation sparks thoughts in my mind: 1) Did Puthoff never truly leave Scientology and instead go undercover for some mission involving Scientology and its belief in extraterrestrial beings? 2) Had he become part of a group within the secret machinery that manipulates information and uses sci-fi stories to cover up the truth? Or 3) Could it be that there are crucial pieces of evidence or notes from those "penetrations" that hold their own importance? And with that, did Puthoff have support within the secretive realm, perhaps in pursuit of disclosure

---

[103] John W. Campbell originally published Hubbard's story in two parts as a serialized format in **Astounding Science Fiction** in 1950. The first book edition of the story, titled **Return to Tomorrow**, was released in 1954 and later reissued as a hardcover in 1975 under the same title.

that he, Ingo, and Price had begun in the 1970s, which gave him the reassurance to reveal this information?

In my opinion, it is prudent to keep all possibilities at the forefront of one's mind and carefully consider each potential combination. Just because one option seems more likely does not mean the others are invalid. That's why I believe it's important to contemplate all probabilities when trying to form a comprehensive perspective, particularly when trying to understand Puthoff's motives[104] for sharing certain documents filled with esoteric ideas and details about thought-transferring aliens and implanting stations on Earth and Mars with an Army Intelligence officer whose main concerns were nuclear war with Soviet Russia and conflicts in the Middle East.

Returning now though to those papers. With the possession of Price's papers thanks to Puthoff, Atwater took charge and decided to challenge RV'ers with what he dubbed "advanced training targets" – a decision made outside the realm of the US Government. These tasks were specifically designed by Atwater himself to test and evaluate Remote Viewers, following strict protocols. In fact, it was Atwater, not Dames as suggested by Schnabel, who oversaw these exercises. This information was revealed when Atwater presented at a conference held by the International Remote Viewing Association (IRVA), where he discussed what he called Project 8200. The presentation's promo stated: "Project 8200 utilized the next generation of STAR GATE remote viewers in an attempt to verify or refute the information provided by Pat Price."

Yet, strict protocols demand feedback for confirmation of a Remote Viewer's success. This raises questions, specifically how can one verify or refute without feedback? Ingo himself wrote, "A 'viewing' (of a distant site or topic) cannot be said to have taken place until positive feedback indicates that it has taken place. This is the formal definition of professional remote-viewing in that unless positive feedback is achieved the 'viewing' must be held as occurring only in the mind or imagination of the alleged viewer." This suggests that some form of feedback existed for these sites.

Per the Project 8200 presentation, Atwater gave his first task in 1982 to ERV participant and former Grill Flame member, Chief Warrant Officer

---

[104] Personally, I believe this viewpoint should be extended/applied to any information circulating in the "contact" and "disclosure" arenas.

Joseph (Joe) McMoneagle (who specialized in altered states RV). McMoneagle successfully RV'ed the Price sites and added that there were more than four sites, including ones located beneath the seabed. What caught my attention was McMoneagle's mention of a significant power source present at Mount Hayes, repeatedly emphasizing the word "power" and describing it as "pulse amplified." He explained the power as being used for long-range communication in low frequencies, without the ability to be disrupted by jamming signals. He noted a sense of unease during the session but could not pinpoint why.

This struck me as uncomfortably like the intense energy used at Scientology's implant stations and electronic weapons that the US Navy showed a keen interest in, not to mention reminiscent of, the devices mentioned by Ingo in **Star Fire** and Persinger's findings.

Next up was McNear, a CRV trainee under Ingo. In May 1984, he was assigned to investigate one of the seabed sites. McNear wrote about an unusual sensation, describing people and an environment with electricity. He noted a secret connection between them, and a strong desire to avoid the place. Feelings of a prison and being trapped in a dark and gloomy place engulfed him so he took an break to clear his head. In the pages that followed, he drew a UFO emerging from the water and flying off into the distance, labeling it as a "flying saucer."

The sites were continually being assigned, with the next one in February of 1985, going to CRV practitioners Ray and Smith, both students of Ingo. During their RV visit to Mount Hayes, they discovered similar anomalies as described in the Price papers. Concerned his knowledge of the papers may have influenced them, Atwater gave the coordinates to Dames, who then enlisted former Grill Flame ERV practitioner and current CRV practitioner Mel Riley to Remote View the area. It seems that the group began using a combination of CRV and ERV techniques – with the former for locating targets and the latter for detailed information. This is significant because ERV relies on altered states and out-of-body methods, while CRV does not. Declassified documents mention two sessions conducted by Riley, with Dames as his monitor. The first session occurred on January 28, 1987, which was an extension of a previous session done in November of 1986; but these files were not part of those declassified by the CIA and instead were found in Atwater's personal files.

During the first Riley session, which took place between 1986-87, a declassified document labeled as "Description of Personnel Associated with 'E.T.' Bases" contained specific tasks for Riley to complete. These tasks involved traveling to Saturn's moon Titan, Mount Hayes in Alaska, and an undisclosed location in either South America or Africa.

During this Remote Viewing session, something strange occurred when Reily focused on Mount Hayes. He began to see images of robots and bizarre-looking people, followed by a tall, dark building that he felt like he was inside of. He described a platform and used words like "darkness" and "empty." Suddenly, he noted a strange sensation in his hand, as if it were being energized. The following drawings show a squiggly line that does not fit with the rest of his sketches, as if his hand had taken control and was creating on its own. He saw more people and then had a vision of zooming away in a vehicle into space. After that, there is no further information recorded. In additional notes, not included in the declassified set, Riley detailed the surroundings of Mount Hayes and where he went inside before zooming away into the darkness.

In the next session, which was recorded in the second declassified document a year later, Riley's task was to Remote View something referred to as the "Galactic Federation Headquarters." This session began similarly to the one from the previous year. He meticulously described and drew the surroundings, which appeared to be like those of Mount Hayes that Riley had sketched the year before. Both drawings depicted a mountain with a cliff platform on the left, a lake below, and mountain ranges to the right. Regardless, Riley believed he was somewhere off-world. As he ventured inside, he wrote "streaming down" and drew arrows descending through what he described as a tall, vaulted room. The arrows pointed down towards a body on a platform – his own body. He noted that place felt familiar. He climbed onto the platform and lay down, immediately being enveloped by a bright beam of white light that seemed to emanate from overhead. Then, a hooded figure approached from behind and stood beside him, with an outstretched hand hovering over his solar plexus. Suddenly, Riley broke away from the session with a strong sense there was something significant he should have remembered about this place.

It was obvious he was physically present in the room with Dames during all of the sessions. The real question is what happened to his soul, being, spirit, astral self, or consciousness? Something definitely occurred; he felt as though a part of him was taken somewhere and examined, not for the first time either since his memory from the previous experience had been erased. Despite this, Riley failed to make the connection between the two events. Still, his subconscious mind seemed to be trying to break through, as shown by his comments about something he should have remembered and the sense of familiarity in the place.[105]

As the RV program was hurtling towards declassification and discrediting[106] in the mid-1990s, it seemed like the UFO "situation" was not about to go anywhere. Under a hide it in plain sight methodology, I believe, on September 20, 1995, just two months before national attention would be drawn to the revelations about RV and nine days before The American Institutes for Research released their damning report on Remote Viewing titled "An Evaluation of Remote Viewing: Research and Applications," a businessman named Robert Bigelow launched a new venture called the National Institute for Discovery Science (NIDS). Despite being a billionaire investor with ties to the aerospace industry and military complex, Bigelow's NIDS flew under the radar as it focused on researching unexplained phenomena.

NIDS was established to investigate unexplained phenomena, with a focus on UFOs. After a few months, Vallée, then a full-fledged UFO investigator, joined NIDS and Puthoff, at that point known for his work on anti-gravity, also became involved with the group. In what I would deem a critical article, Jason Colavita discussed the decline of Remote Viewing and how government interest in UFOs and other paranormal activities may have faded if not for Bigelow's involvement.

In 1996, the year after NIDS was created, Bigelow purchased a piece of land in Utah that had a reputation for strange occurrences. This land became known as Skinwalker Ranch.

Ten years later, Senator Harry Reid helped secure $22 million in secret funding from the Department of Defense (DoD) for Bigelow's company,

---

[105] The CIA reading room, conjunction.world, and ingoswann.com's UFO/UAP page, all have documents that were previously classified but are now available to the public, detailing these Remote Viewing sessions.

[106] In Jim Marrs' **Alien Agenda**, Riley admitted that he began the RV project with hopes of discovering a new paradigm for researching UFOs and aliens. He thought he found it, a program had been meticulously developed over 24 years by a group of dedicated individuals, but unfortunately, it wasn't being used for its intended purpose. Instead, it seemed to have fallen into the hands of reckless individuals, a group Riley referred to as "space cowboys," who were using RV inappropriately. Additionally, Marrs noted that no one with knowledge of the CIA/DIA/Army RV programs has denied that UFOs and aliens were perceived by "all concerned."

Bigelow Aerospace Advanced Studies. This money was used between 2008 to 2011 to manage a program focused on studying UFOs and anomalies, including a specific study at Skinwalker Ranch. Some of this funding went towards researching aerial anomalies, while another portion went towards investigating speculative technology. The program fell under a subproject of the DoD called the Advanced Aerospace Weapons System Applications Program (AAWSAP) also known as the Advanced Aerospace Threat Identification Program (AATIP).

By 2011, Bigelow's government funding had dried up and in 2014, NIDS was shut down. Not long after, a **Vice** article titled "This Is the Real Estate Magnate Who Bought Skinwalker Ranch, a UFO Hotspot" reported that Puthoff and Green, who were still in the game apparently, consultants on a privately funded project involving gravitational physics and exotic propulsion, had suggested to one of the investors in their work, Brandon Fugal, that he purchase Skinwalker Ranch. The two had also been involved in the DoD study at Skinwalker according to Fugal.

They arranged for him to meet with Bigelow and discussions about the sale of the ranch began. In 2016, Skinwalker Ranch was officially purchased by Fugal's company Adamantium Real Estate LLC. This was followed by The History Channel launching a TV show called **Secrets of Skinwalker Ranch** in 2020. The show records a group of experts as they use various technologies to investigate reported UFO sightings and paranormal events on the property.

As I followed the series of events, it became evident to me how closely the show has been linked, from its beginning, to the worlds of Remote Viewing, UFOs, and three lettered agencies. In the larger picture, there was a more significant aspect to consider: in this captivating historical analysis, not once did anyone deviate from attributing this scenario to "aliens," and then, in the year 2000, Ingo drops a bombshell, he calls them human extraterrestrial cooperation bases. Could these bases be utilizing low frequency waves to infiltrate our brains, creating and controlling our behaviors and beliefs – reinforced by human actors operating to push narratives subversively? And so, did Ingo just expose the carefully guarded truth that had been meticulously obscured from the public eye?

No wonder he said, "No one can really diplomatically walk where even angels might fear tread." And why perhaps he urged us to develop what he called "telepathy plus something else," not for sending thoughts out, but for keeping them from coming in?

APPENDIX

LOURDES, FRANCE (1858)
As Excerpted from **The Great Apparitions of Mary: An Examination of Twenty-Two Supranormal Appearances**
(250)

INVESTIGATING THE PSYCHIC RUIN
As Excerpted from **Resurrecting the Mysterious: Ingo Swan's 'Great lost Work'**
(264)

Appendix

Lourdes, France (1858)
As Excerpted from **The Great Apparitions of Mary**

By 1858 the reputation of the great apparition at La Salette was twelve years along, and Emperor Napoleon III had been in power for ten years. Even though he exercised direct dictatorial power, and no one dared go against his will, to the surprise of many he was proving to be an inspiring force.

Under his management, France underwent rapid material progress. Railway building was encouraged, and rail networks for the first time began uniting the nation into an interconnected whole. Cities were rebuilt. Paris was redesigned by the emperor himself, and its now familiar wide boulevards and spacious parks were constructed under his direction. Napoleon authorized the first investment banks, the construction boom gave jobs to thousands, and the economy improved. Napoleon's foreign ventures were also successful at first, and the Second Empire seemed on its way.

Catherine Labouré had not yet died, and her complete story was not yet in the open. The reputation of La Salette seemed secure, and no one imagined that another apparition, even greater than the one at La Salette, would soon occur. The French were therefore astonished when, during February 1858, electrifying rumors began spreading that the Holy Mother was back again, and once more at a place few had heard of.

Lourdes is situated in the Bigorre region of southwest France on the northern slopes of the Pyrenees, the formidable mountain chain between France and Spain. The French side of the Pyrenees receives abundant rainfall and has always been famed for its beautiful scenery, rushing torrents called gaves, and abundant mineral waters. Many of the mineral springs had long been turned into fashionable spas at which the wealthy congregated, bringing money and employment. Yet poverty, even appalling poverty, was still everywhere.

The small town of Lourdes did not have a mineral spring and therefore was deprived of any hope of economic benefits. Even so, it seems to have been an idyllic town on the Gave de Pau joined by the Lapacca Torrent, on the opposite side of which were the hospital and school of the Sisters of Nevers.

On the frigid winter day of February 11, 1858, three young girls bundled in poor garments went outside of town and over a bridge to a rocky promontory at that time surrounded on all sides by the icy waters of the Gave de Pau.

They went there to search for sticks or brushwood to burn and discarded bones to cook into soup, although the area had already been picked clean by others before them. All three were suffering from severe malnutrition.

At the farthest west end of the promontory, but back across the smaller expanse of water, was a towering rock cliff called Massabielle. Into the rock was a quite large hollowed-out area, referred to as a cave or grotto, before which grew some brush and a nearly dead wild rose bush. The older girl went there to search for some sticks.

When the two other girls went to look for her, they saw her kneeling down before the cave, her face turned upward. They ran to her thinking she was injured. Instead they found her transfixed, her eyes dilated, and they were unable to move her arms. They started screaming in fear.

The transfixed girl was Bernadette Soubirous, in two weeks to become arguably the greatest seer ever – while the simple cave was to become the greatest and most majestic grotto in history. In twelve days the poor town of Lourdes, population less than three hundred, was to find itself stampeded by over twenty thousand pilgrims, and by fifty thousand more one month later.

The early years of Bernarde-Marie Soubirous; known to history simply as "Bernadette," comprise a tale of appalling and excruciating poverty. She was born on January 7, 1844, the first of eight children of Francois and Louise Soubirous, in the Boly Mill, where her father worked and in which the family lived.

When she was eight her father lost the sight of his left eye in an accident at the mill. Two years later, when Bernadette was ten, he was fired from the mill, from which the family was turned out, forcing them to live in increasingly impoverished circumstances.

The growing Soubirous family was helped out by a distant relative, one Sajous, a stonemason. He allowed them a ground-floor unit, a "stone cage sweating with damp," called "the dungeon" because it had once been the town's prison.

In 1855, a cholera epidemic broke out in the Bigorre region of the Pyrenees, and Bernadette was taken ill. Many died, but she recovered, although for the rest of her life she suffered from severe asthma. Famine also accompanied the epidemic. For a day's food the family often had to share one loaf or less of bread, or no bread, and a watery soup sometimes stewed from bones picked in the streets or from the surrounding countryside. Francois Soubirous, clearly desperate, was arrested for theft, but the charges were dropped.

The household now began suffering from such grim privation that the fireplace was perpetually unlit. Jean-Marie, the family's eldest boy, was caught going into the local church to eat the soft wax from the candles there and was threatened with jail by the prelate. By February 1858 the family was starving. Bernadette, often coughing and gasping for air, was fourteen. She could neither read nor write.

The apparition to Bernadette Soubirous is particularly well documented, indeed over-documented – which means there are many versions. Four versions, each slightly different in small details, were written by Bernadette herself, the first in 1861, after she had learned to read and write.

In her own words what Bernadette first saw was a "soft glow" about midway up in the cave which she had seen on two earlier scavenging trips. This time a "beautiful girl" appeared within the soft glow. When the beautiful girl beckoned to Bernadette, she "was frightened and didn't respond." However, all the sources agree that her two companions found her kneeling in a trancelike state. The two girls were one of Bernadette's sisters and a mischief-maker named Jeanne Abadie. The two girls managed to shake Bernadette out of her fixated state, and she told them what she had seen.

On the way home, Bernadette apparently met another sister and again recounted seeing the beautiful girl within the soft glow. The sister told their mother. Jeanne Abadie ran through the town with the gossip that Bernadette had seen a vision and was crazy. Various ladies of the town then came to inquire of her mother. Her mother was upset by the stories, and her father also became upset. Bernadette was forbidden to go to Massabielle again. And as a warning precaution, perhaps as a demonstration to the curious women, both girls "were beaten" by the mother for "telling lies." The following evening, though, Bernadette mentioned the matter to the priest at confession and asked him to tell Father Peyramale, the parish priest. Father Peyramale showed no interest.

By Sunday, February 14, somehow Bernadette had achieved her father's permission to visit Massabielle again with the first two girls. Seven more went along with them. But this time they went along equipped with holy water. Bernadette knelt before the cave, prayed, and shortly again saw "Aquero" – meaning "that one" in the local Bigourdan patois. This time she sprinkled holy water on the Lady, which apparently caused Aquero to smile.

At this point, Jeanne Abadie, who had climbed atop Massabielle over the cave, rolled a large rock down which crashed near Bernadette. By then, though, Bernadette had become frozen on her knees in an "entranced state" and no longer responded to her companions' cries.

The inability of the girls to awaken her caused them to panic. Two or more ran back to town, where they found the help of a local miller who returned with them and carried the oblivious Bernadette, "smiling at something no one else could see," back to his mill, where she slowly recovered.

Meanwhile, Jeanne Abadie again gossiped all over town. Bernadette's mother was now terribly upset and worried about her daughter's sanity. The predominant feeling in the town was one of disapproval, and on Monday after school, Bernadette was jeered and mocked in the street and slapped by a woman she didn't know for "putting on comedies."

But a prosperous woman, who sometimes hired her mother as a servant, intervened and under her influence it was arranged to take Bernadette back to the cave early the next day, Tuesday, February 16. This time Bernadette was provided pen and paper and would ask Aquero to write her own name down.

Early on Tuesday, Bernadette visited the cave for the third time, but now accompanied by a much larger group of silent people who jostled for vantage points on the edge of the river in front of the rock of Massabielle. Some of these witnesses carried rosaries, probably to ward off evil.

Bernadette knelt and assumed "ecstasy." No one besides Bernadette saw anything, but in spite of that two adults nearby asked her to be sure to get Aquero's name. In her ecstasy, Bernadette asked them to be quiet. After a time, Bernadette came out of her ecstasy, not having obtained the name.

When asked why, Bernadette said: "I did ask her. But she said it is not necessary." After some silence, punctuated by some grumbling from the gathered witnesses, Bernadette said: "But she asked me, 'Will you have the goodness to come here for fifteen days? I don't promise to make you happy in this world, but in the next.' "

The nameless apparition had spoken! And spoken of this world and the next! Thus began what is sometimes referred to as the "fortnight of apparitions" which were either fifteen or sixteen in number depending on which source is consulted. It is certain that the next apparition was the fourth one.

And it is also certain that when Bernadette again approached the cave, she was accompanied by a hundred or more people. As news of the apparition spread about, the whole population of Lourdes became interested, with a considerable "draw" from surrounding villages.

By the mid-point of this fortnight, the assembling crowd had grown to more than eight thousand, and at one point the crush was of such a magnitude that Bernadette had to be escorted by armed soldiers to the cave by then and forevermore to be called "The Grotto."

Interrogations of seers are part of the dramatic action of the apparitions, but those regarding Bernadette are so well recorded at length that I'll review them only briefly here.

One of the principal facts is that the cantonal vicar of Lourdes, Abbé Peyramale (described as austere, severe, and inflexible), remained aloof from the situation. He referred to Bernadette with "the deepest suspicion" and possibly encouraged the police to threaten her with prison for causing public disorder.

Thus, Bernadette's first inquisitors were the local police. After either the fourth or sixth apparition, Police Commissioner Jacomet ordered her brought directly to his house in the center of town. Most reports state that he found her modest, sincere, not grasping for money or attention, but otherwise "incomprehensible."

Sources provide different versions of the Jacomet interview, but these are largely contrived, since no one was present to write it down directly. It is agreed, though, that either in the first interview, or in the second interrogation, Commissioner Jacomet finally "lost his temper." He subjected her to "humiliating outrage" and finally prohibited the young seer from visiting Massabielle again with the threat of prison if she did.

However, the second Jacomet interrogation came to an abrupt end because of "angry crowds" gathering outside that apparently could hear Jacomet's shouting and began, hooting and demanding the release of the seer.

The next day, Bernadette "ignored the prohibition" and, accompanied by an even larger crowd, went again to Massabielle. But the apparition didn't appear. At the same time, the mayor of Lourdes defied the police prohibition when he realized the growing strength of public opinion in the seer's favor and when arguments also arose. In any event, at the sixth day into the apparition sequence, the town's civil authorities found themselves solely preoccupied with crowd control matters as pilgrims began pouring in.

After the ninth completely stunning apparition (to be described below), Bernadette was again summoned for interrogation, this time by the town's imperial prosecutor, a more serious business. But this interview didn't go very well, apparently because once confronted with Bernadette's "incomprehensible" answers and statements the prosecutor lost the threads of his arguments and became "flustered."

Again, the now vastly enlarged crowds outside demanded the release of the seer and furthermore jeered and ridiculed the prosecutor by broadly gossiping that he was afflicted by St. Vitus Dance (a trembling disease) and that the candles in his house had "lit up by themselves" while Bernadette was there. Shaken, the imperial prosecutor gladly released the child.

Subsequently, Bernadette was again summoned, this time by the examining magistrate and the regional commandant of constabulary from Tarbes, a nearby town. However, it seems that the central topic of this interview was not Bernadette herself or the nature of the apparition, but how to control the crowds which by now had begun to inundate the entire area around Lourdes and Tarbes.

The distance Father Peyramale had engineered between the apparitions and the church began narrowing as a result of the thirteenth apparition (on March 2) in which Aquero asked Bernadette to "tell the priests" that people were to come to the grotto in procession and that a chapel was to be built there. This was electrifying news in a situation that already had become highly charged.

To deliver this message, Bernadette, accompanied by two aunts, her mother's sisters, and a crowd of approximately two thousand ambling along behind, went to Father Peyramale's residence.

Father Peyramale did not like this delegation of three, because he apparently had once expelled the two aunts from the Children of Mary School after both had become pregnant before marriage. His anger so confused and intimidated Bernadette that she and the aunts left his presence before she remembered to give him Aquero's requests.

It was then decided to have a friendly sacristan brave the priest's wrath, and when the sacristan finally presented the Lady's requests to the priest, Father Peyramale was confronted with having to make decisions on behalf of the church.

Father Peyramale demanded that Aquero should give her name. Some sources state that he also demanded that she should cause the nearly dead rose bush at the front of the grotto to bloom at once in the wintry cold. Other sources omit reference to the rose bush or state that it didn't exist in the first place. The existence of the rose bush was probably factual, since mention of it is included in the early reports Jeanne Abadie spread through the town (that the Lady appeared above and to the side of it).

After the fifteenth apparition, however, it is almost certain that no evidence of it could be found largely because anything that could be taken as a souvenir had been snatched up by many of the eight thousand wanting a devotional memento. If the bush had bloomed, it would be certain that its flowers would have been snatched as relics, then its stalks and stems and even the roots.

Father Peyramale's request for the name was put to Aquero during the fifteenth apparition. Again, the name was not forthcoming. It's entirely likely, as many claimed, that Father Peyramale now smiled to himself regarding this anti-climax. In any event, he now considered that no church decisions regarding the apparition were needed and that Bernadette was at an end.

And, indeed, even though Bernadette returned to Massabielle daily the apparitions of the fortnight period now appeared to cease – to the great disappointment of the growing crowds. However, the dramatic action at Lourdes was by no means over with and indeed had just begun.

Popular opinion among the crowds had already decided that the identity of Aquero was that of the Blessed Virgin Mary. Bernadette had begun saying the rosary while kneeling at the grotto and said that Aquero asked for "Prayer for sinners." Who else could Aquero be than the Holy Mother?

Many in the attending crowds claimed they saw the Blessed Virgin at the site and "heard voices" from nowhere, and several children went into fits, ecstasy, or hysterics. By the fifteenth apparition, and in spite of the clergy's objections, the site had become utterly packed with votive images of the Virgin. Believers in the apparition were at that time still called "cultists" having "simple souls" (read "stupid souls"), and these numbered significantly among the crowds.

The cultists had lit vast numbers of candles at the site and left them burning, which the police of Lourdes and Tarbes considered a fire hazard. Even so, the environs of Massabielle "glowed very beautifully at night." Many had tossed money into the cave since there was yet no one in particular to receive it. Thus, the situation had begun to move out of the control of the town's officials and local clerics and pass directly into the hands of popular devotion. Among the arriving crowds were increasing numbers of educated and skeptical people (as distinguished from illiterate peasants and "ignorant believers"). The apparition was not being taken lightly.

But the apparition at Massabielle might have faded into history were it not for the critical ninth apparition during the fortnight period. The ninth apparition took place either on Thursday, February 25, or Friday the 26th. During that apparition, Bernadette unexpectedly arose from her kneeling position, but not from her ecstasy. She first turned away from the cave to face the Gave de Pau. A hush fell over the crowds, numbering at this point about three thousand.

She was seen momentarily to lookback at the apparition, which no one else could see, as if asking for instruction. She then shook her head in some kind of assent. She began to move again, but this time toward the cave, then slightly into it. She knelt at a dry spot and feverishly began digging with her hands.

Almost immediately some muddy water welled up in the shallow depression she had hollowed out. She drank some of this, washed her face with it, and plucked and ate some grass along the edges of the muddy hole. She stood and walked out of the cave with her face covered with mud and still chewing the grass. Some of the observers nearby started giggling, and others hooted that she had finally gone mad. Pandemonium ensued, with shouts to "Arrest her!"

Bernadette had to be escorted to a house on the rue des Petites-Fosses in town. It wasn't until reaching this safe-house that Bernadette said that Aquero had directed her to dig at the dry spot and to "drink and wash yourself at the spring and eat the green you will find growing there."

Later that afternoon, people arriving at Massabielle saw a new stream of water pouring down from the rock grotto and flowing into the Gave. Indeed, the flow increased as they watched. By the next day the spring was producing about twenty-five thousand gallons of clear, fresh water every twenty-four hours.

There was living in Lourdes a "simple quarryman," one Louis Bourriette. According to medical confirmation, he suffered from incurable amaurosis (he was going blind). Louis Bourriette asked that some of the spring water be brought to him. He bathed his blinded eyes with this water – and could see again, a fact confirmed by the town's doctor.

Early the next day this electrifying news inspired a woman, Jeanne Crassus, suffering for ten years from full paralysis of one of her hands, to go to Massabielle. There she dipped her crippled hand into the water for a few moments, and when she again held it up for all to see it had returned to a functional normal hand.

The news of these miracles spread like wildfire. A "roar of acclaim" began among the thousands of witnesses grouped at Massabielle. The ruckus soon spread into the town itself, where church bells began ringing. People were milling and shouting and sobbing in the streets, and the "commotion could be heard at some distance into the countryside."

There were riots at the cave as thousands tried to get at the water. More cures instantly took place. Police, now accompanied by soldiers, arrived to try to restore order. They were overcome by the crowds, and anyway most of them joined the masses attempting to drink the water.

It's quite difficult to comprehend how Abbé Peyramale and his canonical associates, the Fathers Pomian, Serre, and Pene, could have remained aloof from these cures. Yet they did, condemning them as "nonsense," and were assailed for this "stern viewpoint." The first cures, however, caused Father Peyramale to concede that Bernadette "must be honest" after all. But there was yet no theological issue involved, and the clerics remained uninterested.

But during the sixteenth apparition, on March 25, the feast of the Annunciation, an unavoidable religious issue entered into the dramatic events. On the morning of that day, Bernadette awoke very early with a "strong desire" to revisit the grotto. Her parents made her wait until 5:00 a.m., at which time she went along with her family and a large group following her. Bernadette had been to Massabielle daily since the last of the fortnight appearances, but during what is called the "three-week lull" the apparition had not appeared. This time Aquero did.

Although recorded details differ as to why, this time it seems that Bernadette was determined to find out who the Lady was. She put the following question three times to her. "Mademoiselle, would you be so kind as to tell me who you are, if you please?" Aquero began laughing. But when Bernadette repeated the question the fourth time, the Lady stopped laughing, smiled, and said in Bigourdan patois the thunderous words: "Que soy era Immaculada Councepciou."

At this, Bernadette immediately stood up and, with a large train of anxious people following her, hastily went into town repeating the words out loud again and again in order to remember them. Once in town she and a wide-eyed group burst into Father Peyramale's house. Bernadette looked up at him, he down at her, and she simply said: "I am the Immaculate Conception."

Father Peyramale was shocked, for here not only was there a religious issue, but a significant one, and it was one which he knew that the illiterate Bernadette could know nothing about.

This is a complicated, even a bitter issue. Since from at least the fourteenth century the dogma of the Immaculate Conception of the Blessed Virgin Mary had been a source of controversy. It was accepted that Jesus had been immaculately conceived, that is, from the moment of his conception he was sinless. The question was whether Mary herself had been immaculately conceived.

Appendix

The Lady had finally identified herself as the "Immaculate Conception" – which meant that she was, indeed, the Blessed Virgin Mary, Mother of the Savior, and Mother of the Holy Roman Catholic Church as well. There is no doubt that Bernadette understood nothing of this since its meaning had to be explained to her again and again – and she never fully understood its implications until after she entered the local hospice of the Sisters of Nevers, where she learned to read and write.

For some weeks the grotto had been barricaded by the frazzled authorities, not so much to discourage devotion, but to contain the sewage and public health problems brought about by thousands of visitors. An outbreak of cholera was a major concern.

No one really knew what to do about the site, and vigorous battles between the local authorities and cultists began raging about what should be permitted there. As soon as the spring began flowing and cures were reported, local craftsmen had devised a tank to contain the water equipped with outlet pipes, and a board for holding candles.

Crevices were designed in the grotto into which money could be inserted, then gathered and delivered – to the formerly reluctant Father Peyramale. Rosaries were said every day, and over fifty people had claimed to have seen the Virgin. As the cultists got out of hand, in early May the prefect of Tarbes threatened to arrest anyone "seeing visions" and incarcerate them. The police commissioner at Lourdes confiscated all devotional objects, and in June the grotto was boarded up, although the walls were pulled down several times by energetic cultists.

As these difficulties were proceeding unresolved, news of the appearance of the Blessed Virgin and the miraculous water had been circulated throughout France.

The difficulties were finally resolved by a chance occurrence. In mid-August, the imperial family was in summer residence at Biarritz, only some ninety miles from Lourdes. There the prince imperial, son of Emperor Napoleon III, then two-years-old, had "contracted dangerous sunstroke and the threat of meningitis from it."

The emperor, or more probably the empress, sent the imperial infant's governess to Lourdes, where she first interviewed Father Peyramale and then Bernadette. The governess then went to the grotto and in the emperor's name ordered the guards to fill a large bottle with water from as near the center of the spring as possible. This the guards scrambled to do. The royal infant was sprinkled several times with the water. He promptly recovered.

In October, Emperor Napoleon III, in gratitude, personally ordered the officials of Tarbes and Lourdes to permanently remove the barricades from around the grotto which was more than a hint not to interfere with public access to it.

In November a commission of inquiry was appointed by the bishop of Tarbes, whose hearings took four years to complete. In addition to the theological issues involved, the commission doubtlessly considered the emperor's decisive interest, the abundant offerings, and the growing sales of devotional images. The bishop's commission "from the first was deeply impressed" by Bernadette's sincerity and by her "authority and clarity of mind."

In 1862, Monseigneur Laurence, bishop of Tarbes published the expected conclusion:

> We judge that Mary Immaculate, Mother of God, really appeared to Bernadette Soubirous on 11 February 1858, and on subsequent days, eighteen times in all. The faithful are justified in believing this to be certain. We authorize the cult of Our lady of the Grotto of Lourdes in our diocese... [and] in conformity with the wishes of the Blessed Virgin, expressed more than once in the course of the apparitions, we propose to build a shrine on the land of the Grotto, which has now been acquired by the Bishop of Tarbes.

The bishop's document also proclaimed seven of the cures that had taken place in 1858 to be miraculous. Media response, already great, now became enormous.

In 1862, Achille Fould, a Jewish financier and former French minister of finance, purchased an estate near Lourdes which he intended to develop. He quickly convinced the Southern Railway Company to extend through Lourdes and his estate the railway under construction from Tarbes to Pau.

In this way, the poor citizens of Lourdes found themselves directly linked by rail to the rest of the continent – and linked to sources of income forevermore. Organized pilgrimages could now arrive by train, which they did in increasing numbers and have done ever since, and these pilgrims required hotels and restaurants and other amenities.

Appendix

In this way did the greatest healing shrine in European history arise. Thousands of cures have taken place there, although only sixty-four had been officially recognized as of 1970.

While the commission was studying the matter in July 1860, Abbé Peyramale and the mayor of Lourdes prevailed upon the mother superior of the hospital and school of the Sisters of Nevers to take Bernadette in as a boarder.

She was sixteen and still "as ignorant as a baby in the cradle." She thus left her family in some grief a very proud family which, ill provided as they were, refused to accept any form of assistance, except for the healthier house arranged for them by the Abbé.

At the hospice Bernadette had to see many visitors, for inquiries and investigations were going on. The sisters were amazed by her humility and her strength during fatiguing interviews. This seer behaved as a proper vehicle of the Holy Mother should.

She increasingly suffered from asthma attacks, and in the spring of 1862 her lungs became inflamed. As Extreme Unction was being performed she opened her eyes, demanded water from the spring, drank it – and was cured.

She was later transferred to the motherhouse of the order at Nevers over three hundred miles to the north of Lourdes where, as Sister. Marie-Bernard, she remained in humility and obscurity until her death on April 16, 1879, at thirty-two years of age. In the same year, Napoleon's only son, the former prince imperial, nicknamed "Loulou," was speared to death fighting for British interests in the Zulu wars in Africa. He was twenty-one years of age.

Bernadette's body was exhumed for the first time on September 22, 1909. It was found incorrupt, and the process of beatification began. It was again exhumed on April 3, 1919, 40 years after her death, and found in the same incorrupt condition – except for slight discolorations of the face which were corrected with preserving wax.

The body was then placed in a glass coffin and for many years could be viewed by the faithful and sightseers in the chapel of the motherhouse at Nevers. In 1933, she was canonized as St. Bernadette.

In 1906, the grotto and basilica were confiscated from the bishopric of Tarbes by the French state, and in 1910 ownership of it was transferred to the municipality of Lourdes. The first papal visit to the shrine of the apparition of Our Lady of the Grotto at Lourdes took place in 1982.

Conjunction.World

The most famous healing shrine in the world, long since a vast and splendid place, is annually visited by over fifteen million people.

Appendix

Investigating the Psychic Ruin
As Excerpted from **Resurrecting the Mysterious**

Our present concepts of psychic realities, psychic culture, the psychic mind, psychic awareness, psychic abilities, and so forth, are rather fragile constructions built upon an enormous cultural psychic ruin.

It might be helpful to imagine this ruin as a great ancient city that was deliberately destroyed in the past. When parts of the city began to reconstruct themselves, these too were destroyed. This destruction is also taking place today.

This is the most difficult part of this book to write because a finger of accusation must be pointed at the past and present destroyers of the psychic culture in order to throw light upon the disgusting history of psychic destruction. Accusation is always explosive. People get upset and defensive. Upset and defensive people can be very unkind.

Yet no neophytes who have embarked on the path of psychic realization can get very far along on it unless they also realize the larger scope of what they are dealing with. Many beginners adopt the idea that if you ignore negative, destructive affects they will eventually dissolve – that if you even *think* about them, you are feeding them energy. This has to do with an idea that in so ignoring these affects, one is somehow withdrawing their perpetuating energies.

This is sheer psychic lunacy. Yet it is a mistake many beginners do make. It is, for example, being made in our present time by certain prominent New Age thinkers who appear to be depending upon the stability and endurance of our present democratic rights and freedoms. If these mistaken thinkers would examine the social fabric a little closer, they could perhaps espy the many little trenchant totalitarianisms that are flourishing within it – any one of which could flare up at a moment's notice and destroy what totalitarianisms most hate: a resurgence of psychic realization, a resurgence of the truly free and of those liberated from the thrall of humanoid existence.

In what follows, the reader should bear one factor in mind: it is not the way or path of psychic realization to accuse but rather to acknowledge that what is indeed *is*. The urge-force to destroy the growth-principles of psychic realization is not something that belongs to the particular individuals, sects, religions, or sociopolitical machinery *through which the destructive urge-force flows*.

The psychic way is to acknowledge the existence of the destructive urge-forces for what they are, identify *their* dangerous life-units, sources, and centers, and plot a course of development around them. A psychic neophyte gains no real powers of psychic realization and liberation until something like this has been accomplished – after which the beginner is no longer a beginner but a true worker and walker on the path of psychic realization.

There is one slight problem attached to all this. One has to become slightly psychic and partially develop one's powers of psychic realization in order to be able to correctly *perceive* the destructive urge-forces for what they are. Without this initial development the incarnations of the destructive urge-forces will probably look like rational things and the psychic neophyte will continue to exist as a victim or slave to their thrall – for the incarnations of the destructive urge-forces are excellent veil-weavers.

Descriptive accounts of this overall situation leak into culture in literature and art. One of the most recent to accurately portray it occurred with the famous movie **Star Wars**, in which the character of Darth Vader represented the destructive urge-forces, and Obi-Wan Kenobi the achieved psychic master and the psychic neophyte.

Culture is a thing of shifting sands reshaped by winds of fad and fashion and storms of destructive change that develop and manifest in the humanoid level of psychic activity.

Appendix

Life – the greatest psychic principle that is – and its energies are subject to these fads and fashions and storms of destructive change when the great powers of life and its energies are themselves not realized for what they are.

The roots of our present Western culture, as told in history books, are Greco-Roman, Judaeo-Christian, with massive inputs from Arabia that led to the formation of the Renaissance. This led, in turn, to the Age of Enlightenment and the Age of Reason, which loosened the totalitarian grasp of the Catholic Church. To this we must add the Industrial Age, a great destructive change that altered everything ultimately for the worse, and the Age of "Rational" Science that (despite its many positive gifts) at its apex of glory brought into existence the atomic bomb, after which there now follows the Nuclear Age.

At present (and for the last hundred years), our Western culture is absorbing many "New-Age" Eastern cultural factors from India, Tibet, China, and Japan under the completely mistaken conception that these factors represent higher forms of "spirituality." This is such a gross error. And, of course, a lie that has already wrapped veils around many minds.

The Eastern factors are actually psychic philosophical systems that include body management systems (various Yogas), body-mind integrating systems (various Yogas), mind-management systems (various meditations) and psychic realization systems (various techniques than activate and enhance the will and psychic abilities). Hardly anything in these systems equates to what the Westerner conceives spirituality to be.

Prior to the advent of the immense flare up of Pauline Christianity during the first and second centuries AD, the Judaeo-Greco-Roman cultures appear to have been based on philosophies that conceived of existence quite differently from subsequent Christian accounts of them. The ancients (by "ancients" is meant peoples and societies existing prior to the advent of Pauline Christianity) were capable of conceiving of both material (physical) *and* non-material (psychic) aspects of existence as well as the various life energies and forces they perceived as existing *within* each of these realms.

They personified these energies and forces as "divinities." To the ancients, however, the definition of this word was quite unlike the connotations and meanings it subsequently came to have in Christian times. For the last thousand years in our Western culture, definite *religious* Christian connotations have been attributed to the word *divine*, particularly in that these connotations referred to a (one) supreme deity, heaven, godlikeness, and supreme good, and most importantly, in that none of these are integral parts of humans who were cast down in the original sin of Adam and Eve. Humanity must seek salvation, i.e., purify themselves of sin through belief in the Saviour.

To the ancients, however, divinity referred to the qualities of universal energies and forces whose primeval abode was the intangible, non-material cosmos, out of which these energies and forces were reflected in the tangible material realms, specifically but not only in mortal men and women. The material realms were conceived of actually as the past and present <u>products</u> of the workings of the intangible, invisible, nonmaterial forces and energies.

Essentially, the cosmos *thought*. In fact, it thought many thoughts, and each thought set invisible energies and forces in motion, congealing each of them into a semi-solid state still invisible and intangible, but becoming thereby a life-unit – a divinity – emitted by the cosmos. The near-solid, tangible state of these life-units composed the material universe and all physical things in it.

Our modern quantum physics and the new post-quantum physics – hard sciences, both of them – today are theorizing much the same state of affairs. As a result, one of the most important revolutions in how humankind must correctly view the universe is now beginning.

To the ancients, the human being was composed of both visible (physical) and invisible (non-physical) energies and forces through which the divinities "worked" and "expressed" themselves, while, at the same time, being a reflection of themselves. These divinities (energies and forces) could work in harmony (peacefully) with each other or in disharmony (antagonistically) with each other. The divinities were seen neither as "good" nor "bad," but as states of activity that existed, had always existed, and would always exist.

As already mentioned, these divinities were personified (via symbolizing, verbal picturizing, and artistic rendering) by the ancients into a tangible form deemed suitable as an adequate reflection of their invisible qualities. Although these personifications were venerated (i.e., regarded with reverential respect or with admiration and deference) often through rituals, they were almost never religiously worshiped (as we understand *that* word today) through a creed and with extravagant, unilateral deification.

Appendix

The ancients, in fact, tended towards tolerance of and respect for each other's divinities, understanding that whatever the form the different sociopolitical groups chose to represent *their* favourite divinities, the divinities nonetheless represented universal energies and forces. As universal energies and forces, any pictorializing of them showed great similarities no matter the names attached to them, and these similarities were recognized. The major divinities appear still to be alive and well today in the collective unconscious, as revealed by the famous psychologist Dr. Carl G. Jung in his profound book **The Archetypes of the Collective Unconscious**, first published in 1959.

Naturally enough, the ancients set up temples dedicated to this or that divinity at (sacred) sites that seemed to possess certain characteristics or on sites upon which momentous human achievements were attained that appeared to reflect the energies or forces of a given divinity. The purpose for doing so was to honor the divinity *and* to try to obtain from the divinity a continuation of the energies and forces that had at one time manifested on the site.

But the most famous temple sites of the ancients had a totally different and astonishing function. Considering the fact that the ancients understood that the universe was composed of invisible energies and forces that manifested, ultimately, in tangible, physical form, there was a great desire to learn beforehand what these energies and forces (divinities) had in mind.

The ancients appreciated the fact that the divinities revealed themselves and their "purposes," "goals," and "desires" in dreams and that in dreams many psychic scenarios were played out in advance of coming realities. To a limited extent, we understand today that the invisible energies and forces of humanoid psychology *as well as* larger invisible factors do *reveal themselves through dreams*. The ancients established many "sleep" temples whose specific task was to decode dreams.

The ancients also appreciated clairvoyance of many kinds since good clairvoyants could foretell the future as well as "see" at a distance what was happening in present time. Another type of psychic giftedness appreciated by the ancients had to do with augury, meaning to foretell, especially from omens (augury will be detailed later on in this book). Today, history remembers with disdain only two general types of augurs: astrologers and those who "read" entrails (guts of animals, especially chickens). There were, however, many types of augurs (foretellers).

But by far the most important individuals were those who had well-developed psychic abilities by which they could "attune" themselves to the divinities' energies and forces (i.e., could communicate with the divinity or be channeled through by the divinity).

Such an individual (called an oracle), demonstrating a good and long correct track record of accurate foretelling, became individuals of enormous renown and the sites associated with where they lived and worked became even more famous. As this track record grew, so did the importance of the location where the seer lived. The greatest temple sites of antiquity were always those at which a seer-oracle (or a group of successive oracles) lived and worked. Such sites attracted various aspiring oracles who underwent training and eventually replaced deceased or worn-out oracles. Many oracular sites operated for a long time through several "generations" of oracles. When an oracular site failed – that is, when the oracular predictions began to become increasingly inaccurate – they were gradually abandoned in favor of different, more accurate oracles.

The ancient historian, Herodotus, who lived ca. 484-425 BCE, tells that the most ancient oracular site in antiquity was that of the Pelasgic Zeus at Dodona in inland Epirus (Greece), which was, in turn, connected to the oracular site of Ammon in Libya through a brotherhood of priest-oracles. Dodona was founded on a high spot during the deluge by the Deucalion people who took refuge there from the waters. This is the same deluge recorded in the **Bible**, as well as in (among others) the mythology and traditions of the Indigenous peoples of the Americas, Fiji islanders, and Australian Aborigines, and in some ancient paintings still to be found in Mexico.

The Columbia Encyclopedia indicates that archaeology has yielded little trace of the biblical flood, but stories resembling it are found in the record of Berossus (third century BCE) and on a tablet of the Gilgamesh epic of at least 2000 BCE. It is possible that the world myths in agreement that the deluge did occur are more reliable than modern archaeological methods.

It is quite probable that the deluge did occur before the rise of the first of the Old Kingdoms of Egypt (3110 BCE) *after* the construction of the Sphinx, which bears marks of severe water erosion but well before the building of the great pyramids, which do not show any trace of water erosion.

Appendix

The minimum antiquity we can consider for the inauguration of the oracular site at Dodona is thus 3110 BCE – which is to say that Dodona, which was destroyed and abandoned circa 220 BCE, had existed for at least nearly three thousand years.

The oracular site that is remembered best in our conventional history is the one at Delphi in Greece, which earlier had been called Python. Myth holds that it was first the site of the divinity Ge (Earth) and her daughter Themis, who spoke oracles there before the divinity Apollo took possession of it. Experts argue whether the myth is true or not. In any event, for over a thousand years the Delphic oracle was a going concern during which, one succeeding another, the incumbent oracles (Pythias) of Apollo spoke oracles to those who consulted them.

In the modern world of scholarship and research that digs into classical antiquity, opinions about the veracity of the oracles are deeply divided. With regard to Delphi, the most negative of these opinions (the "rational" opinion) holds that the Delphic priesthood managed to keep its many clients (thousands upon thousands of them) satisfied from some prehistoric date to the fourth century AD with a mixture of coincidences, lucky guesses, ambiguities, and judicious interpretations. To believe this, one would also have to believe that all the ancients were incredibly stupid, highly impressionable, infantile dunces having barely evolved up out of the mud.

Nothing seems further from the truth. No one would dare call, for example, Alexander the Great an infantile dunce. Rather he was incredibly clever and insightful. He so appreciated the Delphic oracle's answers to his questions that he built shrines to Apollo wherever he and his conquering legions went.

On the positive side, many oracular researchers are so impressed with the marvelous prophetic skills exhibited at Delphi that these scholars have recourse to psychic powers as the only possible explanation of the phenomena, an opinion that probably more directly corresponds to the ancient realities.

Possibly we shall never really know exactly how the ancients viewed their oracles. Any direct links we may have had with them were, as we shall shortly see, expertly and purposely destroyed. But generally it seems that the ancients were practical men and women living in a tougher world than the one we inhabit today. Their psychic-materialistic outlook (it was neither philosophical nor religious as we use those words today) was rooted in some prehistoric forms of shamanism (shamanism will be discussed later). It is clear they conceived of the cosmos as having both physical and non-physical counterparts. It is clear that they *experienced and realized* contact with the non-physical energies and forces through the means of dream-visions, omens, signs, pronouncements of seers, oracles who voiced the divinities, and statements that the divinities made directly to mortal men and women.

They possessed, therefore, some sort of "idea" that there existed a vast psychic matrix of energies and forces *in which the future was being formed ahead of present time*. It was this future they desired to find out about. There is hardly any other reason to consult an oracle or to interpret a dream vision or an omen – whether this has to do with "Will my plantings grow well this year?" or "Which side will win the war?" or "When will earthquakes and the plague next come?"

Basically, then, the ancients possessed a philosophical outlook that incorporated the invisible, psychic nature of reality – and did so quite seriously judging by their literary remnants and art and architectural wonders constructed solely to reinforce the psychic quotient of their times and places.

None of the above has been told to create the idea that the ancients possessed an ideal way of looking at things or, in fact, of living. Their sociopolitical segments were always in continuous uproar. Even their history, as represented through great art, architecture, and literature, is also marked by pride, passion, revenge, political intrigues, and territorial acquisition.

We can only wonder (and it is worth-while doing so) what human consciousness would be like today if the psychic orientations and realities of the ancients had had the opportunity to fully develop and mature. Alas, this was not to be – for the psychic world view of the ancients (and therefore the ancient psychic heritage of the cultural West) was to be snuffed out as a result of the arising of the cruel monarchy and totalitarian hierarchy of the Pauline Christian religion. Afterward nearly two thousand years had to pass before humanity could feel relatively free to again begin to reconnect to its own psychic nature.

The belief that Jesus founded Christianity has been generally accepted by Christians for almost two thousand years and any claim to the contrary has been considered a serious heresy. In a certain sense, it does not truly matter who founded Christianity. It arose, had its long day in history, and cut its wide swath in many cultures throughout the world.

Today, the future of its main sociopolitical structure, the Catholic Church, is indeterminant. Its hierarchical structure is out of phase with developing humanoid consciousness. Its tenets are being contrasted to other life-supporting tenets found in sources other than Christianity. What will happen will happen.

Many prophets have predicted that its final days are increasingly near.

However, if neophytes on the path of psychic revelation and realization are to survive, they must have a grasp of the anti-psychic sentiments that lurk in certain forms of humanoid consciousness. Christianity as a whole, especially the inquisitional Catholic Church up until near the beginning of the present century, has been the most significant suppressor of psychic consciousness until this dubious position was overtaken by our modern materialistic science.

I think it is fair to state that Jesus was not of the anti-psychic mentality that infects so many other types of humanoid consciousness.

As a Pharisaic Jew, He came from a long line of prophets and as the **Bible** tells (probably quite accurately), psychic revelation and realization were greatly respected in the ancient culture to which He belonged. If "The Gospels" can be taken at face value, these four biographies of His life establish quite clearly that He was an achieved psychic of the superhuman type.

However, the actual origins of Christianity are very obscure, obscured not only by the passage of centuries, but probably very deliberately obscured by the authorities of the early Christian Church. Recent scholarship has shed some light on the origins of Christianity. It is quite probable that Paul, not Jesus, was the founder of Christianity. As a result, many of the structural ideas that came to prevail in Christianity emanated not from Jesus or from his other disciples, but from the mind of Paul and *his* disciples.

It is known in fact that Paul was not a Jew of Pharisaicalee upbringing as he claimed, but came from a Hellenistic Gentile background. Whereas, also known in fact, Jesus and His immediate disciples, Peter and James, were lifelong adherents of Pharisaic Judaism who founded the so-called Jerusalem Church based upon guiding principles laid down by Jesus. Paul was eventually disowned by Jesus's disciples.

Among other scholars, Hyam Maccoby, a Fellow of Leo Baeck College, London, specializing in the relationship between Judaism and Christianity, has given compelling evidence to support his claim that it was Paul alone who created a new religion through his vision of Jesus as a divine Saviour who died to save humanity.[107] Paul's concept – which went far beyond the messianic claims of Jesus Himself – was a blend, an interbreeding of ideas borrowed from several Hellenistic religions, especially from pre-Christian Gnosticism and various mystery cults.

Through several existing, if garbled, other-than-Christian accounts[108] of Jesus's and Paul's times in which both are mentioned, a character study of both can be constructed.

Jesus is revealed as a man of prophetic talents who simply sought to play an accepted role in an existing religion, Judaism, and certainly did not wish to create a new religion.

Paul is revealed to have been a tormented adventurer, threading his way by guile through a series of stormy episodes and ultimately setting up a form of religion that was his own individual creation.

As Hyam Maccoby correctly points out, no religion is based primarily on a theology. First comes the story. Then, when the fires of passions and imaginations about the story have died down, along come the theologians who try to turn the story into a *system*. The system then becomes the religion.

The story Paul created (perhaps only borrowed) can be stated in a few words: humanity is caught up in the powers of evil and rescue has to come from above. This rescue depends on the descent of the divine Saviour.

This story is much the same as that found in pre-Christian Gnosticism, although Gnosticism later took Christian forms. The essence of the Gnostic myth is that the world is in the grip of the powers of evil. This world is regarded as so evil that it cannot have been created by the true God, but created by an evil power called the Demiurge. Escape from this evil can be achieved only through the descent of messengers from the world of Light in order to impart secret knowledge (*gnosis*) by which a privileged few might *escape* (i.e., be saved) from the evil bondage.

---

[107] See **The Myth-maker: Paul and the Invention of Christianity** by Hyam Maccoby.
[108] Editor's note: Perhaps Ingo is referring to **The Antiquities of the Jews** by Flavius Josephus and Tacitus's **The Annual of Imperial Rome**.

Appendix

There is evidence that concepts similar to those of pre-Christian Gnosticism had been incorporated into Judaism. Many ancient Jewish writings have a sense of cosmic evil. But rather than dividing the dualism of good and evil into an extraterrestrial kingdom of God (good) and an earthly kingdom of humanity (evil), Judaism held that the battle between good and evil is within the human psyche. The Jews did not need a saviour from an upper world in order to make human life more viable. In Judaism, the power of evil is broken through the practice of the **Torah**.

In a very direct sense, the division of the universe into only two powers – the duality of good and evil – is an intellectual exercise if for only one reason. Good and evil are only relative values dependent upon circumstances. Yet the intellectual exercise rather naturally demands the establishment of what is the ultimate good and what is the ultimate evil. Since intellectual exercises can readily (nay, almost eagerly) unhinge themselves from reality and trek into myth and fiction about what the ultimate good and ultimate evil are, the intellectual exercise is capable of producing a great variety of ideas that propose to give definition to good and evil – even definitions that are quite insane.

Pre-Christian Gnosticism, Judaism, and budding Pauline Christianity – each seeking to divide cosmic powers into the duality of good and evil – were, then, essentially different from the plurality of the divinities of the ancients. There can be little doubt that the ancients saw some of their divinities as more benevolent or less benevolent. But it appears that the reason for the plurality in the first place was because of the recognition that the divinities were not only *representatives* of powerful cosmic energies and forces but actually *were those energies and forces*. These same energies and forces worked in harmony or collided in the cosmic, supernatural realms, but also, in smaller dramas, within men and women – which is to say, the humanoid psyche.

The ancients, then, saw the cosmos as being composed of manifold energies and forces that, more or less, were equal and that moved in rhythms and in ways that only a truly ascended psychic master might hope to identify.

These manifold energies and forces were not dominated (ruled) by one super-god. No such distinct super-figure was needed since all the energies and forces together *were* that figure.

On the other hand, the reduction of the universals into the duality of good and evil requires the introduction of such a super-figure, who will decide what is good and what is evil and establish priesthoods that would pronounce the will of this super-figure in these matters. It would, therefore, transpire that such a dualistic religious sect eventually would come to the point of claiming that their religion possessed the one true super-figure, thus in their eyes making their religion the *one* true religion.

When this religio-sociopolitical configuration began to manifest in the ancient world, the time of the ancient pluralistic divinity cultures was near its end. The "one god, one religion" intellectual calculation could not possibly tolerate any pluralism and still maintain any self-respect. Furthermore, when such a religion began to get systematized by its theologians, it was certain, eventually, to dawn upon their mentalities that the only way to hold converts was to ensure that nothing else existed that might tempt the converts away. The "one god, one religion" concept also demands the establishment of a sociopolitical pyramid to administer its affairs with a "top man" at the apex, and descending orders of "priests" and subservient workers and – eventually – an army of one kind or another to defend territory (physical and mental) gained and to police the system internally.

Naturally, those outside the evolving religious system might come to view it as a threat to their own ways and preferences, especially if and when the system turns militant or potentially militant.

There is little in history to substantiate why and when anti-Semitic sentiments arose, yet it is known that an intense dislike of Jews was not uncommon in the ancient world. It might be assumed that the theological postulates of the Jews probably did not interest others in the pluralistic divinity cultures of the ancients. Save for one item: that the Jews believed in the supremacy of only one God – *their* God – and that Israel was the election of that God, which is to say that they themselves were the *only* elect people of that God.

However, a radical strain of anti-Semitism can be traced to pre-Christian Gnosticism[109] (and subsequently to some later sects of Christian Gnostics) that was very potent and traces of which, unfortunately, are still being exhibited today. In these sects, the Demiurge (evil) was closely identified with the God of the Jews and it was believed that the ***Torah*** was

---

[109] Israeli philosopher and historian Gershom Scholem once described Gnosticism as "the Greatest case of metaphysical anti-Semitism."

given by this evil deity. The Jews were, in other words, the representatives of cosmic evil – the people of the Devil.

It is, of course, one of the first *duties* of any neophyte on the path of psychic realization to *rise above dualisms, especially those of good and evil, as well as above the dualism of materialism and spirituality.*

In a very precise sense, dualisms are products of false intellectuality. The first great liberation, as it were, is the one that "lifts" humanoid psychic consciousness out of itself and into superhuman psychic consciousness from which all things can be seen in their relative and *manifold* importances. No one can judge anything accurately from within an intellectual dualism. It is a particular effect of intellectual insanity to believe one can do so. Intellectual consciousness, by itself, cannot effect this liberation. Only psychic consciousness at the superhuman level can achieve it. Superhuman psychic consciousness is "equipped" to see through dualisms – in fact, even through pluralisms.

This point is seldom lost on religious systems of the pyramidal one-god-one-religion type. Good and evil are judged simply and easily. Good consists of faith-acceptance of and obedience to whatever theological principles are adopted *and* what supports the pyramidal structure. Evil consists of anything that lies outside the theological principles and, more specifically, any person, motive, belief, or action that does not support the pyramidal structure.

It is well worth while here to point out to the neophyte that a religion can be called a religion only if it possesses a one-god-one-religion theology *and* a pyramidal superstructure set up to try to maintain its purity and integrity. Many other so-called "religions" are not religions at all. For example, Buddhism has no such theology or superstructure and is, rather than a religion, a way of life. Almost none of the ancient cultures possessed theological superstructures, and the divinity "cults," although ritualized, were more akin to "psychic schools," as well as being ways of life.

In fact, Judaism itself is technically not a religion despite the presence of one god and a figurative pyramidal structure whose top-man position is not occupied by a human but by the *Torah*. Judaism is a way of life, the essence of which is mitigated and instructed by the accumulated wisdom of the *Torah*.

At this point, it is perhaps best that we should remind ourselves why we are trudging through this rather lengthy history. The reason is that certain anti-psychic forces exist in humanoid consciousness and that those forces, which exist today, can best be identified when placed against the historical epochs in which they manifested. These existing anti-psychic forces are a danger to the neophyte on the path of psychic realization whether the beginner realizes that such is the case or not.

Understanding now that when the term *Christian* is used, it is referring to Pauline Christianity and not the Jerusalem Church of Jesus and His disciples, we can continue now with our story of the destruction of the ancient psychic arts and crafts (a cultural loss of unbelievable proportions).

There is almost nothing in conventional historical records that completely explains why Christianity should have arisen in the first, second, and third centuries AD to become the dominant cultural force in the West, later extending into many other parts of the world.

However, an astrological-psychic reason can be advanced for those who are prepared to consider it. This has to do with the precession of the equinoxes – the idea that the psychic (invisible) energies and forces of existence are divided into twelve great periods conforming to the signs of the zodiac,[110] and that approximately every two thousand years existence shifts clockwise (backwards) from one astrological sign into the next.

The division of the phases of existence into these twelve periods is so ancient that its actual roots disappear into the depths of vast, pre-flood antiquity.

The two-thousand-year period preceding the beginning of the Christian epoch was "under" the sign of Aries. Before that had been the epoch of Taurus, and before that (lost in prehistory) the time of Gemini.

Some serious preparation is required to comprehend what these signs of the zodiac imply. But generally speaking they have to do with how reality is originating itself and how and in what forms it will manifest.

Because Aries is the first sign of the zodiac, it stands for the original cause, the initial impulse through which the potential (non-material) becomes actual. Aries is understood to be the centre of the cosmic energies and forces (physical and non-material), out of which manifestations realize and achieve themselves.

Pluralism and the toleration of it is "natural" to this sign. It talks of cosmic energies and forces (in the plural) that emanate from an

---

[110] Editor's note: See Ingo's article "The Perils of Erasing Astrology from the Past" on www.chaosastrology.net.

undifferentiated center. Since this center is undifferentiated, it is conceived as neither singular nor plural but simply undifferentiated.

An undifferentiated "something" is quite alien to our Western comprehension in which everything must have a "form" if it is to exist.

But it seems the ancients could and did conceive of undifferentiation and the subsequent manifestations of energies and forces that emanated out of an undifferentiated "source." The pluralistic psychic divinities of the ancients, as well as their general mode of worldview during the two-thousand-year pre-Christian period, do "fit" with the "aspects" of this sign – Aries, whose outer symbol is the head of the Ram.

When the "manifesting" of the undifferentiated whole began its "movement" from Aries into Pisces, a great shift in the forms of the manifestation could be expected. And, indeed, such a great shift occurred, as we well know.

In fact, the original signs, symbols, and manifestations of Christianity clearly, and beyond any doubt, epitomize its close relationship with the zodiacal sign Pisces – whose symbol is the Double Fish.

It is well known that the earliest sign of Christianity was the fish. In fact, when Christianity was being seriously persecuted by the Roman Empire, the fish was the secret code sign by which Christians recognized each other. One traced the outlines of a fish in the sand with one's staff. Any other Christians present completed the Double Fish sign by tracing the outlines of the other fish. The fish appears in much of early Christian art and iconography, clearly relating Christianity's psychic orientation to the energies and forces of Pisces.

What are the "aspects" or "expressions" of the manifesting energies and forces of the astrological Pisces? Modern astrology gives many positive psychic qualities to Pisces that, when compared to ancient, traditional attributions are dubious and some of which do not exist at all. The ancient attributions, coming from an epoch that could and did tolerate pluralisms, are very important when compared to astrological interpretations coming from a period that could and did not tolerate pluralisms.

In his book **The Dictionary of Symbols**, J. E. Cirlot indicates that Pisces, the twelfth sign of the zodiac, when transposed by analogy to the psychic plane, signifies mysticism and the denial of the self and its passions. Further, its manifestations are those of failure, defeat, exile, and seclusion. The keynote of the Pisces psychic-manifestation is the dissolution of all forms that have preceded.

The Pisces of the ancients was closely related and is still related to the Vishnu of India. In Horace Hayman Wilson's translation of **The Vishnu Purana**, we can read, "Who can describe him [i.e., Vishnu], who is not to be apprehended by the senses, who is the best of all things, the supreme soul, self-existent; who is devoid of all the distinguishing characteristics of complexion, caste, or the like, and is exempt from birth, vicissitude, death or decay; who is always, and alone; who exists everywhere, and in whom all things exist. He is the supreme lord, eternal, unborn, imperishable, undercaying; of one essence, ever pure and free from defects."

In this description of Vishnu-cum-Pisces, we can clearly realize a description of the Christian God as well as the Western concept of spirituality. All along Christians have been worshiping through Christ, the Saviour, an ancient Indian divinity – only one of the many in the Indian pantheon of divinities.

In the Piscean epoch, the psychic energies and forces dissolve all things and seek the pure, unadulterated state of the central undifferentiated cosmic center through which to be reborn anew. In a "higher" sense, this means one thing to an achieved psychic master. However, in any lower sense (as when assholes take over the concept) it will mean something else. Intellects will, in the lower sense, almost certainly conceptualize and theologically personify the idea of one god in whose name all the "un-pure" may "justifiably" be destroyed.

Here, then, in the lower form of the psychic energies and forces of Pisces, we can readily espy the essential dogma and archetype of Christianity as it ran its course from approximately the second century AD through the eighteenth century. Vestiges of this archetype are still alive and well.

Astrologers have a fun and furious time of trying to ascertain when one astrological epoch (age) begins and ends. Prior to the Exodus from Egypt, the ancient Jews entertained a respect for many divinities, this well within the ancient pluralistic and Aries-inspired tradition. However, when Moses experienced the "new wisdom" on the mount, he came down and declared that "thou shalt have no other gods before thee." It is clear he foresaw, in a direct, prophetic psychic sense, the ending of the pluralistic-divinity Age of Aries and the commencement of the one-god Age of Pisces.

Appendix

The followers of Moses were quick to respond to their prophet. They disencumbered themselves of their ancient pluralistic heritage and established the Mosaic tradition. This sociopolitical move wielded them into a unified people. It is probable that this move saved Judaism from suffering the same fate its sister ancient cultures experienced when Christianity rose to phenomenal power and commenced its unparalleled destruction of those cultures.

The Christian message was that Jesus, the Saviour, had descended as the Son of God to save not only individuals but the world itself from evil. The appeal of this almost unadulterated Piscean message to certain types of intellects is not lost because we can still see it operating today. The only major ancient sociopolitical life-unit to withstand being overthrown by this new religion was Judaism. The Roman Empire, arguably perhaps the most powerful sociopolitical life-unit that has ever existed in historical times, itself did not withstand being overthrown by Christianity.

The idiocy and cruelty of the Christian sociopolitical system and its hierarchy was soon to be evident (this blanket condemnation certainly does not include all individual Christians, many of whom managed to carry on with a benevolence that was, indeed, Jesus-like). From at least the third century AD well into the eighteenth, Christianity built its dubious "glory" upon a path of unparalleled carnage. This carnage was justified by the general assumption (and this a lie of enormous proportions and abysmal results) that anyone or anything not Christian was evil.

For the first three hundred years of its existence, Christianity was, according to Christian historians, persecuted and in hiding. We shall probably never know the true extent of the claimed persecution since later Christians destroyed any records they could find that were not flattering of them.

We must remember that the first Christians existed in a multi-culture of pluralistic divinities that, however tenuously, on the whole respected multiple divinities. It is understandable, then, that the Christians began to raise great hatred toward themselves with their message of a singular God that did not propose to respect other divinities. Their physical persecution, however, began not because of their unilateral theological stance but because of a rather silly thing.

In the Roman Empire, it was common and expected that all sects would burn incense before the Imperial Purple. This act demonstrated "allegiance" to the state. The Christians refused to burn incense. When the mentally unhinged Emperor Nero ascended to the Imperial Purple, he took great exception to this refusal. Some persecutions began out of which intense propaganda has been made throughout the centuries.

The Christian strategy was to continue to infiltrate the state and they did so until the last great Roman Emperor, Constantine I (ca. 288-337), decreed the Edict of Milan, which established the toleration of Christianity throughout the empire. Constantine moved the empire's capitol from Rome to Byzantium (renamed Constantinople) and was baptized a Christian on his deathbed. This set of events allowed Christians to begin to come out of hiding and the many bishops to begin consolidating the power of Christianity.[111]

As the result of a severe illness in 380, the Emperor Theodosius I (ca. 346-395) was baptized Christian. Under his direction, the First Council of Constantinople (381) cast the Nicene creed practically into its present form and anathematized as heresies all other doctrines. The days of any possible toleration were at an end and the Christian Age of Piscean destruction began in earnest. In another edict of 392, Theodosius forbade all forms of what were henceforth to be termed paganism, which included, in particular, the divinities of the ancients, oracles, and any form of divination or future-seeing and any connection to or utilization of psychic giftedness. This edict effectively closed the door to all the psychic heritages of the ancient past and placed all future psychic manifestations in dangerous jeopardy.

The anti-psychic tradition had begun in the West.

The ancient oracular sites, some having endured for thousands of years, were brick-by-brick, stone-by-stone leveled to the ground. Libraries were burnt and leveled. Sects were extinguished through massive genocides (the deliberate and systematic destruction of racial, political, or cultural groups). This policy of extermination continued well into the 16th century, when the ruthless total destruction of the Incas of Peru and the Aztecs of Mexico was accomplished by the *conquistadores* Pizarro and Cortes of Christianized Spain.

While conventional history focuses primarily on the material aspects of this carnage, not only material artifacts were destroyed, but also the minds of humanoid consciousness – which is to say, the psychic orientations of consciousness. To locate, identify, and destroy these

---

[111] See **The Catholic Encyclopedia**.

psychic orientations, a special process was ultimately required by the Church militant and triumphant. In seeking to guard the Christian faith from any psychic insights that might reveal its severe limitations and abysmally narrow outlook on life, the Church instigated what was to become known as the Inquisitions.

Basically, the inquisitors were empowered to enquire into what individuals were thinking and to correct it if possible – which meant, in the last analysis, to persuade (often through torture) the heretic to reform his or her mind-set again in conformity to Christian dogma. There is little doubt that the Inquisitions got out of control due to a very weak structure of responsibility to superiors. Matters of faith were probably resolved without too much violence, but psychic matters (i.e., psychic intrusions) were handled differently. Psychics were accused of being witches and burnt even after they recanted and promised to desist their psychic activities.

The list of these inquisitional atrocities is abysmally long. The most significant of these destructions was the Albigensian genocide. The Albigensians (i.e., inhabitants of Albi in southern France) comprised numerous people during the eleventh to the fourteenth centuries. Their beliefs were, apparently, semi-Christian, Gnostic, Manichean, Paulician, and Bogomilian. In addition to these beliefs, they apparently also believed in reincarnation, and practiced telepathy, prophecy, and out-of-body travelling. They were subjected to several waves of inquisitional ardour (the Albigensian Crusade). In one last vast carnage, they were killed down to the last man, woman, child, and baby – extinguished.[112]

Eventually, as we shall now see, the waves and events of great psychic change were to catch up with the unadulterated negative side of the Piscean Christian epoch. The wisdom of the ancients included the reality that no energy or force can stay crystallized for very long. Change is inevitable. There is no such thing as an eternal moment, much less an eternal kingdom. Humanoid psychic consciousness often phrases this as "time moves on." But the developed superhuman psychic is more likely to phrase this as "the eternal energies and forces are changing their outward manifestations."

---

[112] See **Inquisition and "The Cathars": Heresy and Authority in Medieval Europe** by Edward Peters.

The Inquisitions of the Catholic Church were forced to dwindle and be abandoned by outer non-Christian pressures. During the 18th and 19th and into the 20th centuries, only a remnant (the Index) of them remained which had to do with what literary works could or could not be read by Catholics.

However, the long, trenchantly enforced anti-psychic sentiment of Christianity became, as might be expected from its duration and pitiless enforcement, a phobic fear (a negative conditioned response) in the psychic systems of humanoid consciousness in the cultural West.

The backbone of the unilateral Christian dominance of the human mind was broken by two cultural developments that heralded the next great shift in astrological psychic energies and forces, the shifting and recrystallizing of these energies and forces from those of the Piscean Age into those of the Aquarian Age.

The first of these developments is known in conventional history as the break between religion and science – yes, yet another dualism. But the roots of Western science lay in the roots of humanism which itself was a backlash against the long dominance of Christian totalitarianism. The original humanist impulse had to do with releasing the minds of individuals from the cloying, cruel forces of the Christian hierarchy, and it succeeded in accomplishing this goal in part.

However, the new humanistic thought was not as free as it envisioned itself to be. When it departed from Christian totalitarianism, it took with it certain Christian traits. Unfortunately, major among these was the anti-psychic phobia long built into humanoid consciousness by centuries of Christian programming.

Since humanism was the fundamental "Earth" upon which scientific scrutiny could erect its eventual scientific edifice, this anti-psychic phobia – perhaps unknowingly, perhaps not so unknowingly – was installed as part and parcel of scientific "dogma."

In the scientific systems, any psychic phenomenologies are referred to as "irrational superstition" and are rejected or attacked (persecuted) with an alacrity reminiscent of the inquisitional "splendors" of Christian dogma. Humanism can be as non-humanistic and science as non-scientific as was the Emperor Theodosius when he unleashed the powers of destruction upon the ancient "pagans."

It is worth pointing out here that anti-psychic humanistic scientific thought is the virtual "ruler" of our present Western culture. It would be a mistake for any neophyte on the path of psychic realization to assume otherwise.

The term *humanism* will be used often throughout this book, so it needs to be understood. A softened-down description of humanism can be found in *The Columbia Encyclopedia*, in which it is said that humanism was, at its outset, a term used for a point of view that probably originated among men of thought during the Renaissance. The application of the term implies that men were now interested in humanity and the humanities – that is, humankind became the chief study of thinkers. This is supposed to distinguish the new thought from that of the Middle Ages, when there was not much interest in the individual but in certain abstractions such as religion, God, and so forth.

But actually humanism was a general uprising aimed at breaking the totalitarian domination of thought long held by force and through terror by the Christian hierarchy. If humankind were to be able to think freely again, it must first, somehow, reduce the power of Christian totalitarianism in all matters. One of the great desires of humanists was to study scientific matters (i.e., the realities of the physical universe and of mind – psychology). The arising of science and humanism thus go hand in hand and it is near impossible to study the origins of humanism and science separately from each other.

At the outset, then, Christian dogma and humanitarian enlightenment thus were not mere opposites as many have thought, but rather foes in competition for the "mind" of humanoid consciousness. This is an important distinction, especially if one views some of the products certain low-life sects of humanists (there are over fifty recorded varieties of humanism) have produced, for example:

- **communism** whose own inquisitions have tortured and dispatched over 250 million people;
- **self-interestism**, which has shattered the interconnectedness of the human fabric;
- **individualism**, which has detached individuals from each other to such a degree that "individuals" feel themselves to be in prison, with a tendency to go psychotic;
- **moral relativism**, which has seriously reduced, perhaps utterly destroyed, the sense of human responsibility and caring in whole societies; and

- **nihilism** (the doctrinaire viewpoint that traditional values and beliefs are unfounded and that existence is senseless and useless) – that peculiar psychological death-beneath-death syndrome that unhinged the minds of many humanist types during the first half of the twentieth century and has left a dreadful heritage among the educational systems of the West.

These examples represent only a few of the disgusting fallouts of humanism after the first nobility it had achieved during the Renaissance had disappeared into the dustbins of mere intellectualisms. None of these fallouts would have been possible had humanism incorporated *the* primary humanistic and humanising factor – that the human so much valued in humanism is not just an "evolved" animal but also a complex *psychic* entity possessing (if only latently) superhuman powers.

But, as we have seen, humanism adopted the trenchant anti-psychic stance of "spiritual" Christianity and (it can just as well be said also) of the more materialistic forms of Judaism. When one speaks of our Western Judaeo-Christian culture, one is actually speaking of the Judaeo-Christian-Humanistic culture – and, basically, the whole mess is devotedly anti-psychic.

Through its minions in science, humanism (in some of its various forms) is actually the real "theological" ruler of the West today. Since this real ruler is also anti-psychic, it is imperative that the neophyte on the path of psychic realization should have at least a minimal understanding of its essential nature.

Each of the various humanisms is usually based upon a set of tenets (usually called manifestos) that propose to be guidelines for how human life is to be viewed and considered. These tenets are specifically not drawn from long experience, since humanists distrust, if not detest, the experience of the Christianized religious (superstitious) past. Instead, these tenets are drawn from the "minds of human beings" since it is a general humanistic belief that humans themselves can better design a set of accurate, fresh life-tenets that do not perpetuate the "mistakes" and "superstitions" of the "religious" past.

Not rooted in past, tried-and-tested experience, the manifestos are based upon a proposed "ideal" human scene and are thus always utopian in nature. Which is to say, they are dream-visions. After a manifesto has been established, the next step is typically Western. Humanists then set about implementing the tenets of the manifesto by destroying all that stands in the way of achieving the utopian dream-vision – a strategy clearly carried over from Christianity, which did the exact, same thing. The grossest form of this implementation came about as the result of the Communist Manifesto, which called for no less than complete and total world revolution and the deliberate destruction of anything that might impede the achievement of the utopian dream-vision envisioned in that particular manifesto.

The various humanisms, then, are sets of utopian dream-visions. Since their basic manifestos are comprised of tenets *not* rooted in past, verified experience, they are instead fantasies, frequently of the crudest types of pseudo-intellectualisms.

Humanists psychologically support themselves and justify their actions by claiming to be *empirical*. This term is, in our present culture, a very important term and very meaningful to the beginner on the path of psychic realization. It has three important definitions: relying on experience or observation *alone* often without due regard for system and theory; originating in or based on observation or experience; and (this is especially important) capable of being verified or disproved by observation or *experiment*. *Empirical*, then, means direct observation.

BUT! The question has to be asked: observation of what *by* what?

This is a question that humanists have consistently failed to ask themselves.

Having as a first priority the rejection of the psychic components, not only of the "human being" but also of the entire cosmos, the humanists relegated themselves to "observing" only the material, physical universe. In fact, the term "empirical science" is equated with "material science," and it is within this "science" that humanistic observational capabilities are, as it were, presently trapped.

But a far worse error has been made and poor Earth is suffering from the results of this error today.

The combined physical and psychic entity called "the human" can really only "observe" what it can comprehend and this has been proved to be the case beyond any shadow of doubt. When the psychic observation systems of the human are shut down, that human is psychically *blind* exactly like the visionless are blind and the deaf are deaf.

As we have seen, humanism rejects the psychic components of the human and the cosmos. As a result, the humanist has not only perpetuated the closure of all the humanoid psychic systems begun by the one-god-one-religion schema of the Piscean Age, but has reinforced this closure within its own sciences.

The humanist scheme for "observation" must then rely *only* on the capacities of intellect as the seat of observation.

As we all know, intellect is a tool for processing what is being observed, and this tool is only as good as what has been programmed into it.

A given intellect may be as piercing as a bolt of light or as dense as a swamp (they are usually the latter). But one thing is for sure: there is no consistency of the powers of intellect. The same "bit" of observational information is processed differently among billions of intellects depending on the scope and peculiar characteristics of programming, state of alertness, or state of torpor. Intellect alone, therefore, represents just so much mental quicksand.

To get past this quicksand, the humanist typically appeals to what is called "reason" or "rationality." Whatever falls outside reason or rationality is termed, by humanists, as *the irrational*. Yes, here again is – another dualism. And as we must have realized by now, dualisms are the fatal flaws in Western thinking: the "either-or" syndrome.

Humanism could be dissected further, but at this juncture its anti-psychic nature has been established. The neophyte on the path of psychic realization will find him- or herself surrounded on all sides by the encultured barriers of humanistic reasoning. When these barriers are encountered, they must be realized for what they are. Otherwise, the beginner, early on, will be defeated.

However, the situation this represents is not as serious as the one-god-one-religion syndrome, though this one humanist anti-psychic factor is dismal and could prevent or delay the psychic reawakening of humanity for quite some time.

The reason this humanist development is not *totally* serious lies in an event of major proportions that occurred in the eighteenth century.

For many people, the American Revolution of 1776 is history and many do not comprehend the enormous shift in consciousness that occurred as a result of it. First of all, the American Constitution and Bill of Rights (the first major products of the Revolution) guaranteed individual rights in a fashion that many humanist sects have abjectly failed to achieve. Granted, these American individual rights may often be felt to be tenuous, but in essence they are upheld by law.

Second, the American revolutionaries reactivated and restored two important traditions of the ancients that were lost as totalitarian Christianity rose to its phenomenal power: democracy and a toleration for "the plurality of divinities" (called in the Constitutional language "freedom of religion").

While it is true that America is otherwise composed of forces that would, if left to themselves and able to empower themselves, seek to suppress democracy and religious freedom, the Constitutional law of the land has actually been maintained as operational for now just slightly over two hundred years.

Americanism is closely identified with these qualities and great care should be taken to remember what these basic qualities are. The American Revolution represented an almost unparalleled shift towards benign consciousness that had been near-extinct for a very long time.

A New Age for humanity thus began in 1776 and not in 1985. Americanism is the great leveler of totalitarianism. Any so-called New-Ager who cannot acknowledge this, or forgets this, is frankly an idiot, and a dangerous one at that.

Today, people are looking forward to the New Age – styled the Age of Aquarius. It is being conceived of as an age of renewed spirituality.

This conception is probably erroneous in the extreme if not only because of the self-limiting factors of how we in the West define spirituality as the antitheses of materialism – which definition, of course, as we have seen above, is pseudo-intellectual garbage. Our present Western conception of spirituality is quite inferior to what the nonmaterial energies and forces actually represent.

The symbol for Aquarius is the ancient sigil (sign) for water. All ancient Western and Eastern traditions relate this sign to the Flood, which may be interpreted as representing a physical flood or as representing a symbolic "flood" among the non-material (psychic) energies and forces of the psychic cosmic consciousness.

Either interpretation portends a rather tough scene ahead since both senses represent the end of a formal universe by the destruction of the power that holds its components together.

In a strict sense, then, Aquarius represents the imminence of liberation through the destruction of the world of phenomena.

Since the psychic (non-material) energies and forces of the cosmos "reveal" themselves in recognizable realities, the psychic qualities of the Age of Aquarius have begun to reveal themselves. The neophyte on the path of psychic realization must <u>realize</u> that the times of psychic energies and forces can be recognized by their "signs."

In the Aquarian sense, then, the following signs have occurred:

- The American Revolution of 1776 destroyed the power that bound totalitarianism potentials together and thus "destroyed" that phenomenal power. The last major holdout of totalitarian power is, of course, the Soviet Union, and its "power" is beginning to unravel rapidly.
- The discovery in the late nineteenth century that materiality was but a superficial construct built upon manifesting non-material forces not only began to restore the ancient cosmic view of existence, but is, at present, beginning to "create" a "new" reality of how the cosmos and its many universes "operate." This is, of course, quantum physics and the New Physics of the 1980s. This century-long acquisition of "new" knowledge effectively "destroyed" the totalitarian hold materialism had maintained since at least the Age of (materialistic) Enlightenment and the Age (secular and humanistic) of Reason, which were mainstreams of thought of eighteenth- and nineteenth-century Europe.
- The most obvious "sign" of the Age of Aquarius, however, was the advent of atomic theory, which ultimately manifested as the atomic and hydrogen bombs. This sign clearly demonstrated that any and all phenomenologies could be destroyed.

The Age of Aquarius is thus somewhat beyond its period of initiation and the signs of dissolution of existing forms are all around us. And it is from the worlds of phenomenal forms that the Aquarian individual must seek to liberate him- or herself. The only way to achieve this is to call forth the psychic superhuman life-units indwelling in the worlds of phenomenal forms – i.e., the resurrection of the psychic person.

This rather naturally posits a new Flood of Consciousness, and the signs show that this has begun and is picking up steam today. This also posits that the psychic person must consciously "work" towards achieving the higher qualities of Aquarius. This means, as a first step, rising above the dualities that trap human psychic consciousness in a destructive "flood" of uncontrolled consciousness.

To bring anything like this off, it is patently clear that the psychic levels of the physical body, the humanoid entity, and the superhuman realms *must be* opened up, realized, and achieved. In the absence of this effort, it is awesomely probable that the "negative" side of Aquarius will manifest in convulsions of a terrific "flood" of upheaval.

The Piscean Age failed utterly to manifest *its* higher qualities and, practically from its outset, descended into what can only be called Piscean gangsterism.

All good prophets make fair warnings. The Aquarian person has a peculiarly difficult task ahead. Be warned. All ages overlap and often rudiments of the passing age get incorporated into the New and cannot be recognized for what they are.

CLOSING THOUGHTS

As far as can be seen today by researchers of antiquity, anyone who consulted an oracle (or sought interpretations for omens, signs, and/or dreams or a seer for pronouncements) almost always did so for practical reasons – *which* is to say, for some help in *realizing* why and what was happening, had happened, and was going to happen and how to act or not to act when the events of the future came to be.

People who consult psychics today (and those who have done so throughout history) almost always do so for much the same practical reasons. But today such activities are decidedly fringe activities sneered at by the main structures of our culture, which is unable to integrate its own psychic components. In antiquity, the psychic components of existence were well integrated and, in fact, constituted the main infrastructure of all ancient societies.

Individuals consulted the invisible energies and forces (divinities) as well as did representatives of cities and city-states. In ancient times, cities were separate sociopolitical units, kingdoms within themselves and the rulers (and peoples concerned) were naturally very interested in the well-being and future fate or destiny of their cities.

SUMMARY

The ancients were comprised of diverse groups of cultures that had formed in the wake of a great, wet catastrophe that is universally referred to in ancient writings and myths as the Flood or the Deluge.

The cause of this flood is unknown. The exact date of this flood is unknown, but several factors would date it somewhere between 9,000 BCE and 11,000 BCE and others would place it even nearer in the past rather than farther.

This Deluge destroyed civilizations, a fact that is affirmed in all ancient records and myths, and even in the **Bible**.

Thus, simply put, civilizations existed *before* 10,000 BCE.

Conventional history has sought to establish that the Egyptian civilization was the largest, oldest post-Flood civilization. The earliest known post-Diluvial *date* marks a calendar in use in pre-dynastic Egypt in 4241 BCE. But it would be ridiculous to assume (as some have) that Egypt was the *only* oldest civilization. It built the largest monuments and its dry climate allowed for the preservation of its cultural artifacts.

The "consciousness" of the ancients was clearly built upon what we, today, call animism and shamanism. Animism is a "system" of reality-recognition. It observes that within every object dwells an individual psychic energy or force that governs its existence. In our present historical times this individual psychic energy or force has been mis-defined and misunderstood as a "spirit." These energies or forces were expressions of a nonmaterial, transcendental "something" that pervades the cosmos.

In our Western languages, we do not have an equivalent word for this "something." The Melanesians of the South Seas refer to it as "mana."

The animism of the ancients did not distinguish between animate and inanimate objects or between physical and mental processes. Everything was thought to have its own individuality. Humans, animals, plants, and stones, as well as emotions, dreams, and ideas alike, were regarded as having indwelling psychic energies and forces. In this present book, all these will be referred to under the general term of *life-units*.

The term animism is applied to the idea (i.e., intuitive realization) that the principle of Life, the transcendental "something," cannot be reduced to the mechanistic laws of physics and chemistry, but is separate and distinct from matter.

Appendix

Shamanism differs from animism only in that animism is a "general theory," whereas shamanism involves the idea that certain people can link into *communion* with the indwelling psychic energies and forces and life-units of all "things." The purpose for doing so is to bring some control into them, divert negative forces and facilitate creative energies, foresee the future, and so forth. A shaman, then, is an embodied, developed psychic, an intuitive connector (so to speak) between the visible, tangible realms and the invisible, intangible realms. Essentially, there is no such thing as shamanism since a shaman is not a special *idea* of or *belief* in how things exist but is always a psychic *person* who facilitates the various psychic "realities" associated with the interconnected, invisible energies and forces, of which the universe of matter is just one manifestation.

The various ancient cultures called these invisible energies and forces divinities and personified them in forms that were artistically and psychically correct for them. It is misleading to call these divinities gods or goddesses because of the peculiar ideas developed of God during the last two thousand years. The divinities of the ancients were not theological models upon which a universal theological theory could be built.

No ancient man or woman would think of subscribing solely to one divinity. No, the cosmos was interconnected by multitudes of non-material energies and forces, and each worked in their own way all together forming a "whole." The idea that only one divinity would dominate the others and *remain dominant forever* was ridiculous.

To try to get some semblance of a correct idea of what the ancients meant by "divinity," we can turn our attention to money, which in our present culture has come to be personified (symbolized) by the dollar sign: $.

In our culture, money has been elevated to the status of a divinity. Its outer symbol ($) signifies a large grouping of invisible energies and forces that work together to bring into existence its physical manifestation (i.e., cash in hand, diamonds around the neck, or gold stashed in safe boxes).

Intuitive money-makers, which is to say, money-makers possessing a few developed psychic life-units, are the only money-makers who ever make lots of money.

To support and enhance their money-making potentials, they are known to consult oracles of all kinds (statistics, projections, futurologists, public opinion, prophets [psychic and otherwise], seers, and astrologers).

Money ($) is an example of a splendid, modern divinity whose chief "temple" is the New York Stock Exchange, with lesser "temples" throughout the world. This divinity is acknowledged as possessing and controlling substantial numbers of invisible energies and forces. It is treated with all the traditional pomp and circumstance the ancients would have given to one of their own divinities.

But money, the main divinity of capitalism, is also acknowledged as only *one* of many other possible divinities – such as the weather, war, peace, Hollywood, human rights, republicanism, the atomic bomb, terrorism, the Democrats, and *PUBLIC OPINION*.

Basically, a divinity is anything that possesses invisible energies and forces that, on a necessity level, have to be accommodated, dealt with, tolerated, controlled, out maneuvered, or gotten out of the way of. The best way to achieve any of these necessities is to get a glimpse of *how they are going to act*, which is to say, a glimpse of the future. The only way to achieve this glimpse is through *psychic revelation*, either one's own or through another psychic.

It is clear the ancients viewed their divinities in this manner since the backbone of most ancient cultures was not worship of divinities, but centers in which the will, direction, plots, and plans of the divinities could be learned. Psychic centers in which augurs augured, seers saw, and oracles oracled.

The only basic difference between then and now is that then the ancients correctly assumed there was an invisible cosmos, in which non-material energies and forces worked in harmony or disharmony and that the "cosmos" of matter and humanity was infused with these same energies and forces, and were in fact their "outer" expressions and manifestations.

Today, through recent discoveries in the New Physics, the existence of this non-material universe has only just been confirmed. And the cutting edge of reality realization now is aware that this "new" non-material "universe" cannot be explored with material tools, but will ultimately have to be explored and revealed – yes – *psychically*.

Psychic abilities, psychic explorations, and psychic prowess were systematically destroyed and eradicated during several centuries in which the lower, destructive forces of the Piscean Age ruled through the front of the Christian Church.

Appendix

The passion, vehemence, and zeal with which these destructive forces went about their rampages brought into existence a new divinity – a humanoid psychological and psychic scar entitled *the Fear of the Paranormal.* The name of this new divinity is *Psychic Skepticism.*

Humanism and science incorporated this divinity and appended it to their new god – material science – and its dogma that answers to everything will ultimately be found in materialism and in materialism alone.

During the reign of the Piscean Negative forces, all psychic explorations and phenomena were forced underground if they were to survive at all. This gave rise to another new divinity – the occult sciences which are most accurately defined as the "hidden" psychic arts and crafts.

The rebirth of psychic consciousness studies can feasibly be attributed to Freud and Jung *and*, importantly, to Velikovsky,[113] as we shall see shortly.

But, actually, that credit should go to the physicist James Clerk Maxwell (1831-1879). In 1873 he observed that the universe was probably not material at all, but just one big *thought.*[114]

At any rate, the only major frontier humankind faces today is the consciousness of humankind itself.

So far, most consciousness researchers have been approaching consciousness research as if it was not psychic at all. Unfortunately for them and their allegiance to humanistic, anti-psychic science and the divinity Skepticism, consciousness is primarily a psychic thing.

All of the above, represents a two-thousand-year history in the West dominated by "religious" forces that were clearly and deliberately anti-psychic.

These anti-psychic forces enacted the lower, negative qualities of the zodiacal Piscean Age.

---

[113] Russian scholar whose works centered on reconstructing the events of ancient history believing that mythology and legend should be interpreted literally.

[114] Called the physicist's physicist, Maxwell's set of four equations explain the science of electricity, magnetism, and light. Einstein acknowledged that he stood on the shoulders of Maxwell.

But the Sayer of Tales said: I can't stay. There are places to go and things to see. But your own minds' eyes can see their own tales if you let them – and can see more than tales if you let them also.

Ingo Swann, **Purple Fables**

BIBLIOGRAPHY

"Advanced Threat Assessment Technique." CIA-RDP96-00787R00050001-2.

Albanese, Catherine L. A Republic of Mind and Spirit: A Cultural History of American Metaphysical Religion. Yale University Press. 2007.

Alberty, Erin. "Severed heads tell a violent mystery at Utah's Dry Fork Canyon petroglyphs." The Salt Lake Tribune. https://www.sltrib.com/artsliving/outdoors/2017/09/12/severed-heads-tell-a-violent-mystery-at-utahs-dry-fork-canyon-petroglyphs/. 2017.

"American Society for Psychical Research." Psi Encyclopedia. https://psi-encyclopedia.spr.ac.uk/articles/american-society-psychical-research.

"An Analysis of a Remote Viewing Experiment of URDF-3." CIA-RDP96-00791R000200240001-0.pdf

Anderson, Kristen. "The Hat Man Is a Shadow Person Who Will Keep You up at Night." Hunt A Killer. https://members.huntakiller.com/blog-articles/2020/12/20/the-hat-man-is-a-shadow-person-who-will-keep-you-up-at-night.

-- "The Hat Man: What's This Shadow Person Got Under His Cap?" https://chillinkristen.medium.com/the-hat-man-whats-this-shadow-person-got-under-his-cap-863c0a12f95c. 2019.

Angebert, Jean-Michel. The Occult and the Third Reich. Macmillan Publishing Company: 1974.

"Any connection?" A sub-reddit discussion linked to @aliens. https://www.reddit.com/r/aliens/comments/192znfk/any_connection/.

Arcane School. Encyclopedia.com. https://www.encyclopedia.com/science/encyclopedias-almanacs-transcripts-and-maps/arcane-school.

"Aos Sí." Wikipedia, The Free Encyclopedia, Wikimedia Foundation. https://en.wikipedia.org/wiki/Aos_S%C3%AD.

Atwater, Skip. "Project 8200: The Untold Story." Presentation at the IRVA Conference, 2009.

Bader, Christoper. "The UFO Contact Movement from the 1950's to the Present." Chapman University. 1995.

Bibliography

Banias, MJ. "This Is the Real Estate Magnate Who Bought Skinwalker Ranch, a UFO Hotspot." Vice. https://www.vice.com/en/article/m7qxyx/brandon-fugal-owner-of-skinwalker-ranch?fbclid=IwAR1aTix3k2ayfOAYiT0p3GbGRQy_gPk8xKtkMqaEL7i_YDIPXYTCiuYJIE8. 2020.

Barrett, David. Sects, "Cults," and Alternative Religions: A World Survey and Sourcebook. Blandford. 1996.

Becker, Robert O. Gordon and Breach. Psychoenergetic Systems, Volume 2. 1977.

Becker, Robert O. and Selden, Gary. The Body Electric: Electromagnetism and the Foundation of Life. William Morrow. 1985.

Becket, Stefan. "What are UAPs, and why do UFOs have a new name?" CBS News. https://www.cbsnews.com/news/what-are-uaps-unexplained-aerial-phenomenon-ufos-new-name/. 2023.

Beckman, Tad. "Notes on the Zuni Origin Myth." https://pages.hmc.edu/beckman/western/zuni.htm. 1998.

Benhorin, Yitzhak. "Operation Paperclip: Nazi scientists in service of CIA." World News: 2014. https://www.ynetnews.com/articles/0,7340,L-4487338,00.html.

Beresford, David. "Snow White's Dirty Tricks." The Guardian. 1980

Bhutani, Risa. "The Uncanny Valley Hypothesis." MSU. https://www.hercampus.com/school/msu/the-uncanny-valley-hypothesis/. 2023.

Bigelow, Michael E. "A Short History of Army Intelligence." https://irp.fas.org/agency/army/short.pdf.

Bille, Mikkel. Being Bedouin Around Petra: Life at a World Heritage Site in the Twenty-First Century. Berghahn Books. 2019.

Blavatsky, Helena. The History of a Planet: Venus: The Light-Bringer Has Nought To Do With Darkness, and Everything With Light." In "Lucifer," September 1887. https://www.helenablavatsky.org/2014/01/the-history-of-planet-venus.html.

-- The Secret Doctrine. The Theosophical Publishing House, Ltd. 1895.

--The Stanzas of Dzyan: From the Secret Doctrine. Edited by Tarl Warwick. CreateSpace Independent Publishing Platform. 2016.

"Blue Ridge Highlands: Mountain Lake Lodge." Virginia is for Lovers. https://www.virginia.org/listing/mountain-lake-lodge/8827/.

Bolin, Robert. "US Army Missile Intelligence Agency, Redstone Arsenal, Alabama." US Department of Defense. 1985.

Bolton, K. R. "The Influence of H P Lovecraft on Occultism." The Irish Journal of Gothic and Horror Studies; Dublin Issue 9. 2011.

Bothwell, Dick. "Debunking the UFO 'Mythology.'" Tampa Bay Times. 1975.

Bowart, W.H. Operation Mind Control. Fontana: 1978.

Boyd, James W. and Crosby, Donald A. "Is Zoroastrianism Dualistic or Monotheistic?". Journal of the American Academy of Religion. 1979.

Bradsher, Greg. "Nazi Gold: The Merkers Mine Treasure." Prologue Magazine. https://www.archives.gov/publications/prologue/1999/spring/nazi-gold-merkers-mine-treasure.html. 1999.

"Briefing for House Permanent Select Committee re OTS Involvement in ESP Research." https://www.cia.gov/readingroom/docs/CIA-RDP96-00787R000500170001-0.pdf.

"Briefing: Project Center Lane." CIA-RDP96-00789R002100180002-8.

Broderick, Lisa. "Time Slips, the Multiverse, and You." Psychology Today. https://www.psychologytoday.com/us/blog/where-physics-meets-psychology/202201/time-slips-the-multiverse-and-you. 2022.

Buckland, Raymond. The Spirit Book: The Encyclopedia of Clairvoyance, Channeling, and Spirit Communication. Visible Ink Press. 2005.

Bullock, Alan. Hitler: A Study in Tyranny. Bantam Books, Books. 1961.

Burr, Harold Saxton. Blueprint for Immortality: The Electric Patterns of Life. Neville Spearman. 1973.

Bibliography

Butler, Richard. Night of Lights, Fatima and The Way. http://web.archive.org/web/20010619193806/http://www.webcom.com/way/night1.html. 1994.

-- The Daughters of Ma, DOMA, Way. https://www.bibliotecapleyades.net/vida_alien/theway/TheWay00.htm.

Caballar, Rina Diane. "What Is the Uncanny Valley? Creepy robots and the strange phenomenon of the uncanny valley: definition, history, examples, and how to avoid it." IEEE. https://spectrum.ieee.org/what-is-the-uncanny-valley. 2024.

Calder, Gordon. "Wartime death of Duke of Kent in Caithness plane crash subject of play reading." Ross-Shire Journal. https://www.ross-shirejournal.co.uk/news/wartime-death-of-duke-of-kent-in-caithness-plane-crash-subje-345837/. 2024.

Charney, Noah. "Hitler's Hunt for the Holy Grail and the Ghent Altarpiece." The Daily Beast. 2017. https://www.thedailybeast.com/hitlers-hunt-for-the-holy-grail-and-the-ghent-altarpiece.

Charroux, Robert. One Hundred Thousand Years of Man's Unknown History. Robert Lafont, Paris. 1963.

Chatterjee, Tara. Knowledge and Freedom in Indian Philosophy. Lexington Books. 2003.

"Church of Scientology of California v. Commissioner of Internal Revenue." https://www.cs.cmu.edu/~dst/Cowen/essays/irslegal/240984.html.

"THE CIA, ANDRIJA PUHARICH & THE COUNCIL OF NINE." World Enlightenment. http://www.world-enlightenment.com/The-Order-of-Things/CIA-Andrija-Puharich-Council-of-Nine.htm.

"C.I.A. Assassination Unit Described." The New York Times. 1975.

"C.I.A. PAPERS DETAIL U.F.O. SURVEILLANCE." New York Times. 1979.

"CIA Special Research Project Bluebird 1952." Public Intelligence: 2012. https://publicintelligence.net/cia-bluebird/.

"Claim of 10,000-year-old Tibet library find not worth paper it's written on." AAP. https://www.aap.com.au/factcheck/claim-of-10000-year-old-tibet-library-find-not-worth-paper-its-written-on/. 2021.

Clark, Jerome. The UFO Encyclopedia: The Phenomenon from the Beginning. Omnigraphics. 1998.

Clark, Paul A. The Hermetic Qabalah. Fraternity of the Hidden Light. 2012.

Clayton, Matt. Native American Mythology: Captivating Myths of Indigenous Peoples from North America. Independently Published. 2019.

Cohen, Daniel. Masters of the Occult. Dodd, Mead and Company. 1971.

Colavito, Jason. The Cult of Alien Gods: H.P. Lovecraft and Extraterrestrial Pop Culture. Prometheus Books. 2005.

-- "How Washington Got Hooked on Flying Saucers: A collection of well-funded UFO obsessives are using their Capitol Hill connections to launder some outré, and potentially dangerous, ideas." The Soapbox. https://newrepublic.com/article/162457/government-embrace-ufos-bad-science. 2021.

Cooper, Helene, Blumenthal, Ralph and Kean, Leslie. "Glowing Auras and 'Black Money': The Pentagon's Mysterious UFO Program," New York Times. 2017.

"Concentrate...Link Mind to Matter." Wichita Eagle, Page 23. 1972.

Cowdell, Fleming, Chris Hodge, Joel, eds. Violence, Desire, and the Sacred. Vol. 2: René Girard and Sacrifice in Life, Love and Literature. Bloomsbury Publishing. 2014.

Cremo, Michael and Thompson, Richard. Forbidden Archeology: The Hidden History of the Human Race. Torchlight Publishing: 2012.

Crowley, Aleister. The Book of Law. Weiser Books. 1976.

-- The Confessions of Aleister Crowley: An Autohagiography. Routledge & Kegan Paul. 1979.

-- Magick: Liber ABA, Book Four. Samuel Weiser. 1997

Bibliography

D'Huy, Julien. "First statistical reconstruction of a Paleolithic ritual: around the dragon motif." New Comparative Mythology. http://nouvellemythologiecomparee.hautetfort.com/archive/2016/03/18/julien-d-huy-premiere-reconstruction-statistique-d-un-rituel-5776049.html. 2016.

Dead of Night Ghost Tours. https://www.deadofnightghosttours.com/.

"Description of Personnel Associated with 'E.T' Bases." CIA-RDP96-00789R003800110001-8 with additional pages from Project 8200.

Desmond, Leslie and Adamski, George. Flying Saucers Have Landed. British Book Centre. 1953.

"DEVCOM Aviation and Missile Center History." https://www.avmc.army.mil/AvMC/History/.

"Did Rudolf Steiner Channel the Masters?" Our Spirit, Come. https://www.ourspirit.com/single-post/2016/07/03/did-rudolf-steiner-channel-the-masters.

Diószegi, Vilmos. Tracing Shamans in Siberia. The story of an ethnographical research expedition. Translated from Hungarian by Anita Rajkay Babó. Anthropological Publications. 1968.

Dirty Dancing. Directed by Emile Ardolino. Great American Films Limited Partnership. 1987.

"Documents Made Public in Case Of Infiltration by Scientologists." New York Times. 1979. https://www.nytimes.com/1979/10/26/archives/documents-made-public-in-case-of-infiltration-by-scientologists.html.

Dowson, Thomas A. "Dots and Dashes: Cracking the Entopic Code in Bushman Rock Paintings." Goodwin's Legacy, Vol. 6. 1989.

Drake, Raymond. "Gods or Spacemen?" Ancient Skies: Official Logbook al the Ancient Astronaut Society. 1989.

-- Gods and Spacemen in the Ancient East. Neville Spearman Ltd. 1968.

-- Gods and Spacemen in the Ancient West. The New American Library, Inc. 1974.

-- Gods and Spacemen of the Ancient Past. The New American Library, Inc. 1974.

"Druid Magic." Down the Forest Path: A Journey Through Nature, its Magic and Mystery. https://downtheforestpath.com/2014/01/24/druid-magic/.

Dulles, Allen W. "Summary of Remarks by Allen W. Dulles at the National Alumni Conference of the Graduate Council of Princeton University, Hot Springs, VA, April 10, 1953." https://www.cia.gov/readingroom/docs/CIA-RDP70-00058R000200050069-9.pdf.

Dunne, Luke. "What Is Plato's Theory of Forms?" The Collector. https://www.thecollector.com/what-is-plato-theory-of-forms/. 2023.

Edmonds III, Radcliffe G. "The Illuminations of Theurgy: Philosophy and Magic." Drawing Down the Moon: Magic in the Ancient Greco-Roman World. Princeton University Press. 2019.

Eichar, Donnie. Dead Mountain: The True Story of the Dyatlov Pass Incident. Chronicle Books. 2013.

"Eileen J. Garrett." First Spiritual Temple. https://fst.org/spiritual-teachings/eileen-j-garrett/.

Elbein, Asher. "Sirens of Greek Myth Were Bird-Women, Not Mermaids." Audubon. https://www.audubon.org/news/sirens-greek-myth-were-bird-women-not-mermaids. 2018.

"Electronic Warfare: NAVELEX Program Information Series." Naval Electronics Systems Command. https://www.navy-radio.com/manuals/navelex-ew-brochure.pdf.

Encyclopedia of Occultism & Parapsychology. Volume 2. Edited by Melton, J. Gordon. Gale Group. 2001.

Evans, Richard J. The Third Reich in Power. Penguin Books. 2005.

"Exploring Ancient Secret Carvings in Skinwalker Ranch Territory." YouTube, uploaded by Carl Crusher, July 17, 2022. https://www.youtube.com/watch?v=9O12rqMKFj8.

"Extra Sensory Perception and Telekinesis – The COMSEC Threat – A Brief: Cryptologic Aspects of ESP." CIA Declassified Document # NSA-RDP96X00790R000100030008-7.

Bibliography

"Fairies: The Mystery of Where They Came From." Formfluent. https://formfluent.com/blogs/blog/fairies-the-mystery-of-where-they-came-from. 2023.

Farley, Dick. "The Council of Nine: A Perspective on 'Briefings from Deep Space.'" https://www.bibliotecapleyades.net/sociopolitica/esp_sociopol_council9_04.htm. 1998.

Febus, Jeff and Knot, Andrew. "The king, his ring and the temple." Calvin University. https://calvin.edu/news/archive/the-king-his-ring-and-the-temple. 2011.

"The Fermi Paradox." SETI Institute. https://www.seti.org/fermi-paradox-0.

Ferre, Lex. "King Solomon." Occult World. 2017. https://occult-world.com/king-solomon/.

"First Spaceship on Venus." Moria. https://www.moriareviews.com/sciencefiction/first-spaceship-on-venus-1959.htm.

Fischer, Benjamin. "The Central Intelligence Agency's Office Technical Service, 1951 – 2001: Celebrating Fifty Years of Technical Support to US Foreign Intelligence Operations." The CIA: 2001.

Fitzpatrick, Alex and Davis, Erin. "America's UFO hotspots, mapped." Axios. https://www.axios.com/2024/02/08/ufo-uap-sightings-us-hotspots-2000-2023. 2024.

"Forced-Choice Remote Viewing." https://www.cia.gov/readingroom/docs/CIA-RDP96-00789R002200280001-7.pdf.

"Foreign Technical Division." Air Force. https://usafunithistory.com/PDF/F-S/FOREIGN%20TECHNICAL%20DIVISION.pdf.

Fort, Charles. The Book of the Damned. Boni and Liveright. 1919.

-- New Lands. Boni and Liveright. 1923.

Foster, Michael Dylan. "Yōkai: Fantastic Creatures of Japanese Folklore." Japan Society. https://aboutjapan.japansociety.org/yokai-fantastic-creatures-of-japanese-folklore#sthash.NExjdL3t.ITUAFIOK.dpbs.

Fritze, Ronald H. Invented Knowledge: False History, Fake Science and Pseudo-religions, Reaktion Books. 2009.

Frost, Cassandra. "Remote Viewing Underground UFO Bases." Rense.com. https://rense.com/general68/remm.htm. 2005.

"Galactic Federation." CIA-RDP96-00789R003800200001-8.

Gates, Robert V. "History of the Naval Laboratory System." International Journal of Naval History. 2016. https://www.ijnhonline.org/history-of-the-navy-laboratory-system/.

Gaume, Johan and Puzrin, Alexander. "Mechanisms of slab avalanche release and impact in the Dyatlov Pass incident in 1959." Nature. https://www.nature.com/articles/s43247-020-00081-8. 2021.

"Gave de Pau." Wikipedia, The Free Encyclopedia, Wikimedia Foundation. https://en.wikipedia.org/wiki/Gave_de_Pau.

"A geological analysis of time slip cases for the presence of quartz." YouTube, uploaded by John-David Butler, April 11, 2021. https://www.youtube.com/watch?v=_-qIDUMEI3A.

Gilbert, Derek. "From Ascended Masters to the Great Old Ones." All Pro Pastors International. https://allpropastors.org/from-ascended-masters-to-the-great-old-ones/.

Gleave, R.M. "Alī ibn Abī Ṭālib." Encyclopaedia of Islam, Third Edition. Flee, Kate, Krämer, Gudrun, Matringe, Denis, Nawas, John, Stewart, Devin J. (eds.). 2008.

"Gondola Wish." CIA-RDP96-00788R002000160011-21.

"Gondola Wish Assessment Report." CIA-RDP96-00788R002000160001-3.

"Gondola Wish" Briefing Memo. CIA-RDP96-00788R002000160011-2.pdf

Bibliography

"Government-Sponsored Research in Psychoenergetics." https://www.cia.gov/readingroom/docs/CIA-RDP96-00789R002200440001-9.pdf

Graves, Robert and Patai, Raphael. Hebrew Myths: The Book of Genesis. Random House. 1986.

Grant. Kenneth. The Magical Revival. Frederick Muller Ltd. 1972.

Greer, John Michael. The New Encyclopedia of the Occult, Llewellyn Publications. 2003.

-- Paths of Wisdom: A Guide to the Magical Cabala. Thoth Publications. 2007.

Griffiths, Sarah. "Unmanned aircraft reveals 2,500 year old petroglyphs in Utah desert." SUAS News. https://www.suasnews.com/2014/03/unmanned-aircraft-reveals-2500-year-old-petroglyphs-in-utah-desert/. 2014.

Gross, Lauren. UFO's: A History 1953: August-December. 1990.

"A Guide to Deciphering the Differences Between a Yeti, Sasquatch, Bigfoot and More." Newsweek. https://www.newsweek.com/bigfoot-sasquatch-yeti-legend-myth-403932. 2016.

Guiley, Rosemary Ellen and Imbrogno. The Vengeful Djinn: Unveiling the Hidden Agendas of Genies. Llewellyn Publications. 2011.

Håkan Blomqvist´s blog. https://ufoarchives.blogspot.com/2017/04/through-curtain.html. 2017.

-- The Edith Nicolaisen - George Adamski Correspondence. https://ufoarchives.blogspot.com/2019/01/the-edith-nicolaisen-george-adamski.html. 2019.

Hall, Manly. Secret Teachings of All Ages: An Encyclopedic Outline of Masonic, Hermetic, Qabbalistic and Rosicrucian Symbolical Philosophy. Being an Interpretation of the Secret Teachings concealed within the Rituals, Allegories, and Mysteries of all Ages. H.S. Crocker and Company, Inc. 1928.

Harrigan, Fiona. "The Feds Spent $22 Million Researching Invisibility Cloaks, UFOs, and a Tunnel Through the Moon." The Reason Foundation. https://reason.com/2022/04/20/the-feds-spent-22-million-researching-invisibility-cloaks-ufos-and-a-tunnel-through-the-moon/. 2022.

Harris, Ruth. Lourdes: Body And Spirit in the Secular Age. Penguin Books. 2000.

"Has Radar Found 'Lost Gold.'" Intelligencer Journal. 1977.

Hatto, Arthur. The World of the Khanty Epic Hero-Princes: An Exploration of a Siberian Oral Tradition. Cambridge University Press. 2017.

Haze, Xaviant. Aliens in Ancient Egypt: The Brotherhood of the Serpent and the Secrets of the Nile Civilization. Simon and Schuster. 2013.

Heidelberg, Aimee. "The Grim Theories Behind the Dyatlov Pass Incident." This History Collection. https://historycollection.com/the-grim-theories-behind-the-dyatlov-pass-incident/. 2023.

Helland, Christopher. "UFO Religions Online: Prophetic Failures and the Narrative Techniques of the Ground Crew." The Encyclopedic Sourcebook of UFO Religions. 2003.

Herbert, Frank. Dune. Chilton Books. 1965.

Higdon, Margery. Alien Abduction of The Wyoming Hunter: First Person Story of Carl Higdon, October 25, 1974. CreateSpace Independent Publishing Platform. 2017.

"Hinduism: Rebirth and the Law of Karma." Ramakrishna-Vivekananda Center of New York. https://ramakrishna.org/problemofsuffering.html.

"History of the U.S. Army Research, Development and Engineering Command (RDECOM)", RDECOM, October 2008.

"Hmong Minority: History, Religion and Groups." Facts and Details. https://factsanddetails.com/asian/cat66/sub417/item2744.html#chapter-8

"Hmong Rituals." The Split Horn: PBS. https://www.pbs.org/splithorn/shamanism1.html.

Hoffberger, Rebecca. Text Messages. 2024.

Holmes, Rachel. "The Mystery Of The Council Of Nine." Medium. https://medium.com/@RachelHolmees/the-mystery-of-the-council-of-nine-fc3c1a2b6dab. 2023.

Bibliography

The Holy Bible, English Standard Version. Crossway Bibles. 2011.

Hopkins, Budd. Missing Time: A Documented Study of UFO Abductions. R. Marek Publishers. 1981.

Homer. The Odyssey. Translated by Robert Fagles. Penguin Classics. 1999.

Horowitz, Mitch. Occult America: The Secret History of How Mysticism Shaped Our Nation. Bantam. 2009.

"How Prevalent is Violence in Missing and Unidentified Persons Cases?" National Institute of Justice. https://nij.ojp.gov/topics/articles/how-prevalent-violence-missing-and-unidentified-persons-cases. 2022.

Hubbard, L. Ron. Scientology: A History of Man. Bridge Publications, Inc. 2007.

Hunt, Linda. Secret Agenda: The United States Government, Nazi Scientists, and Project Paperclip, 1945 to 1990. St. Martin's Press. 1991.

Huyghe, Patrick. "U.F.O. Files: The Untold Story." New York Times: 1979.

Hynek, J. Allen. The Hynek UFO Report. Dell Publishing Co., Inc. 1977.

Hynek, J. Allen and Vallée, Jacques. The Edge of Reality: A Progress Report on Unidentified Flying Objects. Contemporary Books, Incorporated. 1975.

"The Indecipherable Judaculla Rock." Ancient Origins. https://www.ancient-origins.net/unexplained-phenomena/judaculla-rock-00605.

"Interview with Patrick Price." CIA-RDP79-00999A000400050006-0.

"Invasion on Chestnut Ridge - Full Documentary (2017 Bigfoot Sasquatch Paranormal Movie)." YouTube, uploaded by Small Town Monsters, May 7, 2023. https://youtu.be/H0lp0GUdJrw?si=jB4SQxQqXR1fZxw5.

"Invited to Secluded Indian Reservation (Zuni Pueblo Tribe)." YouTube, uploaded by Peter Santenello, December 25, 2022. https://youtu.be/g5C0qQMsiBY?si=cL3Qok7I0d4OtObB.

Jacobsen, Annie. Operation Paperclip: The Secret Intelligence Program that Brought Nazi Scientists to America. Back Bay Books: 2015.

-- Phenomena: The Secret History of the U.S. Government's Investigations into Extrasensory Perception and Psychokinesis. Little, Brown and Company: 2017.

"JEMI observes the passing of Sandra Wright, former board member." http://johnemackinstitute.org/2009/12/jemi-observes-the-passing-of-sandra-wright-former-board-member/. 2009.

Jenkins, Phillip. Mystics and Messiahs: Cults and New Religions in American History. Oxford University Press. 2000.

"Jinn of Solomon." https://jinnat.tumblr.com/Jinn%20of%20Solomon.

Joe, Jimmy. "Fairies Magic: What Can They Do With Their Magic?." Timeless Myth. https://www.timelessmyths.com/mythology/fairies-magic/.

"Joe Rogan Experience #2152 - Terrence Howard." YouTube, uploaded by PowerfulJRE, May 18, 2024. https://www.youtube.com/watch?v=g197xdRZsW0.

"John Keel: A Paranormal Pioneer." Mufon of Ohio. https://www.mufonohio.com/mufono/jk.html.

"John Keel, 1930-2009, Tributes from Ingo Swann, Jacques Vallée, Phyllis Benjamin, Marc Coppola, Dwight Whalen, and Patrick Harpur." The Fortean Society. http://forteans.com.s3-website-us-east-1.amazonaws.com/keel.html. 2009.

Johnstone, Ryn. "The Uncanny Valley: What Unknown Thing Hunts Us?" https://rynjohnstone.com/the-uncanny-valley/. 2021.

Joseph, Frank. Atlantis and Other Lost Worlds: New Evidence of Ancient Secrets. Arcturus Publishing Limited. 2008.

Josephy, Marcia Reines. Magic & Superstition in the Jewish Tradition: An Exhibition Organized by the Maurice Spertus Museum of Judaica. Spertus College of Judaica Press. 1975.

"Judaculla Rock." Discover Jackson County North Carolina. https://www.discoverjacksonnc.com/attractions/culture-heritage/judaculla-rock/.

"Judaculla Rock." North Carolina Ghosts. https://northcarolinaghosts.com/mountains/judaculla-rock/.

Bibliography

Kachuba, John B. Shapeshifters: A History. University of Chicago Press. 2019.

Kadane, Lisa. "The true origin of Sasquatch." BBC. https://www.bbc.com/travel/article/20220720-the-true-origin-of-sasquatch. 2022.

Karagulla, Shafica. Breakthrough to Creativity: Your Higher Sense Perception. DeVorss & Co., Inc. 1967.

Keel, John. Anomaly No. 1, May 1969.

-- Jadoo: The Astounding Story of One Man's into the Mysteries of Black Magic in the Orient. Julian Messner, Inc. 1957.

-- Our Haunted Planet. Futura Publications Limited. 1975.

-- "UFO Agents of Terror." SAGA Magazine. October 1967.

-- Why UFOs: Operation Trojan Horse. Putham. 1970.

Keel, John and Colvin, Andrew. The Big Breakthrough: Confronting UFOs, Men in Black, Mothman, and Mysterious Humanoids - Trojan Horses of a Breakaway Civilization? CreateSpace Independent Publishing Platform. 2017.

Keys, David. "The thousand-year-old mystery of the giant snake found in drawings across the world." The Independent. https://www.independent.co.uk/news/science/archaeology/colombia-venezuela-rock-art-giant-snakes-b2556860.html. 2024,

Kin, L. The Pied Pipers of Heaven: Who Calls the Tune? VAP Publishers. 1994.

King, Francis. Modern Ritual Magic: The Rise of Western Occultism. Prism. 1989

"King Solomon and the Jinn." Darvish. https://darvish.wordpress.com/2006/07/13/king-solomon-and-the-jinn/.

Klass, Philip. "The MJ-12 Crashed-Saucer Documents. Part 2" The Hundredth Monkey: and Other Paradigms of the Paranormal. Edited by Kendrick Frazier. Prometheus Books. 1991.

Klein, Shelley. The Most Evil Secret Societies in History. Michael O'Mara Books. 2005.

Kleinfeld, N. R. "What Inquiring Minds Want to Own." The New York Times. https://www.nytimes.com/1989/05/07/business/what-acquiring-minds-want-to-own.html. 1989.

Knapp, George. "I-Team: Skinwalker Ranch and the 'hitchhiker effect.'" 8News. https://www.8newsnow.com/investigators/i-team-skinwalker-ranch-and-the-hitchhiker-effect/. 2022.

Kosior, Wojciech. "The Fallen (Or) Giants? The Gigantic Qualities of the Nefilim in the Hebrew Bible." Jewish Translation - Translating Jewishness. Walter de Gruyter. 2018.

Krebernik, Manfred. Mondgott A.I. in Mesopotamien. De Gruyter: 1995.

Kress, Kenneth. "Parapsychology in Intelligence: A Personal Review and Conclusions. CIA-RDP96-00791R000200030040-0. 1977.

Kurlander, Eric. Hitler's Monsters: A Supernatural History of the Third Reich. Yale University Press. 2017.

-- "How Mysticism and Pseudoscience Became Central to Nazism." Jacobin. https://jacobin.com/2021/11/supernatural-thinking-occultism-esotericism-nazism-adolf-hitler-world-war-two-border-science. 2021.

-- "One Foot in Atlantis, One in Tibet: The Roots and Legacies of Nazi Theories on Atlantis, 1890-1945." 2000.

Layne, Meade. The Coming of the Guardians: An Interpretation of the Flying Saucers as Given from the Other Side of Life. Third Edition. The Boarderlands Sciences Research Associates. 1957.

LeCouteux, Claude, King Solomon the Magus: Master of the Djinns and Occult Traditions of the East and West. InnerTraditions. 2022.

Lees, David James. "Trusting Your Inner Guide and Why It Matters." Wu Wei Wisdom. https://www.wuweiwisdom.com/trusting-your-inner-guide/.

"The Legend of Fairies: A Brief History." Paykoc Imports. https://www.paykocimports.com/blog/the-legend-of-fairies-a-brief-history/. 2022.

Lewin, Moshe. Stalinism: Essays in Historical Interpretation, edited by Robert C. Tucker. W.W. Norton & Company: 1977.

Bibliography

Lewis-Williams, J. David and Challis, Sam. "Truth in error: an enigmatic 19th century San comment on southern African rock paintings of 'lions' & 'shields'." Hunter Gatherer Research. 2010.

Lewis-Williams, J. David and Pearce, David. "FRAMED IDIOSYNCRASY: METHOD AND EVIDENCE IN THE INTERPRETATION OF SAN ROCK ART." The South African Archaeological Bulletin. 2012. https://www.jstor.org/stable/23631394.

Lévi, Éliphas. Dogme et ritual de la haute magie Rituel (Transcendental Magic: Its Doctrine and Ritual, Volume II). 1856.

Lindon LaRouche. Wikipedia, The Free Encyclopedia, Wikimedia Foundation. https://en.wikipedia.org/wiki/Lyndon_LaRouche.

Loendorf, Lawrence. "Vision Quest Structures." The Pryor Mountains. https://pryormountains.org/-archaeology/vision-quest-structures.

Lovecraft, H. P. "The Call of Cthulhu." Weird Tales. 1928.

"Lucifer is Christos." Inner Light. https://www.philaletheians.co.uk/study-notes/secret-doctrine%27s-proposition-3/lucifer-is-christos,-inner-light.pdf.

Luhrssen, David. Hammer of the Gods: The Thule Society and the Birth of Nazism. Potomac Books. 2012.

Lymer, Kenneth. "Shimmering Visions: Shamanistic Rock Art Images from the Republic of Kazakhstan." Expedition Magazine: Penn Museum. https://www.penn.museum/sites/expedition/shimmering-visions/. 2004.

MacGowen, Roger A. and Ordway III, Frederick. Intelligence in the Universe. Prentice-Hall, Inc. 1966.

MacIsaac, Tara. "Ancient Race of White Giants Described in Native Legends From Many Tribes." Ancient Origins. https://www.ancient-origins.net/myths-legends/ancient-race-white-giants-described-native-legends-many-tribes-005774. 2016.

Mallen, Lara, Pearce, David, Arthur, Charles, and Mitchell, Peter. "The Rock Arts of Metolong: Paintings, Archaeology and Cultural Resource Management in Western Lesotho." Journal of African Archeology. https://brill.com/view/journals/jaa/20/2/article-p176_3.xml?language=en. 2022.

Margaritoff, Marco. "The True Story Of The Dyatlov Pass Mystery — And The Chilling Potential Explanation." All That is Interesting. https://allthatsinteresting.com/dyatlov-pass-incident-solved. 2024.

Mark, Joshua J. "War in Ancient Times." World History Encyclopedia. https://www.worldhistory.org/war/. 2009.

Marrs, Jim. Alien Agenda: Investigating the Extraterrestrial Presence Among Us. Harper Collins Publishers: 1997.

-- Psi Spies: The True Story of America's Psychic Warfare Program. New Page Books. 2007.

-- The Rise of the Fourth Reich: The Secret Society that Threaten to Take Over America. HarperCollins. 2008.

Martin, Jonathan. "Judaculla Rock." North Carolina History. https://northcarolinahistory.org/encyclopedia/judaculla-rock/.

"Mary Moody Northen | Mountain Lake Lodge History." YouTube, uploaded by Mountain Lake, January 4, 2021. https://www.youtube.com/watch?v=hOYTVK5fT7o&t=302s.

May, Edward. "SAIC Memorandum." CIA-RDP96-00791R000200190034-0.

"Meet the Mesopotamian Demons." The Getty Center. https://www.getty.edu/news/meet-the-mesopotamian-demons/.

Mekemson, Curt. "Jellyfish-like pictoglyph at Sego Canyon." https://wandering-through-time-and-place.com/2017/08/04/a-canyon-of-mystery-and-magic-sego-canyon-rock-art/jellyfish-like-pictoglyph-at-sego-canyon/. 2017.

"Memorandum for the Assistant Director for Scientific Intelligence. FC Durant, 'Report of Meetings of the Office of Scientific Intelligence Scientific Advisory Panel on Unidentified Flying Objects, January 14–18, 1953,' 16th February 1953." https://www.cia.gov/readingroom/docs/CIA-RDP81R00560R000100030027-0.pdf.

"Memorandum for the Secretary of Defense." File: 02-A-0846_RELEASE. https://upload.wikimedia.org/wikipedia/commons/5/5f/02-A-0846RELEASE-mk-ultra.pdf.

Bibliography

Milner, Terry. "The Very Strange Death Of Top Remote Viewer Pat Price." Rense.Com. https://rense.com/general9/stranged.htm. 2011.

"Missing 411: The UFO Connection | David Paulides | Ep 154." YouTube, uploaded by Rick & Bubba University, March 18, 2023. https://youtu.be/QQCWawGtQSs?si=f1XqF0AdfC1UO1uv.

Missing 411: The U.F.O. Connection. Directed by David Paulides. 2022.

"Missile and Space Intelligence Center." https://www.dia.mil/About/Organization/MSIC/.

Mitchell, Janet Lee. Out-of-Body Experiences: A Handbook. McFarland & Company, Inc. 1981.

Mjohnsonewtn. "The Message of Lourdes Premieres This Week on EWTN." Inside EWTN. https://insideewtn.com/2022/12/08/the-message-of-lourdes-premieres-this-week-on-ewtn/. 2022.

Montgomery, M. R. Many Rivers to Cross: Of Good Running Water, Native Trout, and the Remains of Wilderness. Simon & Schuster. 1996.

Mooney, James. "Myths of the Cherokees." Journal of American Folklore. 1888.

Morgan, James. "Decoding the symbols on Satan's statue." BBC. https://www.bbc.com/news/magazine-33682878. 2015.

"Morteros Trail." The Reader. https://www.sandiegoreader.com/news/2014/feb/12/roam-morteros-trail-anza-borrego/.

"Mountain Lake." Virginia Places. http://www.virginiaplaces.org/watersheds/mountainlake.html

"Mountain Lake Hotel Investigation: Full DVD." YouTube, uploaded by SuperNatural-Media, July 4, 2012. https://www.youtube.com/watch?v=I9LPfBLO3sE.

Mountain Lake Lodge website. https://www.mtnlakelodge.com.

Mumford, Michael D., Rose, Andrew M., and Goslin, David A. "An Evaluation of Remote Viewing: Research and Applications." The American Institutes for Research. https://irp.fas.org/program/collect/air1995.pdf. 1995.

Murphy, Ronald L. Unexplained World of The Chestnut Ridge: A Hile through the Goblin Universe of Western Pennsylvania. Camonica Books. 2016.

"Mysterious Judaculla Rock And The Slant-Eyed Giant Of The Cherokee." Ancient Pages. https://www.ancientpages.com/2021/05/08/mysterious-judaculla-rock-and-the-slant-eyed-giant-of-the-cherokee/. 2021.

"The Mystery of the Lake." YouTube, uploaded by Mountain Lake Lodge, March 17, 2015. https://www.youtube.com/watch?v=C9Ui8TCJKoY.

"Mythic Humanoids." Wikipedia, The Free Encyclopedia, Wikimedia Foundation. https://en.wikipedia.org/wiki/Mythic_humanoids.

NamUs Case Reports. https://namus.nij.ojp.gov/library/reports-and-statistics.

"National Air and Space Intelligence Center Heritage." National Air and Space Intelligence Center. https://www.nasic.af.mil/About-Us/Fact-Sheets/Article/611728/national-air-and-space-intelligence-center-heritage/.

Neal, Viola Petitt and Karagulla, Shafica. Through the Curtain. DeVorss & Co., Inc. 1983.

Nechumazqfarren. "Operation High Jump: US Scientific Expedition Led by Admiral Richard Bird Departs for South Pole on August 26th, 1946." Medium. https://medium.com/@nechumazqfarren82/operation-high-jump-us-scientific-expedition-led-by-admiral-richard-bird-departs-for-south-pole-on-dd234140f39a. 2023.

Nichols, Jake. "Alien Abductions Of 2 Wyoming Men In The 1970s Remain Unexplainable." Cowboy State Daily. https://cowboystatedaily.com/2023/09/30/alien-abductions-of-2-wyoming-men-in-the-1970s-remain-unexplainable/. 2023.

O'Sullivan, Michael. "Art review: 'The Visionary Experience' at American Visionary Art Museum in Baltimore." The Washington Post. https://www.washingtonpost.com/goingoutguide/museums/art-review-the-visionary-experience-at-american-visionary-art-museum-in-

Bibliography

baltimore/2014/11/06/dcd1067c-6119-11e4-91f7-5d89b5e8c251_story.html. 2016.

Oktaviana, A.A., Joannes-Boyau, R., Hakim, B. et al. Narrative cave art in Indonesia by 51,200 years ago. Nature. https://doi.org/10.1038/s41586-024-07541-7. 2024.

"Otto Rahn – Otto Skorzeny Raiders of the Found Ark?" https://otto-rahn.com/otto-rahn-otto-skorzeny-raiders-found-ark.

"Our Lady of Betharam." Roman Catholic Saints. https://www.roman-catholic-saints.com/our-lady-of-betharam.html.

"Paula Roberts papers." University of West Georgia. https://aspace-uwg.galileo.usg.edu/repositories/2/resources/488.

Pauwels, Louis and Bergier, Jacques. The Morning of the Magicians: Secret Societies, Conspiracies, and Vanished Civilizations. Destiny Books. 2008.

Pearce, Q. L. Native American Mythology. Greenhaven Publishing LLC. 2012.

Pendergrast, Mark. Mirror, Mirror: A History Of The Human Love Affair With Reflection. Basic Books. 2004.

"Penetration: Special Edition Chapter." 21st Century Ratio. 2020.

Persinger, Michael A.. "The neuropsychiatry of paranormal experiences." The Journal of Neuropsychiatry and Clinical Neurosciences. 2001.

Peterson, Joseph H. Editor. The Lesser Key of Solomon: Lemegeton Clavicula Salomonis, Detailing the Ceremonial Art of Commanding Spirits Both Good and Evil. Weiser Books. 2001.

Picknett, Lynn and Prince, Clive. The Stargate Conspiracy: The Truth about Extraterrestrial life and the Mysteries of Ancient Egypt. Penguin Publishing Group. 2001.

Praamsma, Saskia and Block, Matthew. The Urantia Diaries of Harold and Martha Sherman: Volume One: 1898-1942. Square Circles Publishing. 2016.

Price, Patrick. "UFO Bases." October 1973.

Pringle, Heather. The Master Plan: Himmler's Scholars and the Holocaust. Hyperion. 2006.

"Probe of the AFSA CIA's 'Occult' O." CIA-RPD75-00001R00100050017-4.

"Project Moondrop." Ingo Swann papers, University of West Georgia, Irvine S. Ingram Library, Special Collections.

"Project SCANATE: Exploratory Research in Remote Viewing." CIA-RDP79-00999A000400050002-4.

"Project Sun Streak." CIA-RDP96-00789R002100240001-2.

Pruitt, Sarah. "Why the Mormons Settled in Utah." The History Channel. https://www.history.com/news/why-the-mormons-settled-in-utah. 2023.

"Psychic Gravity Manipulation." SuperpowersWiki. https://powerlisting.fandom.com/wiki/Psychic_Gravity_Manipulation.

Puharich, Andrija. The Sacred Mushroom: Key to the Door of Eternity. Doubleday & Company, Inc. 1974.

Puthoff, Harold. "Letter to Ken Kress." CIA-RDP79-00999A000200010059-1.pdf. 1973.

-- "ULTRATERRESTRIAL MODELS." Journal of Cosmology. https://thejournalofcosmology.com/Puthoff.pdf.

Puthoff, Harold and Targ, Russell. Advanced Threat Technique Assessment. https://www.cia.gov/readingroom/docs/CIA-RDP79-00999A000400050012-3.pdf.

-- Mind Reach: Scientists Look at Psychic Abilities (Studies in Consciousness). Hampton Roads. 1977.

Raynes, Brent, "An Interview with William Henry Belk: One of the original pioneering giants in the paranormal field." Alternate Perceptions. 1998. http://www.apmagazine.info/index.php?option=com_content&view=article&id=215. 2021.

"Readings in Intelligence." CIA-RDP87M01007R000400810001-4.pdf.

Bibliography

Recluse. "The Office of Security Meet The Nine: Even Stranger Things." VISUP. http://visupview.blogspot.com/2016/08/the-office-of-security-meet-nine-even.html.

Regardie, Israel; et al. The Golden Dawn: An Account of the Teachings, Rites, and Ceremonies of the Order of the Golden Dawn. Vol. 3–4. Llewellyn Publications. 1982.

Reigle, David and Reigle, Nancy. Blavatsky's Secret Books. Wizards Bookshelf. 1999.

Remnick, David. "25 Years of Nightmares." The Washington Post. 1985. https://www.washingtonpost.com/archive/lifestyle/1985/07/28/25-years-of-nightmares/cb836420-9c72-4d3c-ae60-70a8f13c4ceb/.

Remote Viewing/Penetration Conversation between Art Bell and Ingo Swann. Coast to Coast AM Radio Show, March 2000. https://youtu.be/FnybFp9jFwE?si=DExC-7h3LmywpQSP.

Rennie, Daniel. "Heinrich Himmler Thought Germans Were Descended From Nordic Gods – So He Tried To Prove It." All That is Interesting. 2018. https://allthatsinteresting.com/ahnenerbe.

"Report on the Historical Record of U.S. Government Involvement with Unidentified Anomalous Phenomena (UAP) Volume I." The Department of Defense. https://media.defense.gov/2024/Mar/08/2003409233/-1/-1/0/DOPSR-CLEARED-508-COMPLIANT-HRRV1-08-MAR-2024-FINAL.PDF. 2024.

"Report of the Meeting of Scientific Advisory Panel on Unidentified Flying Objects Convened by the Office of Scientific Intelligence, January 14 - 18, 1953." https://www.cia.gov/readingroom/docs/CIA-RDP81R00560R000100030027-0.pdf.

Rivlan, Robert and Gravelle, Karen. Deciphering the Senses: The Expanding World of Human Perception. Simon and Schuster. 1984.

"Roadside Attraction Sego Canyon Rock Art." Road Trip Ryan. https://www.roadtripryan.com/go/t/utah/moab/sego-canyon-rock-art#beta_photos.

Robinson, Timothy. "Scientology Raid Yielded Alleged Burglary Tools." The Washington Post. 1977.

Rolleston, Thomas William. Myths and Legends of the Celtic Race. Constable. 1911.

"Root Race." The Free Encyclopedia, Wikimedia Foundation. https://en.wikipedia.org/wiki/Root_race.

Rotondi, Jessica Pearce. "Five Secret Societies That Have Remained Shrouded in Mystery." The History Channel. 2019 and 2023. https://www.history.com/news/secret-societies-freemasons-knights-templar.

Rust, Renée. "The Rock Art of the Anysberg Nature Reserve, Western Cape: A Sense of Place and Rainmaking." University of Stellenbosch. 2020.

Sadowski, Piotr. From Interaction to Symbol: A systems view of the evolution of signs and communication. John Benjamins Publishing Company. 2009.

"Sandy Wright Obituary." The New York Times. 2009.

Sarbazi, Naveed. "Abductions and Trials by Djinn." https://www.academia.edu/41464268/Abductions_and_Trials_by_Djinn?auto=download.

Schiffman, H. R. Sensation and Perception: An Integrated Approach. John Wiley & Sons. 1976.

Schnabel, Jim. Remote Viewers: The Secret History of America's Psychic Spies. Dell. 1997.

-- "TINKER, TAILOR, SOLDIER, PSI: When the Cold War was at its height, the Soviets and the Americans would stop at nothing to gain an edge in intelligence. But psychic spying? According to the cognoscenti, yes. But, says Jim Schnabel, putting the ESP into espionage was not without risks..." The Independent. https://www.independent.co.uk/arts-entertainment/tinker-tailor-soldier-psi-1598203.html. 1995.

Schrader, Helena. "The Poor Knights of the Temple Solomon." 2015. http://defendingcrusaderkingdoms.blogspot.com/2015/10/the-poor-knights-of-temple-of-solomon.html.

Schwarz, S. L. "Reconsidering the Testament of Solomon." Journal for the Study of the Pseudepigrapha, https://doi.org/10.1177/0951820707077166. 2007.

Bibliography

Scott-Elliot, William. The Story of Atlantis and the Lost Lemuria: With Six Maps. Percy Lund, Humphries & Co. 1925.

"Seabed Remote Viewing Session." CIA-RDP96-0078R001900700003-3.

"Secret Funding Over, CIA Director Says." The Daily Illini. 1977.

"Seduction by Fairies." CMU's A Midsummer Night's Dream. https://amidsummerscasebook.wordpress.com/2010/09/30/seduction-by-the-fairies/

"Sego Canyon Rock Art Interpretive Site." The American Southwest. https://www.theamericansouthwest.com/sego-canyon-rock-art-interpretive-site.

"Sego Canyon Rock Art Petroglyphs and Ghost Town." Moab Adventures Condo. https://www.moabadventurecondo.com/post/sego-canyon-rock-art-petroglyphs-and-ghost-town.

Sender, Pablo. "Mahatmas versus Ascended Masters." Quest Magazine. https://www.theosophical.org/publications/quest-magazine?start=845. 2011.

Severo, Richard. "Lyndon LaRouche, Cult Figure Who Ran for President 8 Times, Dies at 96. New York Times. 2019.

Seyffert, Oskar. A Dictionary of Classical Antiquities: Mythology, Religion, Literature and Art. Translated and Edited by Henry Nettleship and J. E. Sandys. William Glaishner, Ltd. 1891.

"The Shaman and The Spirit Master." Misfits and Heros. https://misfitsandheroes.wordpress.com/2014/06/13/the-shaman-and-the-spirit-master/. 2014.

Sheldon, Natasha. "The Fontinalia: Celebrating the Roman 'Festival of Springs.'" History and Archaeology Online. https://historyandarchaeologyonline.com/the-fontinalia-celebrating-the-roman-festival-of-springs/. 2019.

"The Shermans and the Urantia Book." https://haroldsherman.com/urantia/.

Shia Chat. https://www.shiachat.com/forum/topic/235069382-within-you-is-enfolded-the-entire-universe-%E2%80%94-imam-ali-

%D8%B9%D9%84%D9%8A%D9%87-
%D8%A7%D9%84%D8%B3%D9%84%D8%A7%D9%85/

Shklovskii, I. S. and Sagan, Carl. Intelligent Life in the Universe. Holden-Day. 1966.

"The Shocking Kholat Syakhl Story – The Dyatlov Pass incident." Young Pioneer Tours. https://www.youngpioneertours.com/kholat-syakhl-story-dyatlov-pass/

The Silent Star. Directed by Kurt Maetzig. DEFA Studio for Feature Films | Film Studio Wroclaw (Poland). 1960.

Silverfox57. "Shadow People." Brickthology. https://brickthology.com/category/lakota/.

Sinaiee, Maryam. "Archaeologist Finds Striking Similarities Between Prehistoric Rock Art In Iran And America." Radio Farda. https://en.radiofarda.com/a/iranian-archaeologist-finds-striking-similarities-between-prehistoric-rock-art-in-iran-and-america/30607822.html. 2020.

"Siren." Encyclopedia Britannica. https://www.britannica.com/topic/Siren-Greek-mythology.

Sofia, Hannah. Trip Advisor Review of Judaculla Rock. https://www.tripadvisor.com/Attraction_Review-g49070-d144401-Reviews-Judaculla_Rock-Cullowhee_Jackson_County_North_Carolina.html.

Spence, Richard. Secret Agent 666: Aleister Crowley, British Intelligence, and the Occult. Feral House. 2008.

-- "Aleister Crowley and the Link Between Occultism and Espionage." Wondrium Daily. https://www.wondriumdaily.com/aleister-crowley-and-the-link-between-occultism-and-espionage/. 2020.

Spiegel, David. "Dissociative Subtype of Posttraumatic Stress Disorder." Merck Manual. https://www.merckmanuals.com/professional/psychiatric-disorders/dissociative-disorders/dissociative-subtype-of-posttraumatic-stress-disorder. 2023.

Springett, Bernard H. Secret Sects of Syria and the Lebanon: A Consideration of Their Origin, Creed sand Religious Ceremonies, and Their Connection with and Influence upon Modern Freemasonry. George Allen & Unwin Ltd. 1922.

Bibliography

Stafford, Charles. "Old-time religion? Forget it." St. Petersburg Times. 1979.

Steiner, Rudolf. Atlantis and Lemuria. Anthroposophical Publishing Company. 1923.

Stewart, Jude. Patternalia: An Unconventional History of Polka Dots, Strips, Plaid, Camouflage & Other Graphic Patterns. Bloomsbury. 2015.

"Stop Rockefeller Nazi Doctors." National Caucus of Labor Committees. CIA-RDP88-01315R000300590040-4. 1974.

Story, Ronald. The Space-Gods Revealed: A Close Look at the Theories of Erich von Däniken. Harper & Row. 1976.

Stothers, Richard. "Unidentified Flying Objects in Classical Antiquity." The Classical Journal. 2007.

Straudenmaier, Peter. Between Occultism and Nazism: Anthroposophy and the Politics of Race in the Fascist Era. Leinden: 2014.

Strickland, Ashley. "Half-animal, half-human hybrids depicted on oldest discovered cave art." CNN. https://www.cnn.com/2019/12/11/world/oldest-rock-art-humans-scn/index.html. 2019.

"Sts'Ailes people." Wikipedia, The Free Encyclopedia, Wikimedia Foundation. https://en.wikipedia.org/wiki/Sts%27Ailes_people.

Sturrock, P.A. "UNCERTAINTY IN ESTIMATES OF THE NUMBER OF EXTRATERRESTRIAL CIVILIZATIONS." National Aeronautics and Space Administration, Grant NGR 05-020-668, SUIPR Report No. 808, March 1980. https://ntrs.nasa.gov/api/citations/19800014518/downloads/19800014518.pdf.

Suliman, Adela and Goldman, Paul. "Former Israeli space security chief says extraterrestrials exist, and Trump knows about it." NBC News. https://www.nbcnews.com/news/weird-news/former-israeli-space-security-chief-says-extraterrestrials-exist-trump-knows-n1250333. 2020.

Swann, Ingo. The Agony and Ecstasy of the Signs of the Zodiac, unfinished. Ingo Swann papers, University of West Georgia, Irvine S. Ingram Library, Special Collections.

-- Anacalypsis: A Psychic Autobiography, unfinished. Ingo Swann papers, University of West Georgia, Irvine S. Ingram Library, Special Collections.

-- Biographical detail and other materials prepared for Everybody's Guide to Natural ESP but not included. Ingo Swann papers, University of West Georgia, Irvine S. Ingram Library, Special Collections.

-- Biographical detail prepared for Resurrecting the Mysterious but not included. Ingo Swann papers, University of West Georgia, Irvine S. Ingram Library, Special Collections.

-- Biographical detail and other materials prepared for To Kiss Earth Goodbye but not included. Ingo Swann papers, University of West Georgia, Irvine S. Ingram Library, Special Collections.

-- "Can Remote-Viewing Penetrate the UFO-ET Enigmas." 1992. Ingo Swann papers, University of West Georgia, Irvine S. Ingram Library, Special Collections.

-- Correspondences and Notes. Ingo Swann papers, University of West Georgia, Irvine S. Ingram Library, Special Collections.

-- E-Meter/RV Sessions. Ingo Swann papers, University of West Georgia, Irvine S. Ingram Library, Special Collections.

-- The Great Apparitions of Mary: An Examination of Twenty-Two Supranormal Appearances. Swann-Ryder Productions, LLC. 2017.

-- Jimmy Wings, unfinished. Ingo Swann papers, University of West Georgia, Irvine S. Ingram Library, Special Collections.

-- Letters between Ingo and L. Ron Hubbard. Ingo Swann papers, University of West Georgia, Irvine S. Ingram Library, Special Collections.

-- Master of Harmlessness. Swann-Ryder Productions, LLC. 2021.

-- Maverick Starbuster. Swann-Ryder Productions, LLC. Unpublished.

-- "New Scientific Discoveries Regarding the Existence of Certain PSI Faculties Synopsis." Swann-Ryder Productions, LLC.

-- "On Remote Viewing, UFOs, and Extraterrestrials." FATE Magazine. 1993.

-- Penetration: A Question of Human and Extraterrestrial Telepathy. Swann-Ryder Productions, LLC. 2017.

-- Penetration: A Question of Human and Extraterrestrial Telepathy: Special Edition, Updated. Swann-Ryder Productions, LLC. 2020.

-- Pink Neon. Swann-Ryder Productions, LLC. Unpublished.

-- Psychic Literary & the Coming Psychic Renaissance. Swann-Ryder Productions, LLC. 2018.

Bibliography

-- Psychic Warfare. Ingo Swann papers, University of West Georgia, Irvine S. Ingram Library, Special Collections.

-- Purple Fables: Quartet. Swann-Ryder Productions, LLC. 2017.

-- Reality Boxes and Other Dark Holes in Human Consciousness. Swann-Ryder Productions, LLC. 2017.

-- Remote Viewing: The Real Story. Swann-Ryder Productions, LLC. https://www.biomindsuperpowers.com. 1996.

-- Speech at Edgar Cayce's A.R.E: "Experiences from my Past, Paths to the Future". 2003.

-- Star Fire. Swann-Ryder Productions, LLC. 2017.

-- "The UFO Extraterrestrial Problem." FATE Magazine. 1992.

-- Waking Dream Work. Ingo Swann papers, University of West Georgia, Irvine S. Ingram Library, Special Collections.

-- The Windy Song. Swann-Ryder Productions, LLC. 2020.

-- The Wisdom Category. Swann-Ryder Productions, LLC. 2017

-- Your Nostradamus Factor: Accessing Your Innate Ability to See into the Future. Swann-Ryder Productions, LLC. 2017.

Swann, Ingo and Cook, Nick. Resurrecting the Mysterious: Ingo Swann's 'Great Lost Work.' Swann-Ryder Productions, LLC. 2020.

Tabler, David. "Judaculla Rock." Appalachian History. https://www.appalachianhistory.net/2019/09/judaculla-rock.html. 2019.

Talbot, David. The Devil's Chessboard: Allen Dulles, the CIA, and the Rise of America's Secret Government. Harper Perennial. 2016.

"Tap Into Your Dark Side With Shadow Work." Cleveland Clinic. https://health.clevelandclinic.org/shadow-work. 2023.

Tawfiq, Idris. "The Story of Solomon and the Queen of Sheba." About Islam: 2022. https://aboutislam.net/reading-islam/understanding-islam/the-story-of-solomon-and-the-queen-of-sheba/.

Taylor, Thérèse. Bernadette of Lourdes, Her Life, Death and Visions. Burns & Oates. 2003.

"Technical Memorandum." https://www.cia.gov/readingroom/docs/CIA-RDP79-00999A000300030030-6.pdf.

Teller, Joanne and Blackwater, Norman. The Navajo Skinwalker, Witchcraft, and Related Phenomena: Spiritual Clues: Orientation to the Evolution of the Circle. Infinity Horn Publishing. 1999.

The Worthless One. X Direct Messages and Emails. 2024.

"Then and now ~ Carl Higdon talks about his alien abduction during hunting, Wyoming, October 25, 1974." YouTube, uploaded by Eyes On Cinema, August 20, 2022. https://www.youtube.com/watch?v=zXvwYBEZH2I.

"Theosophy: Religious Philosophy." Britannica. https://www.britannica.com/topic/theosophy.

"30 Best Charles Fort Quotes With Image." Bookey. https://www.bookey.app/quote-author/charles-fort.

Thompson, Ken. "21 Best Buddha Quotes Showing The Power of Your Mind." A Panda's Journey. https://coacht.blog/2020/06/10/21-best-buddha-quotes-showing-the-power-of-your-mind/.

Tierney, Jacob. "Derry's Livermore Cemetery steeped in history, even if 'Night of the Living Dead' legend isn't true." Trib. https://archive.triblive.com/local/westmoreland/derrys-livermore-cemetery-steeped-in-history-even-if-night-of-the-living-dead-legend-isnt-true/. 2018.

Trench, Brinsley Le Poer. Men Among Mankind. Neville Spearman 1962.

-- The Sky People. Saucerian Books. 1960.

"To the Stars." Wikipedia, The Free Encyclopedia, Wikimedia Foundation. https://en.wikipedia.org/wiki/To_the_Stars_(novel).

Tooze, Adam. The Wages of Destruction: The Making and Breaking of the Nazi Economy. Penguin. 2007.

Torbay, Jordan. "The work of Donald Ewen Cameron: from psychic driving to MK Ultra." History of Psychiatry. 2023. https://journals.sagepub.com/doi/full/10.1177/0957154X231163763.

Bibliography

Tumminia, Diana. Alien Worlds: Social and Religious Dimensions of Extraterrestrial Contact. Syracuse University Press. 2007.

Turner, Ben. "James Webb telescope confirms there is something seriously wrong with our understanding of the universe." LiveScience. https://www.livescience.com/space/cosmology/james-webb-telescope-confirms-there-is-something-seriously-wrong-with-our-understanding-of-the-universe. 2024.

"Two Thousand and Five." Wikipedia, The Free Encyclopedia, Wikimedia Foundation. https://en.wikipedia.org/wiki/2005.

"2009 Remote Viewing Conference." International Remote Viewing Association. 2009.

"UAP." NASA. https://science.nasa.gov/uap/.

"UFO Captives." In Search of…. Season 3, Episode 1. Created by Alan Landsburg. 1978.

"UFO vs. UAP: What's the difference?" News Nation. https://www.newsnationnow.com/space/ufo/ufo-vs-uap-whats-the-difference/.

"UFOlogy and Rosicrucianism: A Roundtable with Paul Hynek." https://absurdbydesign.wordpress.com/2020/11/04/ufology-and-rosicrucianism-a-roundtable-with-paul-hynek/. 2020.

"Uncover CAI-Police Plot to Take Over U.S." New Solidarity. CIA-RDP88-01315R000300590056-7. 1974.

Under Canvas Moab website. https://www.ulumresorts.com/moab/.

"Unidentified Aerial Objects: Project Sign." Headquarters Air Material Command, Wright-Patterson Air Force Base.

"Unidentified Flying Objects and Air Force Project Blue Book." US Air Force. https://www.af.mil/About-Us/Fact-Sheets/Display/Article/104590/unidentified-flying-objects-and-air-force-project-blue-book/.

"United States of America v. Jane Kember, Morris Budlong, Sentencing Memorandum."

https://en.wikisource.org/wiki/United_States_of_America_v._Jane_Kember,_Morris_Budlong,_Sentencing_Memorandum.

"UPDATE: NASA Shares UAP Independent Study Report; Names Director." NASA. https://www.nasa.gov/news-release/update-nasa-shares-uap-independent-study-report-names-director/. 2023.

Urban, Hugh B. "Scientology." Handbook of UFO Religions, edited by Benjamin Zeller. Brill. 2021.

-- New Age, Neopagan and New Religious Movements. University of California Press. 2015.

Ussishkin, David. "Solomon's Jerusalem: The Text and the Facts on the Ground." Jerusalem in Bible and Archaeology: The First Temple Period. Atlanta. 2003.

V., Jayaram. "The Meaning and Significance of Pāshupata." Hinduwebsite.com. https://www.hinduwebsite.com/hinduism/concepts/pashupata.asp.

Vallée, Jacques. Confrontations: A Scientist's Search for Alien Contact. Ballantine Books. 1991.

-- Forbidden Science, Volume 2: California Hermetica, The Journals of Jacques Vallée 1970-1979. Anomalist Books. 2017.

-- Passport to Magonia: From Folklore to Flying Saucers. H. Regnery Company. 1969.

Verma, Vicky. "Ancient Library Of Tibet With Over 84,000 Secret Manuscripts: Only 5% Is Translated." How and Why's. https://www.howandwhys.com/ancient-library-of-tibet-with-over-84000-secret-manuscripts-only-5-is-translated/. 2022.

Violatti, Cristian. "The Meaning of European Upper Paleolithic Rock Art." World History Encyclopedia. https://www.worldhistory.org/article/787/the-meaning-of-european-upper-paleolithic-rock-art/.

"Vision Quest." Encyclopedia Brittanica. https://www.britannica.com/topic/vision-quest.

"Völkischer Beobachter, German Nazi Newspaper." Britannica. https://www.britannica.com/topic/Volkischer-Beobachter

Bibliography

von Däniken, Erich. Chariots of the Gods? Unsolved Mysteries of the Past. Econ-Verlag. 1968.

"Vsigoth People." Encyclopedia Britannica. https://www.britannica.com/topic/Visigoth.

Wacks, David A. "Fairies and pagan mythologies in the medieval Spanish ballad." University of Oregon. https://davidwacks.uoregon.edu/2017/12/31/fairies/. 2017.

Wagner, Dan. "The Haunting Rock Art of Sego Canyon." The Great American Hikes. https://www.greatamericanhikes.com/post/the-haunting-rock-art-of-sego-canyon.

Wakefield, Margery. The Road to Xenu: Life Inside Scientology. Lulu.com. 2009.

Walker, Andrew "Project Paperclip: Dark side of the Moon." BBC News. 2005.

Walters, Jennifer. "Magical Revival: Occultism and the Culture of Regeneration in Britain, C. 1880 – 1929." https://dspace.stir.ac.uk/bitstream/1893/323/1/Thesis.pdf.

Warner, Laura. "Utah Lake story changing with times." Desert News. https://www.deseret.com/2004/5/31/19832108/utah-lake-story-changing-with-times/. 2004.

Warnock-Matthews, Abbie. "Utah's Ancient Six Fingered "Bigfoot" Petroglyph." Stargate Voyager. https://stargatevoyager.com/2023/04/15/utahs-ancient-six-fingered-bigfoot-petroglyph/.

Webb, James. The Occult Underground. Open Court. 1974.

Weiss, Daniel. "Snake Guide." Archeology. https://www.archaeology.org/issues/439-2109/digs/9917-digs-finland-snake-figurine#:~:text=Contemporaneous%20rock%20art%20from%20the,guided%20shamans%20to%20the%20underworld. 2021.

Wells, H. G. War of the Worlds. Harper & Bros. 1898.

Welsh, Mary. "AFTAC Celebrates 50 Years of Long Range Detection." https://web.archive.org/web/20110717073938/.

"WHAT IS MEANT BY OPERATING THETAN (OT)?" Scientology. https://www.scientology.org/faq/operating-thetan/what-is-ot.html.

"What is Yeti? By Express Web Desk." https://indianexpress.com/article/what-is/what-is-yeti-himalayas-abominable-snowman-indian-army-5703282/. 2019.

"Where did they all go? How Homo sapiens became the last human species left." The Guardian. https://www.theguardian.com/science/2023/nov/18/where-did-other-human-species-go-vanished-ancestors-homo-sapiens-neanderthals-denisovans. 2023.

Whispering Oaks Ranch website. https://www.whisperingoakslodging.com/.

"Wild Horse Canyon." ADVENTR.co. https://adventr.co/2010/11/wild-horse-canyon/.

Williamson, Hugh Ross. The Challenge of Bernadette. Burns & Oats. 1958.

Wise, David and Ross, Thomas B. The Invisible Government. Random House: 1964.

Wistrich, Robert. Who's Who in Nazi Germany. Bonanza. 1984.

Wood, Ryan. Majic Eyes Only: Earth's Encounters with Extraterrestrial Technology. Wood Enterprises. 2005.

"Wunderwaffe." The Free Encyclopedia, Wikimedia Foundation. https://en.wikipedia.org/wiki/Wunderwaffe.

Yadav, Gaurav. "Mythical Beings: Gandharvas." The New Indian Express. https://www.newindianexpress.com/lifestyle/spirituality/2023/Oct/28/mythical-beings-gandharvas-2627280.html. 2023.

Yeadon, Glen and Hawkins, John. The Nazi Hydra in America: Suppressed History of a Century: Wall Street and the Rise of the Fourth Reich. Progressive Press: 2008.

Zeller, Benjamin. Handbook of UFO Religions. Brill. 2021.